20 WAYS
TO MANAGE
BETTER

Andrew Leigh is a director of Maynard Leigh Associates, the development and consultancy service. MLA's clients include Airmiles, Safeway, SAP, Hewlett Packard, Cape Gemini, Ernst & Young, Campbells and the London Stock Exchange. The author worked as a business journalist on the *Observer*, was for many years a senior manager in the public sector and now advises companies on management development. He is an expert on teams and leadership. He has written many other books and is a Fellow of the Chartered Institute of Personnel and Development.

The Chartered Institute of Personnel and Development is the leading publisher of books and reports for personnel and training professionals, students, and for all those concerned with the effective management and development of people at work. For details of all our titles, please contact the Publishing Department:

tel. 020-8263 3387

fax 020-8263 3850

e-mail publish@cipd.co.uk

The catalogue of all CIPD titles can be viewed on the CIPD website:
www.cipd.co.uk/publications

20 WAYS TO MANAGE BETTER

Andrew Leigh

Third Edition

Chartered Institute of Personnel and Development

For my parents,
George and Rene Leigh

© Andrew Leigh, 1984, 1995, 2001

First published 1984
Reprinted 1985, 1987, 1991, 1992
Second edition 1995
Third edition 2001

Phototypeset by The Comp-Room, Aylesbury and printed in the UK by
the Short Run Press, Exeter

British Library Cataloguing in Publication Data
A catalogue record for this book is available from the British Library

ISBN 0-85292-879-3

The views expressed in this book are the author's own, and may not
necessarily reflect those of the CIPD.

Chartered Institute of Personnel and Development,
CIPD House, Camp Road, London SW19 4UX
Tel: 020-8971 9000 Fax: 020-8263 3333
E-mail: cipd@cipd.co.uk
Website: www.cipd.co.uk
Incorporated by Royal Charter. Registered charity no. 1079797.

CONTENTS

INTRODUCTION

How has the management role changed since *20 Ways to Manage Better* was first published nearly two decades ago? Certainly no one spoke Internet then, and computers were only beginning to make serious inroads into work and living.

While each new generation of managers faces different challenges, the fundamental role remains: to get the best out of resources. The emphasis, though, has clearly shifted firmly towards 'people', rather than mainly machines, capital, technology or other so-called 'hard' assets.

There is less talk now about 'management' and management science, and far more about leadership. This reflects a realisation that what makes the difference to organisational competitiveness, creativity, profitability and survival ultimately rests on people and how they think, act and, above all, relate.

In nearly two decades, the management role has naturally undergone many transformations, from an obsession with management by objectives through to downsizing, from balanced scorecards to treating the organisation as an organism rather than a machine.

20 Ways tries to reflect the reality of organisational life, without allowing the endless succession of management fads to distort its focus. The latter has been and remains distilled wisdom. It is the book I would have wished to receive as a new or relatively inexperienced manager. Having passed through that phase of my life, it remains a great place to share personal experiences of what seems to work well.

I have agonised over whether to alter the 20 topics for this new edition. Should it have chapters on creativity and innovation, being entrepreneurial, managing diversity, knowledge management or even how to outsource? Should there still be separate chapters on stress and time management, or should these be incorporated into a single chapter on objectives and time management?

That the chapter headings have been left relatively unchanged, rather than the content, merely underlines the enduring nature of management. For example, being a good presenter is even more relevant today than it was when the book was first published. If you master the basics of project management or networking, they will serve you well into the foreseeable future.

The reading list has been completely revised, although I confess that a few classics have stayed, simply because they remain so well worth your time. I have also added some Internet sites where these seem appropriate, but the list is not as complete as I would wish. Any suggestions will be gratefully received.

It is a privilege to offer *20 Ways* in yet another edition. My thanks go to the CIPD for its longstanding faith in this book. Thanks are also due to Jo Sovin for additional research assistance. I trust that you find this book enriches the challenge you have set yourself of managing better.

Andrew Leigh

SETTING OBJECTIVES

The Millennium Dome says it all. Choose the wrong objectives and see where it gets you. Nobody really knew what the Dome was for. Originally hired to define the contents, design guru Stephen Bayley wanted the Dome filled with 'the best' but was eventually dismissed for his pains as 'an out-of-touch elitist'.

So, they filled the Dome with trivia and many stayed away. History's verdict on the Dome will surely record that it was a blatant case of 'build it first, decide what it's for later.'

'Objectives' is a fancy word for 'aims' or 'goals'. These are not always identical to targets, since you can have both. For example, you can aim to be chief executive of your company, and have the target of doing it before you are 30.

Once there was a whole movement pompously called 'management by objectives' (MBO), and it created a wondrously confused bureaucratic mess. Now there are process systems that purport to define all that the company does. These manage to tie everyone in knots filling in forms and trying to control just about everything.

Simple, understandable objectives are important for managing well. They help steer companies, individuals and teams. Setting them is a core management skill that continues to move through numerous iterations.

MBO failed, for example, because it tried to be too comprehensive and corporate planners rather than managers ended up deciding what a company did. More recently, objective-setting has evolved from being a top-down, 'tell them' process, into a more participatory approach.

No matter how you do it, though, you can only make sense of your management role, and your own use of time, when you know what you are trying to achieve – both at work and in the rest of your life.

Ask successful managers what they are trying to achieve and they can almost certainly tell you, usually in a few words. Equally important, they usually keep a list. It may be a 'to do' list, or a 'what I will achieve next week' list. But somewhere, on some piece of paper or on a computer, there will be a list.

Writing down objectives is nothing new. What is interesting is that documenting them seems to possess a curious power of its own. When you write down an intention or aim, this helps to crystallise it, giving it a hard-to-explain momentum. By itself, of course, the writing is nothing more than just that. Yet, since so many effective managers attest to the power of writing down aims as part of achieving them, it would be sensible to take notice.

■ Write down your objectives – somewhere!

If you are going to help others set their objectives, rather than hand them out as tablets from the mountain, you need to first clarify your own aims as a manager. Doing this will be an important guide to using your time well.

Write down in a few sentences what you want to achieve in the next:

■ six months
■ two years
■ five years
■ 20 years.

Nobody else needs to see your jottings. Nor do they have to be 'right'. More important is that you attempt to articulate what the future should look like. This reflects the established principle that:

■ If you want to know the future, help define it.

When you state what you want to achieve, you immediately influence where to put your attention.

If you detect in yourself a natural reluctance to carry out the above task, you are not alone! Most people, faced with a demand to say what they want in the next 20 years, for example, find it a challenging, sometimes painful puzzle. Who knows what the world will look like in two decades?

Yet, once again, the act of writing down aims has a power of its own. The experience of trying to define what you want sets in motion both a conscious and unconscious thinking process that does not stop once you have listed a few aims.

No matter how insubstantial your thoughts may be, try to write something down. The act of recording these ideas, no matter how vague they may be, contributes to making better sense of the day-to-day use of your time.

How much time is there?
What scope do you really have to achieve anything? Rather less than you may think. You probably spend one-third of your life asleep, and one-third away from work. Even putting in a regular 12-hour day does not leave much time in which to achieve what you want. Yet, it can be more than enough if you are clear about what you want and use your time well.

In most companies, managers and leaders spend less than 3 per cent of their time focused on the future of the organisation.

Most time goes on running the business on a day-to-day basis.

Objective-setting

Objective-setting is an art, not a science. Yet, how they are established is also a critical factor in making them useful.

To survive as a manager in the twenty-first century, you need to build objective-setting into your daily way of working. This is not about doling out goals to everyone else. It is about creating a process in which you and others choose goals for which you both want to be held accountable.

When you stop trying to set goals for everyone else, you make room for choosing your own goals. You have more time to focus on the important tasks of helping others reach their goals.

The right ones?

No matter how brilliantly you create objectives, though, they can still be fundamentally the wrong ones. When Christie's, the auctioneers, set up its web-based service, experts urged the managers to adopt a system of showing three-dimensional images of items for sale. These would turn 360 degrees and could be viewed from different angles. Rightly, the management rejected this proposed objective as technically overambitious. Instead, the decision was to go for simple, attractive illustrations that would do the job perfectly well.

Getting clear

Organisations tend to have their own language about goals, objectives, aims and targets. Rather than make fine distinctions between the various terminologies, let's focus instead on:

■ What are you, another individual, a team, or the company, trying to achieve?

Organisations adopting formal objective-setting usually adopt rules for creating, documenting and monitoring them. These may be large statements of intent and include specific targets. For example, to:

- double our turnover in two years
- reduce complaints to three per five hundred customers
- increase our profit margin by 20 per cent within 18 months
- obtain a 30 per cent market share by next June
- shut this production line with minimum disruption to other lines
- improve the retention of staff by 15 per cent within one year
- open a branch office in New York within five years.

To be useful, though, many objectives are best broken into smaller chunks. These chunks become targets, which are the details of the whole process.

While practically anyone can set a broad aim, the managerial skill is converting it into a series of practical steps that mesh to produce the overall result. So, for example, an objective such as 'improve our profit margin' may need converting into several smaller targets:

Target 1 Increase our sale price to the customer by 10 per cent.
Target 2 Identify all overheads and their proportion of the total.
Target 3 Reduce overheads by 30 per cent within one year.
Target 4 Launch at least one high margin new product this year.

Organisational targets in turn may need to be converted into still smaller ones that ultimately relate to a person's own job. They become milestones for judging progress.

Develop your objective-setting skills and you will almost certainly increase your personal effectiveness as a manager and manage your own time better.

Others will see you as someone who is organised and efficient. It really pays to model good behaviour and show the way with objective-setting.

A formal objective-setting system

- helps achieve specific results that are defined in advance
- provides a way of co-ordinating action
- focuses on the kernel of a manager's job – to get results
- improves communication between a manager and others
- acts as a tool for clarifying results
- explains what is expected from people
- provides a control and monitoring mechanism.

What's happening?

An important part of using objectives is knowing whether they are being achieved. This means gaining feedback on:

- at what rate the aim is being achieved
- how close the result is
- anything getting in the way of reaching the result
- what still needs to be done.

Smart objectives

How do you set useful objectives that make sense of your use of time? An excellent system is called the SMART method. SMART goals are:

Stretching; **M**easurable; **A**cceptable; **R**ecorded; **T**ime-limited

Stretching

Choose objectives that use your own and other people's full potential. Such aims are not necessarily attainable, or in some cases realistic. With a *stretching* objective you may not always know whether it will definitely be achieved. Such an objective is therefore risky. Only in trying to reach it will you eventually know whether it was realistic. So, stretching goals:

- pose a challenge
- excite
- tap creative and inner resources.

Measurable

A *measurable* objective is specific and the opposite of 'woolly'. It is measurable if you can answer the simple question:

- Will I know whether this goal has been achieved?

Measurability means deciding by how much the desired objective has been reached. For instance, the objective 'to increase my sales quota' is vague. The essentials are unclear: by how much and by when?

You will make an important contribution to objective-setting by constantly seeking measurability. Some senior managers have even argued that 'if you can't measure it, you can't manage it'. This is an extreme position but it certainly focuses on the importance of making objectives specific.

Acceptable

An *acceptable* objective gains your or other people's commitment. For an individual, team or company it means choosing goals that excite or interest. Even when you face imposed goals, it is always worth asking the question:

- Is there any part of this objective that really interests me?

Similarly, if you or your team receives top-down objectives to pursue, look at these together and explore what seems interesting about them. When you dig into a stated objective, you can usually find some angle to promote interest or enthusiasm. Without these, objectives have little point or chance of being achieved.

What do you do, though, when you receive an imposed goal

that you find uninteresting? If no amount of exploration pro-duces any excitement, it is time to become assertive. Share your reservations.

SEE CHAPTER 20 ON *ASSERTIVENESS*

Most people love a challenge. Devising demanding goals that grab their interest is part of being an effective manager. Often it does not even matter whether the objective is ultimately unat-tainable, so long as you can somehow convince yourself and others that it is therefore worth striving for.

However, beware of:

■ setting clearly impossible objectives
■ constantly changing the goalposts.

Since people so often rise to a challenge, inexperienced man-agers can be tempted to set impossible or unfair objectives. When this happens people soon switch off.

It is therefore important to either find ways to convince people that a goal is indeed feasible or allow them time to conclude that it might be. For example, Motorola senior managers sug-gested to its engineers that it was possible to produce a range of mobile phones with virtually no rejects.

Initially the engineers regarded the objective as unachievable. Yet, the objective would not simply go away. So, the engineers began asking themselves how it might be possible to achieve zero defects. Eventually they triumphed, reaching the apparently unachievable objective of creating a production line with virtu-ally no failed phones.

Recorded
While you can retain a single objective in your head, it is harder with five or six. First for yourself, and then for others, develop a

reliable way of keeping track of each goal by recording:

■ What are you aiming to achieve?
■ Is it being achieved – how far or near is the result?

Record objectives and their detailed targets in a file or notebook, or create a special documentation system. You may also be able to use an existing system within your company.

While recording and monitoring goals encourages clarity about what is happening, often there is far too much detail involved. List the more detailed information about complex goals on separate schedules, while keeping track of broad goals on a single A4 page, on screen, or on a wall chart.

Time-limited
Make your objectives *time-limited* so that you and others know when they must be reached. Time boundaries:

■ rationalise effort
■ clarify urgency
■ focus team energy
■ communicate goals to non-team members
■ set standards of performance.

Without time boundaries, objectives rapidly degenerate into a mere wish list. Without some sense of urgency, the natural human tendency is to tackle other, more pressing matters.

Select time boundaries to which you and others can relate. Broad corporate objectives, for example, may refer to a decade, yet to be useful at the individual level they must be converted to shorter, more meaningful periods.

There is no point in selecting time-limited objectives if the deadlines are ignored or constantly changed. Encourage a culture in which the deadline for objectives being reached are maintained and only altered after much soul searching.

An utterly rigid time boundary is unlikely to survive.

RECRUITMENT AND RETENTION

- Is George Soros, the international financier, mad, hypocritical or highly perceptive?
- How long would it take to move Mount Fuji? What information do you need to arrive at a credible answer?

You could be asked one of these questions if you try joining either *The Economist* or the consultancy Booz-Allen & Hamilton.

The first question is used by *The Economist* to learn how well candidates express themselves and whether they are good at expressing their opinions. In the second, Booz-Allen wants to know whether applicants can think on their feet.

Both of these companies take recruitment extremely seriously. It is also a basic management skill, which you will need throughout your career. You do not need to know all the right questions, or how to conduct tests for weeding out applicants.

What matters is understanding the essentials of recruitment and making sound hiring judgements. It is equally important to know and use ways to retain people once they have been hired.

Reeling them in

Recruitment is like fishing. You need a good bait to bring your prey to the surface, but it may take more skill to make it bite.

In 2000, for example, Arthur Andersen hung a lucrative welcome sign to recent graduates willing to start as trainee accountants. Every person joining received a massive £10,000 golden hello. It was yet another indication that recruiting the right talent had reached a new level of intensity.

In the developed world recruitment is increasingly about talent and managing it. Shortages of IT staff, telecom experts and financial specialists are just some of the areas where recruitment is changing.

With ageing populations in many advanced nations, the talent shortage is likely to worsen. Nearly two-thirds of 255 senior managers in a UK survey found it hard to recruit people with particular skills, such as strategic awareness or innovativeness.

The situation is made worse by poor recruitment practices, particularly a continued reliance on mainly the interview as a way of hiring. Interviews – when used as the main method of selection – are notoriously poor predictors of recruitment success.

Recruitment is ceasing to be simply an advertisement and is becoming a sophisticated hiring process. The people you want will probably not even consider joining your company unless they see clear signs that you know how to respect, nurture and retain talent.

Give recruitment and selection a fair share of your attention and it will certainly repay you. You will reduce the amount of time and energy spent on trying to deal with 'square pegs' stuck in round holes.

Finding the right people used to be solely about identifying applicants with the right skills and experience. Now it is just as important to find people who bring suitable personal qualities and character traits. So an important shift in the recruitment process is checking out applicants' values and finding out how they have behaved in the past.

Ben & Jerry's, the ice cream company, uses tests, interviews and checks to screen out managers who do not share the company's social goals.

Toyota runs five-day testing for values such as teamwork, quality orientation.

Online recruiting

The big shift in recent years has been online recruiting. Many companies use their own website to avoid expensive mailings of information and to speed up the whole process.

British Airways' strategy, for example, is to direct candidates to its graduate recruitment site. A tracking system holds details of people who narrowly missed being appointed. These applications are revisited and often save BA from having to re-advertise.

There is conflicting evidence about just how online recruiting is really altering how people job hunt. In 1999 the IPD found that about one in three employers had placed job ads on the Internet. Yet, a year earlier, an NOP poll found that less than 1 million people used the Internet to find jobs. What is clear, though, is that online recruiting is now a realistic way to attract certain types of candidate.

One of the most popular sites is Monster.com, which carries 3,000 job vacancies and a database of 40,000 CVs. It also claims to receive 130,000 hits each month. These job sites can be a source for recruitment, but you also need to be webwise:

- Use websites because they will make recruitment easier, or shorten the time it takes to find the right person, not because everyone else is doing it.
- Follow the job-seeker to the appropriate site.
- Experiment with different sites and check pre-screening and monitoring services.

- Write effective online ads that are concise and answer the question: why should I consider your organisation?
- Consider print ads too, as a way of directing people to your site where they can learn more.
- Make your own site easy to navigate and reach the jobs quickly.

The Internet is also offering new ways of assessing possible job candidates through:

- *Online testing before interviewing* – Asda used an online multiple choice quiz to find graduates who are passionate about retailing – 60 per cent of the candidates were weeded out. Amusingly, it is reported that those who failed this test were then automatically transferred to the Sainsbury's website.
- *Telephone interviews before face-to-face meetings* – Jamba Juice, a US retailer of health drinks, targets managers through the Internet and then conducts telephone interviews to select the best.
- *Interactive testing* – candidates are shown a video clip on screen and asked to deal with a situation, often work related. Companies using this approach say it brings out personality and speeds up the recruitment process.

Why recruit?

As a manager you need to view recruitment and selection in the wider context of the organisation's future:

- What does the organisation want to be?
- What are its aspirations?
- What is its strategic intent?
- What capabilities will the enterprise need in the future?

Taking a short-term and narrow view of recruitment and selection may fill a vacancy, yet it may not necessarily help the organisation to thrive.

So, an important strategic issue to consider is how your recruitment and selection activity can contribute to longer-term business goals. This more far-reaching vision will set you apart from managers who take a more myopic view of their job.

Are you recruiting:

- for today or tomorrow – a cohesive approach is to link recruitment with succession planning
- to preserve or challenge the status quo – unless you know which, you are likely to end up with someone who does not deliver what you need
- for what people know or who they are – great personalities will not make up for lack of ability; highly informed people who do not fit your culture are equally useless.

Increasingly 'the job' is being replaced by a more fluid concept of work to be done. Job descriptions, once the heart of employing people, are giving way to more flexible ways of describing broad tasks and skills, attitudes and responses to changing situations.

Choosing

Placing her crystal ball on the boardroom table, the fortune-teller stared into the murky depths: 'You would be unwise to employ Mr Johnson as your sales director; he has a dark secret not declared on his CV.'

A smartly dressed man who entered holding a clipboard followed her. Using the handwriting on Mr Johnson's letter and application form, he revealed that: 'He's an outgoing sort of chap, likes to eat and drink, probably a bit of a womaniser. He is a latent homosexual and is a bit too insensitive for this job.'

So far, no company admits to employing a fortune-teller for staff selections and virtually none, in Britain at least, use graphology.

Yet given the poor record of accomplishment of many company appointments, they might just as well have resorted to such dubious measures. A poor recruitment choice could cost your company dearly.

For example, if someone leaves within the first six months it can cost more than three times their annual salary in finder's fees, advertising and the whole appointment process. Worse, a bad recruitment decision may ultimately affect your own career prospects.

If part of your management role is to obtain results from people, selecting the right ones is essential. Even with personnel experts to support you, recruitment and selection is a prime management responsibility. Many managers enter the recruitment process as a knee-jerk response to an empty slot. As we saw previously, though, by being strategic you will tend to stand out from the crowd, especially when you ask questions such as those described below in relation to the business plan.

The business plan of the company or a particular division is ideally the starting point for recruitment decisions. From this flows the rest of the recruitment process, as shown in the box.

The process

Stage 1	Create the business plan – identify company aims
Stage 2	Resource analysis – identifying numbers and types of people, skills and other human resource requirements, using the succession planning
Stage 3	Work analysis – specify the new work and decide content; prepare descriptions of the work
Stage 4	Candidate specifications – describe the sort of person who would fit the job
Stage 5	Attract candidates – publicise existence of vacancy

Stage 6 Sorting – initial matching of candidates to the requirements, shortlisting – choosing whom to take to the next stage

Stage 7 Selecting – meeting candidates, interviewing and testing

Stage 8 Deciding and making the appointment

Stage 9 Induction

The business plan (stage 1)

It is hard to make any sense of recruitment needs if you are unsure where the organisation is heading. You can only respond to specific vacancies and take a short-term view.

Effective managers, as we have seen, use a longer-term horizon. Even if you do not have direct access to the company's business plan, you can certainly push to find out issues that will make more sense of the need to recruit.

Resource analysis (stage 2)

Even without professional help with resource analysis, give attention to:

- recruitment avoidance
- recruitment need.

The former is when you systematically check whether there is any way to do without extra employees by asking questions such as:

- Why do we need to recruit – is an appointment essential?
- Could the work be reallocated to existing staff?
- Can the work be divided up or eliminated?
- Are existing staff using their full potential?

You may also need to explore why a previous employee left and whether simply hiring a replacement will work. Ask questions such as:

- What is the resource requirement now and for the next few years?
- What is the nature of the work that needs to be done?
- What kind of person would do the work (fill the job)?
- Where could we find the right kind of recruit(s)?
- What will we need to pay to attract the right candidate(s)?
- What special training will be necessary?

Work analysis (stage 3)

Work analysis helps you select employees that are more productive by identifying the main themes in the tasks to be done. It also lists what attributes people need.

This is where you systematically explore the nature of the work itself. For existing jobs, obtain information by asking those doing them to write down in detail their duties and categorising them in some way.

Alternatively, ask someone else to study the person doing the work and produce a detailed report on what is involved. You may need information on:

- work requirement such as basic education and pre-job training needs, on-the-job training required, skills required, physical effort needed, mental demands etc
- responsibility for materials, equipment, decisions, supervision of others, safety, contact with the public etc
- working conditions such as weekend or late night working, location and other issues such as hazards.

There are many ways to obtain information for work analysis including film, written records, observation, structured and open-ended questionnaires, diaries, interviews and job shadowing.

Work analysis is a field in its own right, and includes techniques such as studying critical incidents, repertory grid and occupational analysis. Though you will probably never conduct these studies yourself, you may need to use specialists to provide the information, so get a feel for what is involved.

Job descriptions – on the way out? (stage 4)

The next step within work analysis is to create a written description of the work. This normally consists of several pages summarising the purpose, scope, grade, duties and responsibilities, and relationships that form the job. It usually excludes information about the skills or personality required.

SEE *CANDIDATE SPECIFICATION (STAGE 5)* BELOW

Job descriptions are a statement of what the job is about. Yet, in fast-changing organisations these are increasingly regarded as inflexible and soon outdated. You can write down as much as you like, yet reality soon makes such material look irrelevant.

It is often better to describe broad activities and areas of responsibility, such as 'manages the help desk and ensures it runs smoothly to high standards', rather than a detailed specification as to what this involves. A short clear work description lies at the heart of good recruitment practice.

Candidate specification (stage 5)

You now need to clarify the sort of person you need in a candidate specification. This lists the essential attributes required, such as a university degree, a high level of manual dexterity or an ability to use a spreadsheet. Distinguish between:

■ essential candidate requirements
■ desirable candidate requirements.

Avoid using vague 'management speak'. For example, saying you want someone keen and well motivated has little value. No one is likely to want someone who is idle, apathetic and unmotivated.

Attracting candidates (stage 6)

It is usually easier to attract candidates than to select the right one. Before looking outside, check if there is already someone suitable in-house. Even with extra training this will be cheaper than recruiting an outsider.

If you know the sort of person you want – for example, a new graduate – find out what will attract and retain them. Pay, for example, may be less critical than whether the job is interesting and has good prospects.

> One large food company lost half its new graduates within six months of hiring them because it was recruiting extroverts and sending them unsupported to remote places.

Think carefully about your desired candidate and advertise in a medium he or she is likely to see. For instance, you may obtain rather different candidates by advertising on the Web than in a newspaper.

Successful job advertisements clarify the nature of the job and the person you are seeking. Take a personal interest in the job advertisement and do not leave it entirely to personnel specialists.

Offering the name of a person to write to also encourages replies. Avoid using box numbers, as this tends to deter people from applying.

To avoid a mountain of applications, give enough information for people to exclude themselves. Make sure the copy is legal and without racial, sexual and other forms of discrimination. Be wary also of unnecessary ageism creeping in as this may cost you some effective candidates.

Recruitment adverts
Give priority to:

- the work being interesting
- advancement and prospects
- earnings and security
- personal involvement
- relationships and working with colleagues
- education and training prospects.

Give less priority to:

- holiday entitlement
- travel opportunities
- sports and social facilities
- status symbols
- fringe benefits
- prestige of the organisation.

CVs

What kind of CV do you want from someone you might manage? Traditionally CVs were long and boring; more recently they have become shorter as people have reduced the amount of material to go on Internet recruitment sites.

The trouble with CVs, though, is not just missing material, but misleading or even false information. Studies have shown that CVs show job applicants claiming to be working abroad when actually they were in prison, or others claiming to be accountants and solicitors without even having a qualification.

About a quarter of all CVs contain lies. People lie about their qualifications, salary, previous experience, job title, references, criminal past, age, and even their address. The commonest falsehood is about previous experience and the next is lying about higher education and salary.

Checking CVs can be dreary but worth it, as the cost of recruiting the wrong person runs into thousands. Look particularly carefully for:

- what is missing
- gaps in employment history
- very short length of employment for each job
- lengthy descriptions of so-called 'responsibilities'
- exaggerated claims about personal abilities.

Sorting and listing (stage 6)

An attractive job advert can pull in dozens, maybe hundreds of applications. In self defence the larger companies are developing increasingly sophisticated screening methods to find the candidates to shortlist.

The response of candidates to these methods is to ensure that their CVs contain a large number of key words that the computer system might be seeking. The fact that these companies need to rely on such soulless means of recruitment often reflects a failure to nail down sufficiently the type of person they want.

With more than half a dozen applicants you can develop a:

- preliminary shortlist
- reserve list
- reject list.

Treat everyone who applies with respect. They all deserve a courteous reply if they have taken the trouble to contact you. Even if the reply is a general rejection, make it friendly. For example, wish the person good luck with searching for a job.

Consider involving others in the job of drawing up these lists. Not only will it allow you to delegate some of the work, it also helps ensure that suitable candidates do not slip through the net.

To successfully screen your applicants you need to be clear about what you are looking for. Think about:

- key organisational values
- the danger of cloning – recruiting more 'people like us' and losing diversity
- job-specific competencies.

Selecting (stage 7)

The three ways favoured by most organisations are:

- job application form
- references
- interviews.

However, there are plenty of other methods to consider, including:

- psychological tests
- ability tests
- assessment centres
- group exercises
- work sample tests.

Accuracy of recruitment methods ranked from highest to lowest

- assessment centres for promotion
- structured interviews
- work samples
- ability tests
- assessment centres for performance
- biodata
- personality tests
- unstructured interviews
- references.

Three relatively new forms of making people reveal themselves include:

1 *Computer simulation* – this is an extension of role play in which candidates strap on a headset and, for example, chair a meeting, handle an irate customer and so on.
2 *Dynamic assessments* – instead of assessing what candidates already know, these tests assess what they learn. Candidates who answer a question wrongly or do not have the knowledge are given training or feedback then re-tested to assess whether they have learned.
3 *Virtual screening* – these may use software to assess someone or tape interviews, which are then watched to look for revealing signs. However, candidates may have the legal right to challenge a decision made solely by automatic means, such as electronic screening of CVs.

Assessment centres
These are both a place and a process. An assessment centre can improve your whole recruitment process and counter a dangerous reliance on interviews. The essence of a centre is that candidates experience a microcosm of the job and are tested on work-related activities. Interviewers review how a candidate handles the assignments and they predict future job performance.

Well-run assessment centres can save you time as a busy manager and are not as expensive as they seem. Their cost needs to be compared with the price paid for recruitment mistakes.

Unless you are already a personnel expert, outsource the job of running an assessment centre to a specialist. It is time-consuming to set up relevant tests, conduct them and analyse the results.

The interview

Three things most managers think they do well in life are: drive a car, make love, and interview. Interviews, though, are generally a poor way to predict recruitment success, particularly if they are unstructured.

To maximise your chances of success in using interviews:

- avoid relying solely on it as your main means of selection
- structure interviews into a logical sequence covering key areas
- use behaviour and situation questions rather than mainly attitude questions – for example, 'What would you do if . . .?', 'How would you deal with . . .?'
- identify critical questions that can rapidly exclude or include someone, for example, 'If you were offered this job would you take it?'

Tests

Psychological tests, individual and group exercises can sometimes increase your knowledge of a candidate and improve the selection process. However, you will usually benefit from professional help in using such methods. Many tests for example require a licensed administrator.

Psychological testing has many supporters yet these seldom do better than an insightful, experienced assessor. Because they tend to be expensive and time-consuming, restrict these kinds of test to the final group of candidates.

Work sample tests

These are a sound way of checking whether people can do what they say they can do. For example, if someone says he or she can type using WordPerfect, let him or her demonstrate and you will soon know whether it is true.

Try giving the candidates examples of real work problems and ask them how they would tackle them.

Avoiding bias

- **Primary effect.** You jump to conclusions about a candidate – research does not support the idea that interviewers accept or reject candidates in the first few minutes.
- **Expectancy effect.** Your initial expectations about someone stem from the application form and prejudices your final decision.
- **Confirmation effect.** You ask questions that mainly tend to seek information confirming your initial impression; this prevents you asking more probing and important ones.
- **Fixed views effect.** Because you have a preconceived notion of your ideal candidate, you try to match candidates to this notion; it prevents you from selecting someone who is excellent yet different.
- **Halo effect.** You consistently interpret information and rate candidates too positively or too negatively.
- **Contrast effect.** Your decisions are affected by candidates you saw earlier and by pre-set employment quotas.
- **Negative bias.** You are more influenced by negative information from candidates than positive information.
- **Clone syndrome.** You keep looking for candidates who are like you in terms of background, education, personality and attitudes.
- **The Liking effect.** You select candidates because you personally like them and are consequently less objective in your ratings of ability.

Spot the liar

It is said that the body cannot lie and you certainly do not need a lie detector to see through many candidate cover-ups. There are plenty of clues that suggest someone is being untruthful during the recruitment process. For example:

- Listen for negative statements, for example, 'I am not an anxious person' rather than 'I am a calm person'.
- Watch for missing detail, for example not volunteering names of people or places.
- Catch the short answers. For example, in response to 'What do you know about our company?', 'Quite a lot' may hide ignorance if there is no elaboration.

Other signs you can look for include physical clues such as squirming in the seat, a lack of hand gestures, excessive touching of the nose, too much eye contact and a general increase in the number of speech errors and nervous ticks.

Verbal clues also provide a good source of information to root out deception during recruitment. For example:

- the length of time taken to answer questions – liars generally take longer
- slow and very considered speech – the candidate is thinking ahead, perhaps to avoid self-revelations
- very fast and high-pitched speech as an attempt to gloss over something
- anxiety to fill in pauses between questions as if they have something to hide.

Generally the less prepared someone is for an interview the more telltale signs he or she will give off.

Decision and appointment (stage 8)

Two-thirds of British employers always take up references and only a handful never do. Better still may be a chat with the person's present employer: you will often learn far more than from any written reference. However, not all organisations permit this practice. References can prove a deciding factor when you are having to decide between two closely matched candidates.

If you are faced with several evenly matched candidates, you may be unsure who to appoint. Rather than toss a coin or make an instinctive decision, try a second or even third interview. This may seem excessive but the cost of a wrong decision is high.

If you still cannot choose between two equal candidates, this may suggest that neither is really what you want since by now you should have learned quite a lot about them and their personalities. Try giving a job-related task to perform that uses some clear criteria for how you will assess the results.

When you are finally ready to make your decision, try asking the candidate: 'If we offer you the job will you take it?' Surprisingly, you may sometimes uncover hesitation or even a plea for time to think it over. That may prove a decisive clue as to whether to actually offer the job when you have two or more candidates you are prepared to employ in the role.

Take up any references and conduct any security checks required in your organisation. Before confirming the appointment, be sure the person has accepted the normal terms of employment and the pay on offer.

Induction (stage 9)

The final stage is helping the person settle into the new job. Careful attention to induction can:

■ establish a favourable attitude towards the employer
■ help the person reach maximum effectiveness in the shortest time.

Induction is a key part of retaining people (see below). Once someone has accepted the job offer, develop a lively celebratory 'newcomer kit' that gives a good picture of the company so that the new employee feels he or she has made the right choice.

For technical people, establish a partnership between the professional and the line manager. They should meet on the first day to clarify the role, the manager's style and priorities and the employee's needs.

You can seldom invest enough in the induction process. It can save time in bringing someone up to speed and ensure that he or she has a good attitude towards the new job.

Retention

Once you have recruited someone, losing him or her is costly, disappointing and disruptive. Hewlett-Packard, for example, calculated that the cost of recruiting and retaining an employee is nine times higher than retention.

Small companies can ill afford the loss of skills, knowledge and experience, and too often resignations come as a surprise. Watch for signs that people are taking single days off, checking holiday entitlement or scanning adverts. But if you really care about motivating people, you will soon realise when someone has lost the enthusiasm for a job.

People do not necessarily leave for financial reasons. According to a survey by a UK government department, almost two-thirds of employees would choose a job paying 5 per cent less than another if the employer provided formal training opportunities.

Abbey National, with various call centres, found from exit interviews that staff wanted more coaching and promotion opportunities. Consequently, it added an extra supervisory layer to provide both.

Stress may be one factor behind a retention problem. (See also

Chapter 16.) UBS Warburg, for example, created a concierge scheme in which employees get washing machines fixed, shopping picked up and nannies organised. Meanwhile at PricewaterhouseCoopers, managers track employee time sheets to identify overworked, workaholic individuals.

> At Sun Microsystems, the top contributors to both recruitment and retention have been identified as:
>
> ■ work challenge
> ■ career development
> ■ financial opportunity
> ■ work variety
> ■ organisational commitment to people.
>
> There is also one-to-one career counselling. These measures have reduced attrition rates by 1 per cent, saving the company $1 million. And while the industry had turnover rates of over 15 per cent, Sun had voluntary turnover in single figures.

A survey by recruitment company Top Jobs on the Net revealed that 'bad relationship with the boss' is a common motive for moving jobs, and it is often the 'last straw'. So, ensure that you have plenty of ways to 'listen' to how people are feeling about their work.

For example, anonymous online 'chats' with senior managers via a company website can give real information on employee satisfaction.

External pressures that threaten the retention of your staff include:

■ greater labour mobility
■ new employment psychology – under-35s, for example, expect to change jobs often, perhaps every two to three years

- allure of dot.coms or fast-growth start-ups
- strategic poaching – whole teams may move employers if the price is right.

Inside companies, desire for greater retention is driven by:

- business growth – for example, in 2000, ABN AMRO announced plans to recruit around 500 investment bankers to cope with the business opportunities
- value of top executives – the company may be more vulnerable to losing a client than losing its top directors
- skill shortages – some posts may take many months to fill
- cost of attrition
- culture and knowledge – departures of people damage company cohesion and lose intellectual capital.

Only around a third of all companies have an employee retention strategy and only about 40 per cent even measure retention.

> Prudential's Building Management Capability uses a sophisticated planning model to assess how long it wants different employees to stay. Managers can develop highly targeted retention programmes, create contingency plans for filling potential gaps in skills and measure the impact of HR decisions.

To retain people means paying attention to how they are feeling and reacting. Your most important people are often the most difficult ones to retain, especially if they are technical professionals whose skills are in demand. They want hard to deliver fun and engaging environments in which they can work intensively yet unwind.

Communications Company Marconi employs around 600 new graduates a year in the UK. They are mainly technical specialists in software, engineering, telecom and electronics. The company runs a two-year global development programme aimed at retaining the most able professionals by providing them with a wide variety of career opportunities.

'We have to be flexible and responsive to their needs', explains the manager who introduced the scheme.

Keeping people on board

Retaining staff starts at the recruitment stage. You need to enthuse these candidates and capture their imagination in the first interview. 'Techies' in particular will be influenced by:

- opportunities for personal and career development, growth and achievement; this includes autonomy and control over their work and independence
- challenges such as the chance to earn respect and contribute in innovative ways to key business goals
- being at the leading edge of their field and keeping their skills up to date.

Because they are often highly focused individuals, you also need to check out that they really understand your organisation's mission, values, reward structure and commitment to work–life balance.

Retention may not seem a particularly exciting area for your managerial attention. In fact, it is as much a creative challenge as any other area of your work.

Holding on to the creatives

Creative people are an inspiration to work with but they are challenging to manage and can leave for what may seem perverse reasons.

These people are not usually motivated by promotion up the ladder or traditional corporate benefits. They are high maintenance and can be emotional, defensive, passionate, egotistical and oversensitive.

To hold on to creative people be willing to:

- **Help them develop their work** – what matters to them is quality, so shelling out for an extra photo shoot or a better piece of art gear can make all the difference.
- **Reward them so that they can play** – paying them matters, but so do the latest gadgets such as specialist software.
- **Let them flock** – creatives are heavily self-motivated, so they will want to report to someone who is either like them or really understands what they need.
- **Stroke and appreciate them** – nominate them for awards, celebrate their achievements and generally help them gain public recognition.
- **Keep them energised** – encourage them to get out and see the latest ideas at key events or in stores. They need lots of outside stimulus.
- **Make their work important** – give them challenging, important and urgent assignments; they love to do the impossible.
- **Get out of their way** – creatives work best when they are allowed to get on with it, so keep the monitoring and checking to a minimum, and learn to trust them.

Further reading

CAPPELLI P. 'A market-driven approach to retaining talent'. *Harvard Business Review*. Jan/Feb 2000.

CIPD. 'Recruitment on the Internet'. www.cipd.co.uk, originally issued in December 1999; minor revisions July 2000.

'Effective selection tools: adapt and survive'. *IRS Employment*

Review, No. 702, April 2000 – Employee Development Bulletin. pp5–10.

KNEELAND S. *Hiring People*. Oxford, How To Books, 1999.

MACDONALD J. *and* RILEY J. *Successful Recruitment in a Week*. London, Hodder and Stoughton, 1999.

NEWELL D. 'How to retain technical professionals'. *People Management*. 8 June 2000.

ROBERTS G. *Recruitment and Selection: The competency approach*. London, CIPD, 1997.

APPRAISAL

Chapter 3

Is appraisal a disaster? Research from around the world suggests that managers universally hate doing appraisals, do them badly or are under the illusion that they are naturally good at them.

The history of appraisal schemes is abysmal. Vast effort often goes into launching these complex arrangements, with mountains of paper and endless checking. Return a year or so later, though, and you will find that the scheme is either being revised, dumped or is drifting aimlessly. A 13-country European survey in 1999, for example, found that most of the 460 organisations were busily making changes to their appraisal systems.

Faced with this reality, some companies have abandoned formal appraisals. Yet despite the negative image of appraisals, it is a basic part of your job as a manager to give people systematic feedback on their performance.

Every employee is entitled to know the answer to the question:

■ How am I doing?

Looking at performance is entirely sensible. But many managers are reluctant to deal with performance issues and are worried about the possibility of confrontation or conflict. New, more imaginative ways of assessing performance that may reduce one-to-one conflict include:

■ Ask a whole team to share responsibility for appraising individual members' performance – particularly relevant where it is a self-managed team.

■ Hold a development meeting that focuses only on helping someone achieve results without linking this directly to pay or promotion.

■ 360-degree feedback – feedback stems from a variety of sources, such as peers and subordinates, other managers, and even customers and suppliers.

Whatever form the appraisal takes, it needs to happen regularly, so that employees know how they are doing and whether they need to improve their performance.

Why conduct appraisals?

■ make decisions about rewards
■ achieve an improvement in performance
■ show people where they fit in and motivate them
■ identify potential and develop the individual
■ succession planning
■ promote people
■ identify and communicate poor performance.

The commonest reasons for appraisals are to:

■ improve performance
■ identify training needs
■ encourage a manager/worker dialogue.

The commonest benefits from appraisal are:

■ better individual performance
■ improved employee communications
■ stronger employee commitment.

You are the owner

As a manager you will be expected to conduct appraisals yourself, or be part of a group assessing performance. Usually it is your responsibility to organise it and arrive at these judgements about employees reporting directly to you. In this way you 'own' the process.

Appraisal that only involves you commenting on another person's performance, though, is best avoided. Such a one-to-one session is charged with emotion, which neither party may be equipped to handle.

It is easy to understand why managers everywhere seem uncomfortable about conducting appraisals. When you work with someone on a near-daily basis, a formal appraisal can easily harm what may anyway be a difficult relationship.

With flatter organisations, fewer layers and less direct supervision, different and rather healthier attitudes towards appraisal are emerging. Rules, and obedience to them, are playing a less important part in many successful enterprises. With a more organic, less mechanistic view of organisations, a well-run appraisal:

- helps a person maximise his or her potential
- links individual performance to the achievement of corporate goals

Performance management

While appraisals need to focus on the individual's immediate work performance, they should also be about whether the person is demonstrating through actions:

- support for the company culture, values and aspirations.

Instead of asking 'Are you doing what I asked?', you are assessing 'What are you doing to support our vision and our values?'

This wider view of appraisal often generates a more powerful conversation. During it you concentrate on obtaining results from someone, rather than passing judgement. You do this by:

- giving direction
- recognising and rewarding
- discovering employee concerns
- offering and receiving feedback
- increasing job satisfaction
- sharing knowledge.

This approach is just as demanding as the more traditional form of judgemental appraisal, but in many ways far more satisfying for both parties.

In the new-style performance management appraisal, you may play many roles, including leader, facilitator, negotiator, counsellor and even researcher.

Unlike old-style appraising, which tends to be problem-centred with you the manager saying how the individual can improve, performance management is more future-orientated.

During this meeting you hold a genuine dialogue with the other person: you are enquiring, receiving and encouraging. Here appraisal is not something 'done' to someone. Instead, it is based on mutual respect, more like a partnership.

Damned by Deming

The arch high priest of 'quality', W.E. Deming, condemned performance appraisal as one of the seven deadly sins of management practice. He saw it as damaging because it blamed variations in company performance on individuals rather than on the system of management control.

Deming argued that by dealing with the individual's performance, management merely creates morale problems. Yet, individual responsibility within a team setting is also at the core of
the new approach to running organisations. Increasingly managers realise that many important aspects of the organisation
are not entirely measurable and that effort and behaviour are
just as important as more hard-edged, quantified results.

Performance management demands a definite link between pay
and performance in appraisals. This is a controversial aspect of
appraisals and many companies have abandoned trying to cram
this issue into the process. Instead, remuneration is handled sep-
arately, taking into account performance reviews.

Annual appraisals are far too infrequent to make much impact.
Effective appraisal involves more regular assessments and feedback sessions. This is because it no longer makes sense to see a
person's self-development as narrowly restricted to organisational life. Instead, you can assume that if you help to develop
the individual you will eventually grow the company.

Methods

You can appraise someone by:

- assessing personality
- reviewing job-related abilities
- using rating scales
- evaluating individual results
- testing competencies.

Mixing these methods is not necessarily effective. A better
approach, the essence of performance management, is focusing
on goal-setting combined with an open discussion about personal development.

360-degree appraisal

For most managers, appraisal still implies assessing someone who directly reports to them. Yet there is an increasing awareness that peer appraisal is also powerful. Moreover, downward assessment needs to be supplemented by allowing the appraisee to do some appraising of the manager.

Upward appraisal

Upward appraisal has been gaining favour at American Express. It is separated from pay and other annual assessments. Managers are shown questionnaires completed by peers and subordinates. The combined scores produce a set of company norms. These allow managers to compare themselves to their equivalents in the organisation. As one manager explained:

> *The first time it's quite daunting. You don't know what you are going to hear. The perceptions of people around you are pretty accurate; they know your weaknesses.*

At Federal Express, too, all managers are annually appraised by their subordinates. The results are fed into a system for assessing the manager's own performance. Someone who receives a negative upward appraisal is required to change and faces a reappraisal six months later.

At WH Smith, staff were asked to rate their managers on 32 attributes, including: communicates relevant information to me; plans the work effectively; inspires me to do well; does not impose unrealistic objectives; is courteous.

To make upward and peer appraisal work, it almost certainly has to be done anonymously.

With organisations increasingly valuing teamwork, the role of individual appraisal is being challenged. Appraising someone in isolation from the rest of the team makes only limited sense and the implications are clear. Meaningful appraisals must include a wider perspective.

Rather than relying solely on 'manager analysis' to decide someone's effectiveness, you may need to obtain a broader range of information supplied by team members and others outside it.

Performance management moves appraisal away from a historical look at someone's work with its inevitable emphasis on what went wrong. Instead you give more attention to the future:

■ setting key objectives – what the person is accountable for
■ agreeing measures and standards to be obtained
■ assigning timescales and priorities.

Coaching and counselling

To help employees achieve their performance targets, you should also develop your supportive skills. Instead of being just a directing, controlling, delegating person, you will need to offer practical help and advice to people for achieving results.

The appraisal meeting then becomes more like a coaching or counselling session. By focusing on the longer term, rather than immediate outcomes, the dialogue with the employee may be more equal and more of a two-way conversation.

FURTHER DETAILS OF THIS APPROACH CAN BE FOUND IN CHAPTER 4.

The appraisal meeting

Poor interviewing skills are a major cause of failed appraisals. If you feel unconfident about conducting these meetings:

■ attend a short development course
■ work with a more experienced interviewer
■ obtain help through one-to-one coaching.

Give some thought to what you call the meeting. In the

appraisee's mind, there is likely to be a difference, for example, between a 'discussion' and 'an interview'.

A discussion implies that you are mutually exploring the challenge of the person performing even better. In that sense it is a genuine sharing of information and ideas. You can learn, too; it is a two-way process. For example, the appraisee may reveal that the way you handle certain issues is not entirely helpful. As part of the conversation you might therefore agree to do certain things differently.

By contrast, 'an interview' suggests that the appraisal is something you will 'do' to the other person. Calling it an interview underlines the subordinate position of the other person, which may make a useful conversation much harder.

Before the appraisal meeting
Prepare for an appraisal by gathering formal and informal information. You may use a questionnaire and feedback, such as views and opinions of those who have been in contact with the person you are meeting.

Whatever way you conduct appraisals in your company, you need solid information, not just feelings or hearsay. Good appraisals are based on well-understood criteria.

Structure
Your appraisal meeting needs a definite structure so that both parties know what territory you are going to cover and in what order. A typical structure is:

- introduction
- discussing performance strengths
- reviewing areas for personal development
- developing specific plans
- summarising key points and agreed actions.

You need:

■ a convenient time for both parties to meet
■ at least 60 to 90 minutes for the discussion
■ a comfortable setting with no interruptions
■ a written agenda
■ a written report of what was decided
■ a clear review strategy.

Appraisal meeting strategies

■ **Tell and sell:** you judge the person's performance and convey your opinion. You aim to persuade the person to adopt specific solutions for action:

> *Here's what I think about your work and I'd like you to try my suggestions for action.*

■ **Tell and listen:** you describe objectively the person's performance but say nothing further. You listen carefully to what the other person says about it:

> *I'll explain how I see your work, after that it's up to you to say what you think.*

■ **Joint problem-solving:** you jointly review performance focusing not on the individual but on the entire work situation. Together you identify actions:

> *We'll discuss work problems and possible solutions; together we'll work out what to do.*

■ **Self-appraisal:** you prompt the other person to give a personal audit to identify strengths and development needs. The person offers suggestions for change and you add your ideas:

> *Tell me how effective you are being. You'll be much
> tougher on yourself than I'd ever be; I'll add my
> thoughts to yours for further action.*
>
> ■ **Goal-setting:** together you define the person's future
> objectives and how performance will be assessed against
> these aims. Any agreed actions are concerned with achiev-
> ing the aims:
>
> *We'll set some mutually acceptable goals and decide
> how we'll monitor progress. If you wish, I'll suggest
> ways of achieving these goals.*

Standards

Performance criteria are essential for making sense of appraisals.
Unless people know how they are being assessed, they are likely
to conclude that the whole process is arbitrary and unreliable.

It can take weeks or months to create credible standards and
these may need updating regularly. It might be helpful to obtain
outside advice on devising these criteria, but the best source is
probably the person being appraised.

Performance standards should rely on observable facts, rather
than mere opinion. You and the employee may need to discuss
specific standards jointly, if these have not already been established. Three main types of performance criteria to consider are:

■ measurable or quantifiable results, such as profit per quarter,
sales per month, customers contacted, jobs completed etc
■ actions that reflect agreed policies and cultural norms – these
might be anything from demonstrating customer care to personal time-keeping and minimising absences
■ personal qualities and work characteristics – these might
include such intangibles as self-confidence, co-operation,
leadership and showing initiative.

During the appraisal

Make sure you start the appraisal promptly and have a clear time in which to do it. Imagine how an appraisee feels waiting while you grandly conclude something that seems more important. To that person the appraisal meeting may be the most important event of the month.

Start the meeting by putting the person at ease. If you are weak on small talk, find something to break the ice without being too contrived. Avoid long rambling introductions; these can cause confusion or anxiety as the person wonders why you do not get to the point.

Explain the purpose of the discussion and what will happen. Encourage dialogue through open-ended questions, rather than closed ones that produce a yes or no response.

Start by asking the person to talk about his or her performance since the last appraisal. If you agree with the assessment say so. Otherwise, remain quiet until he or she has finished and only then start to share your own perceptions.

It is important that you are specific and use real examples to support any adverse comments you make. When you use real issues, you may well touch nerves and turn a normal conversation into one that is more tricky to handle. This is why you need to develop your personal communication skills so that you can approach the situation in a positive and productive way.

Unpalatable truths

For some managers appraisals are an opportunity to dole out criticism for past behaviour. While the meeting is certainly a chance for some home truths, it is seldom effective to deliver these in a spirit of punishment and revenge.

Without pulling your punches, take care how you deliver

criticism and unpalatable facts. Always assume someone wants to do a good job.

SEE CHAPTER 11

If you criticise, do so with kindness, offering specific examples, not generalities.

■ The secret of giving adverse feedback is offering it with care and respect.

Rather than talking about what kind of person he or she is, focus on behaviour and actions. Do not cast doubts on someone's motives or integrity unless you have absolute proof, and even then think whether this will really achieve your purpose.

Also, avoid apologising for giving adverse feedback. The other person is entitled to know when he or she is not meeting your expectations.

During the conversation:

■ do plenty of listening
■ summarise regularly
■ take detailed notes.

Listening
Active listening is essential in any appraisal encounter.

SEE CHAPTER 18

If you speak for more than about a fifth of the time, this is not appraisal, it is lecturing. Reflect back to the other person your interpretation of what he or she is saying and feeling. Feelings are an important part of the appraisal experience and you need to carefully tap into what the other person is experiencing.

As a result of the discussion the appraisee will probably be making most of the changes, rather than you. So encourage the person to put forward ideas for change, rather than just saying what to do. That way the person is more likely to 'own' the changes and take responsibility for making them.

Summarise

Regularly pause to sum up where the conversation has reached. When you do the summing up it shows you are really listening. When the appraisee sums up, it helps that person show an understanding of the performance issues.

Try to share the summing up task between you.

Notes

Take notes as you go along. Otherwise, you may soon forget what occurred. Also, this helps to show the appraisee that you are interested and involved.

Once you reach some agreed aims for the next appraisal period, it is time to end the discussion by summarising the key points. Agree the next review date and explain what happens next. Thank the person for participating.

Ending it

Be sensitive to how the other person may feel by the end of the discussion. No matter how enjoyable you may have found the interchange, the appraisee may be only too glad to depart. Avoid too much more small talk, leaving the other person feeling 'If only I could get away'.

Follow-up

After the appraisal meeting, either you or the appraisee should complete a report showing the:

- original purpose of the meeting
- points discussed
- conclusions reached
- objectives set
- training and development actions required
- matters left unresolved.

Both parties should agree the contents with enough space to add comments. Parts of the report may need to be kept confidential, for example when there are issues of promotion or career changes. Keep such items to a minimum, as secrecy does not build trust.

The other person will be more committed to pursuing a goal, making a change or behaving differently if you show that you take the appraisal seriously. For example, if during the appraisal you agreed to undertake an action, complete your side of the bargain.

Consider asking the other person to comment on the appraisal experience to you or an independent third party. This will help you develop your own appraisal technique.

Ensure that the event concludes on a positive note with the person feeling up rather than down. You halve the chances of improvement if the appraisee departs in a state of gloom.

Team appraisal

An emerging trend is the move from appraising individual performance towards assessing the performance of an entire team. The impact of team appraisals can be considerable. However, these sessions are no substitute for meeting with each team member to review personal work performance.

In an effective team appraisal system, all members comment on the group's performance and sometimes on each other's contribution. For example, the team may offer its collective views on the effectiveness of the current leader. This kind of appraisal needs to be handled with care. It may be sensible to start such a process with an outside specialist's help.

Further reading

FLETCHER C. *Appraisal: Routes to improved performance*. London, CIPD, 1997.

GILLEN T. *The Appraisal Discussion*. London, CIPD, 1998.

GROTE D. 'Performance appraisals: solving tough challenges'. *HR Magazine*. Vol. 45, No. 7, July 2000. pp145–50.

HUNT N. *Conducting Staff Appraisals: How to manage the process for the benefit of both the organisation and its individual members*. Oxford, How To Books, 1997.

WYNNE B. *Performance Appraisal: A practical guide to appraising the performance of employees*. Hitchin, Technical Communications (Publishing) Ltd, 1995.

COACHING

Chapter 4

Coaching brings out the best in people. It is about using insight and creativity to improve performance. We are used to the idea of coaching in sport but the sort of coaching that makes a difference in business situations is more complex and often more demanding.

Through direct, one-to-one conversations, coaching can range from straight instruction to good listening and encouragement, from planned one-on-one sessions to working with a group to help it tackle a hard task.

The kind of coaching you need to do as a manager will almost certainly involve one-to-one conversations. These are part of the normal day-to-day work and are informal and spontaneous. You may also be expected to coach in formal, planned sessions.

Coaching has become a core management skill because increasingly people expect to receive solid management support for their work. They now look to managers not just for direction and decision-making but for stimulus, understanding and help in thinking about their work in creative and inspiring ways.

It is part of the job

Coaching is now built into virtually every manager's job, although not always explicitly. Every day, supervisors, managers and team leaders coach colleagues to be more effective, without necessarily calling it coaching. They focus on changing behaviour that alters performance.

With the shift of management away from command and control, coaching is no longer just about giving instruction or demonstrating a particular skill to the 'trainee'. Now it has a far wider remit, including:

■ stimulating people to find their *own* way to perform more effectively; it means helping a person to identify and begin to use personal resources and natural talent, in new, more creative ways.

The rise and rise of coaching as a management requirement also stems from the shift to expecting employees to take more responsibility for their own development. This makes greater demands on managers to be effective coaches.

Coaching is also a high-profile management skill, partly because organisations are facing constant change and growing complexity. Often, there is no 'right way' to do something, no unique solution that the manager can point to with superior knowledge or experience.

> *It can be no dishonour to learn from others when they speak good sense.*
>
> **Sophocles**

Increasingly, organisations need people to experiment, be creative, invent new answers to difficult questions, and take responsibility for solving a problem. In these situations, managers are no longer the source of all knowledge. Instead, others may have far more knowledge or skills.

So when managers coach, they are:

■ developing people's potential to perform well
■ using a strategic tool for ensuring that the organisation has the capabilities it needs to handle the future
■ passing on their knowledge and enthusiasms.

In essence, it is an empowering tool and a vital link between learning and doing.

Coaching differs from:

- training – which mainly uses formal learning processes and structured feedback
- counselling – which is a process for overcoming a specific situation or problem and often starts by looking at the past
- mentoring – which focuses mainly on career planning
- appraisal – which is usually a formal process conducted only a few times a year, often linked directly to issues such as promotion, objectives, meeting targets, stretching and multi-skilling.

What makes coaching special is the relationship with the person being coached. The ideal session is a conversation between equals, one of whom may happen to have more knowledge or skill. If you were to listen to one of these sessions you would notice that a common characteristic is there is strong mutual respect between both parties. Creating this respect begins with how the coach treats the other person.

While you may use coaching techniques to help someone solve a problem, or use specific information, the big push is for:

- performance coaching.

This is when you do most of the listening. You set up a learning environment where it is safe to fail – some cultures only allow failure within the actual coaching session, not on the job.

Such an environment needs to actively encourage:

- experimentation – talking about what gets in the way of higher levels of performance

- exploring new ways of working
- new forms of commitment
- changes in behaviour and new ways of approaching work.

When you concentrate on performance coaching, you do not need to be an unbeatable expert in a subject. After all, many successful tennis coaches have never actually won Wimbledon.

Acceptance

You cannot make someone accept coaching. A person reluctant to engage in the coaching process makes it an uphill struggle, distressing for both parties. So, an important early issue to face as a management coach is to:

- check that the person is really willing and motivated to accept coaching.

How do you get someone to accept coaching? It may, for example, require a separate conversation about the person's performance and the need to improve or develop. It may arise directly from some problem that has arisen, such as the person failing in some way, feeling stressed or unclear about how to prioritise. Or, it could arise because the individual concerned directly asks for help.

It is often sensible to separate the identification of the need for coaching from doing the coaching. That is, you help the person to first see that there is a problem that needs to be worked on. Sometimes this part may be done by someone else, for example by another manager, or by colleagues.

The process

Coaching involves:

- understanding

- practice
- feedback.

For this you need to:

- prepare
- meet
- follow-up.

Developing understanding is about being an insightful coach, someone who sees beyond the superficial problem or issue and goes beneath the surface. Where does this insight come from?

It mainly stems from a mixture of:

- being totally present – really 'seeing' what is happening and what is needed
- practice at working with people in a coaching situation
- learning to dig down and ask the right questions
- being in touch with what you are feeling and how you are being affected by the other person.

Framework

Each coach develops a personal style and may use a highly individual framework for tackling a particular performance issue. A useful one we sometimes use for our management coaching sessions is:

Assessment

■ Identify areas for change, put issues in context and jointly identify what seems to sabotage success.

■ Establish a clear baseline from which to start coaching by discovering what the person knows about the issue or his or her attitude to improving performance. Often you will be surprised by how much the person already knows. Inexperienced coaches plough ahead regardless, causing boredom or frustration.

■ Make the coaching environment as pleasant as possible and stop incoming phone calls and interruptions.

■ Allow learners to describe their current situation or skill in their own words. Offer open questions such as 'Tell me about . . .', 'How do you think you communicate?' This encourages learners to expound on what they know and may give you something highly relevant to work with.

■ Listen actively, without making judgements. This is no time to criticise or boast about your own skills. Concentrate instead on clarifying what exactly the person knows, can do and might want to learn.

Aims

■ Choose goals; reveal obstacles – what is getting in the way of you achieving them? Agree action to overcome them.

■ Ask the person to define personal development aims. Since you cannot readily impose learning objectives on someone else, encourage the person to take ownership of the process.

■ Explain how the coaching will work and agree a standard or result for the person to achieve. Treat the discussion of what is to be learned as a partnership, in which you both work together to define the outcome. Once this has been determined, summarise the learning objectives, preferably in writing.

■ Discuss learning objectives as if you are dealing with success, not faulty behaviour.

Explore

■ Create new possibilities for behaviour and action, using practical and creative techniques to stimulate further insight.

■ This is when you encourage the person to think of alternative behaviour, ways of acting or being not previously considered.

■ It is a creative session in which anything might be suggested or tried, so long as it is about doing things differently. If absolutely necessary, share what works for you without saying: 'This is the right way'.

■ Avoid overloading the learner with constant advice. Let the learner get on with it and grow through making mistakes.

Some performance coaching questions

■ How do you see yourself achieving that?
■ When do you see yourself achieving this – what is the timetable?
■ What would you like to do?
■ When do you think you will complete that?
■ How do you see that working?
■ What resources will you need?
■ Who else will be working with you on this?
■ How could you do that better next time?
■ What would success look like?
■ How could you make that happen?
■ Where do you plan to do this?
■ What are the choices facing you?

Rehearse

■ Practise new actions and behaviour, improve and experiment. You create a safe place in which the person tries new ways of performing. It is an environment in which failure reveals as much as success and where people are congratulated for trying.

■ This is when you may need to exercise patience, allowing the other person to struggle, without providing the answer. It can be agonising and frustrating, knowing someone is not performing well, yet only by failing in a safe place will the person grow and develop.

■ Identify learning opportunities to practise. For example, you may want to help someone improve how he or she handles meetings. Before running a real meeting, though, you may be able to create some simulated meetings in which the person practises chairing skills and receives honest feedback.

Perform

■ The person takes agreed actions and new learning into life and work.

■ You may also need to offer hands-on opportunities where the person knows what authority he or she has to act and that there is freedom to make mistakes. It may require ingenuity on your part to create such an environment.

■ Remind the learner that you are available to help if needed and clarify when the next coaching situation will occur.

Review

■ Reflect on the effects of action, absorb feedback and adjust goals where necessary.

■ Good coaches monitor and work to sustain development and growth. There needs to be plenty of praise and encouragement at this stage. Use open and probing questions such as: 'What did you discover from doing it that way?'

■ Avoid conducting a cross-examination – aim to be a 'mirror' for a person rather than a critic.

■ Encourage the learner to try again, perhaps offering a few tips. Rather than demand wholesale changes ('you are going to have to do it entirely differently'), suggest an adjustment before the learner goes off to try again.

■ Avoid words like 'wrong', 'bad', and 'incorrect'. Instead, leave room for people to assess themselves. Ask questions rather than pass judgement. Refrain from showing the person entirely what to do, instead encourage a return to another hands-on attempt.

■ Constantly recap, summarising learning points and the agreed action.

■ Use questions to prompt discussion about progress and to check the learner's understanding.

■ Give praise while looking for more good points to reinforce.

Complete

■ Acknowledge achievements and make plans for the next steps while maintaining the change.

■ Coaching works best when there is a clear start and finish to the work. Avoid allowing the coaching to drift into endless sessions that cover absolutely everything.

■ Jointly agree ways in which the new learning and behaviour can be reinforced.

■ Ask the person to take responsibility for reporting back, which could lead to celebration of success.

■ Give credit where it is due. Be willing to congratulate the person on achievements and acknowledge the changes that have occurred.

Other frameworks

The above framework is only a guide; you may not need to adopt all of it. Nor is it necessarily one that will work best for you. However, it does cover the broad steps used in a coaching programme.

A popular coaching framework used by experienced coaches is the GROW model. This four-stage approach is easy to remember and a powerful tool in the right hands.

The GROW Model: A simple framework for steering an individual coaching session
Goal
What would you like to discuss?
What would you like to achieve?
What would you like from this session?
If I could grant you a wish for this session, what would it be?
Can we do that in the time available?
Reality
What is happening now?
How do you know that is accurate?
When does it happen?
How often does it happen?
What effect does this have?
What have you tried so far?
Options
What could you do to change the situation?
Are there alternatives to that approach?
Who might be able to help?
Would you like suggestions from me?
Would you like to choose an option to act on?
What I will do (wrap-up)
How will I monitor progress?
What evidence will demonstrate that things are different?
What are the next steps?
When exactly will you take them – the timetable?
What might get in the way?
What support do you need?
How will you obtain this support?

Based on *The Tao of Coaching* by Max Landsberg (Harper Collins, 1997).

Success as a coach

---

10 coaching tips from those on the receiving end

- Treat me as a person in my own right.
- Set me a good example.
- Encourage and support me.
- Praise me when I do well.
- Back me up with your superiors.
- Do your own job competently.
- Do not pull rank on me.
- Keep me informed about what I need to know.
- Take time from your normal duties to coach me.
- Never underestimate what I can do.

Successful coaches get satisfaction from the success of others and make time for the coaching role. The gain is not one-sided. It is a learning experience for you too because you:

- develop your own leadership skills
- give people a chance to contribute their ideas
- create results while learning
- enhance your skills and competency of coach and learner
- bring a focus on quality
- generate ownership and commitment.

What do you need?

If you treat coaching as a drain on your time then it is better to avoid coaching altogether. People soon detect that your heart is not in it. But it can be one of the great satisfactions of being a successful manager. When you coach, you do not rely on using your formal authority. Instead, you are influencing and persuading, drawing the best from the other person, devoting your best efforts to stimulate excellent performance.

You will almost certainly have to rearrange your priorities and make space for the coaching sessions. This will ultimately save you time as people become more confident, proactive and better performers.

> *We simply cannot afford the luxury of managing people in the same way as we have in the past. All managers have had to become more of a coach and counsellor, leaders who are receptive to the notion of empowerment.*
>
> Stephen Croni, Group Personnel Director, Rank Xerox

Managers who demand high levels of control seldom make good coaches, since this tends to reduce people's sense of ownership about the learning. Your own management style, priorities and attitudes affect how people respond to you as a coach. Adapt your approach to different people by listening to what they need, which might include:

- opportunities to gain experience
- reflecting on their personal development and performance
- a chance to develop ideas and guidelines about what to do
- experimenting with new skills and methods.

10 coaching techniques

- Acknowledgement – catch the learner doing something right
- Examples – use immediate situations to point out learning
- Model good practice – show by example
- Challenge – warn him or her first, and then play 'devil's advocate'
- What has changed? – find differences since the last meeting
- Focus on *how* to resolve an issue, rather than the issue itself
- Limit alternatives – avoid deflection from the main point
- Goal review – how far have aims been achieved?
- Positive reframing – taking another perspective
- Scaling – rate changes or effectiveness from 1 to 10.

Most of the time staying cool and dispassionate as a coach helps learners to think things through for themselves. Yet if you stay too 'managerial' and distant, you may be seen as impersonal and uncaring. Successful coaching depends on building a relationship and you cannot easily do that if you stay too detached.

It can be extremely satisfying to have someone hanging on your every word, but good coaches are wary of this happening. For example:

■ Are you creating dependency, rather than independence and confidence?
■ Are you infantilising the person by assuming that he or she cannot take responsibility or exercise personal power?
■ Are you directing and giving answers, rather than forcing the person to think for him or herself?

There are few greater management challenges than learning to coach well. Be willing to experiment with your coaching style and most of all – be a learner!

Do you need coaching?

You may also sometimes need coaching for yourself. An increasing number of managers find that having a personal coach is a good way to:

■ handle stress
■ think through problems
■ re-examine goals and values
■ be more creative in their leadership.

Private executive coaching is growing fast, particularly in the USA, and the trend is strongly upwards in Europe too. It is sometimes hard to convey the benefits, but as one manager facing a stressful mid-career move put it, her year of coaching was 'like a grenade in my life that's still going off'. It taught her 'people have to take more responsibility for their own growth and development. Coaches can help people come to grips with huge change.'

Coaches are everywhere these days, often on the phone, rather than doing it face-to-face. Companies hire them to shore up executives or sometimes to ship them out. Many managers, fed up with minimal advice from inside the company, are taking matters into their own hands. They are enlisting coaches for guidance on how to improve their performance, boost their profits, and make better decisions about everything from personnel to strategy.

You are just as entitled to have a personal coach as someone much more senior in the organisation. Some would argue that it is essential.

Choosing a coach

■ Check that the coach is really experienced – speak to some people who have used that coach before.

■ Before you have the first meeting, establish what you specifically want from the relationship.

■ If you intend to use telephone coaching, have at least one or two face-to-face meetings first to establish the relationship.

■ It is less important that the coach knows your own industry or your job than that he or she has a good coaching track record.

■ Make it a time-limited programme, rather than one that drifts on for months or years with no end date in mind.

■ Your own coaching sessions are a way of bridging the gap between what you are being asked to do and what you have been trained to do.

Further reading

ATHERTON T. *How to be Better at Delegation and Coaching*. London, Kogan Page, 1999.

LANDSBERG M. *The Tao of Coaching*. London, Harper Collins, 1997.

LEIGH A. *Coaching with Confidence*. London, Maynard Leigh Associates, 1998.

LEIGH A. *Creating a Coaching Culture*. London, Maynard Leigh Associates, 1998.

PARSLOE E. *The Manager as Coach and Mentor*. London, CIPD, 1999.

YEUNG R. *The Things that Really Matter about Coaching People*. Oxford, How To Books, 2000.

NEGOTIATING

Negotiation is the polite word for bargaining. And bargaining simply means haggling. People do it in bazaars and in multinational trading corporations. You cannot avoid it in your job if you are to be effective.

The Internet has dramatically altered both how people bargain and the variety of situations where it is possible. Individuals can negotiate with each other, with a single supplier or a whole group of them. Companies now combine to bargain with other companies to obtain everything from office supplies to machine parts.

Whether you work in a large company or sell your services as a freelancer, you will end up bargaining in some way. If you outsource your IT services, the cost will finally come down to a bargaining situation.

Most managers negotiate through:

■ informal bargaining
■ formal bargaining with trade unions and other bodies
■ commercial bargaining.

Informal bargaining occurs so often that we hardly think twice about it. For example, when you ask a team to complete a job by mid-week and they respond that the end of the week would be preferable, you are both negotiating. If you mention to your boss that you think it is time you got a pay rise and you get a non-committal answer, that is bargaining too.

Formal negotiating usually involves a trade union or other representative body. While it may be amicable, it can still demand hard bargaining. This might encompass issues such as annual pay agreements, working practices or introducing new technology.

Commercial bargaining is about making business deals. For example, negotiating a new contract with a supplier, completing an important sale or agreeing a takeover.

Effective negotiators possess:

- a quick mind
- a strong reserve of patience
- an ability to conceal without lying
- a capacity to inspire trust
- an ability to know when to be assertive and when to be self-effacing
- knowledge of the issue
- an ability to see the broader picture.

Large companies resort to specialist negotiators who they hope will be expert bargainers. For example, procurement departments do little else but bargain to get the best deals.

Even if you delegate the bargaining job to an expert, you will not escape becoming involved in issues such as power, strategy, tactics and fallback positions.

Effective negotiators:

- ask twice as many questions
- give 40 per cent less information away
- do more than twice as much testing, understanding and summarising
- use few support arguments – they stick to just one or two good reasons, rather than relying on a whole string of them.

What you negotiate for is even more important than how you negotiate. There is no point in doing it brilliantly if you are negotiating about the wrong things. Successful managers conduct their negotiations in the wider context of the organisation's strategic intent. They bargain in order to build the future.

Power

Ultimately power decides the result of a bargaining situation. Your bargaining power depends on the:

■ strength of your negotiation position once all bluffing has ended.

If one side holds total power, there is no scope for bargaining. It only happens at the margin, where both sides believe they can obtain something of what they what.

So bargaining occurs when there is a slight imbalance of power. In this situation, each party tends to try to minimise the disadvantages rather than maximising their gains. If you attempt to do both simultaneously, you may not optimise the outcome.

Know your bargaining power

How much bargaining power you possess depends on:

■ the losses you would suffer if you were to agree or disagree with what the other party wants
■ the losses the other party would suffer by agreeing or disagreeing with what you want.

> **Know your bargaining power**
>
> ■ Calculate roughly how much power you possess.
> ■ Apply knowledge of your position to the bargaining situation.
> ■ Analyse the situation to see how power is spread between the parties.
> ■ Use your knowledge of the power situation to formulate a strategy.
> ■ Exercise your power to get what you want.

Despite the many unknowns in most bargaining situations, you can almost certainly improve your ability to negotiate by analysing your bargaining power. It is not enough to just rely on instinct. There is a natural temptation to plunge into negotiations simply to test the reality of your bargaining power. However, this is usually a weak negotiating stance and will probably not help you get the best result. Before starting any actual negotiations:

■ spend time assessing your bargaining power.

For example, you may be able to strengthen your position by basing it on facts, rather than speculation or wishful thinking. This will enable you to create a sound negotiation strategy and bargain with more confidence.

Conflict v co-operation

At some point, negotiating comes down to resolving conflict. If you hate conflict or always tend to avoid it, you will probably not enjoy negotiating. To improve your negotiation skills you will need to become more comfortable with facing up to and resolving conflict.

Negotiating implies that both parties are initially some way apart in their positions. Sometimes, this emerges into the open, as with an industrial dispute. Everyone involved knows it exists and the main issue is how to resolve it satisfactorily. Occasionally the conflict is beneath the surface of the discussions. No one alludes to it, yet it exists.

You can improve your negotiation results by taking into account the different types of result you can achieve:

- win/lose – one party gains and the other loses
- win/win – both parties gain a mutual benefit
- lose/lose – neither party gains a benefit.

When you think about a particular negotiation situation, which outcome do you want? Effective negotiators usually try for a win/win situation where both parties leave feeling good about the outcome.

In some commercial negotiations, though, the aim is to achieve gains at the other party's expense. Seeking a win/lose position often occurs when managers deal with trade unions or those with relatively less power. The trouble with seeking a win/lose result is that it may not be the best possible outcome for either side.

In commercial bargaining or informal negotiations between departments and divisions, or between you and individuals, both sides usually need to emerge with a sense of victory.

It is important to unravel the exact nature of the conflict, since there may be many elements creating it. You can clarify the nature of conflict if you:

- state the issue about which you will be negotiating
- list the points you and the other party are most likely to raise
- for each point, state the most likely settlement
- decide how close the results are that each side wants.

69

Big differences in desired results create win/lose situations

A traditional view of negotiation is that it is always confrontational, in which win/lose is inevitable. If you are a highly competitive, driven individual, for example, then you may relish treating all your management negotiations as based around conflict.

Increasingly managers need to treat negotiation more as a form of collaboration where you look for a win/win situation. It seldom makes sense, for example, to always move rapidly to litigation, or to humiliate your opponent. Instead, it may be more effective to avoid stalemate and achieve fairness.

Negotiation stages

Management negotiations consist of several distinct stages:

- prepare
- offer
- clarify
- negotiate
- close
- implement.

Sometimes these are combined, occurring rapidly with little or no time gaps between them.

Prepare

Prepare in depth when the stakes are high. Too often managers face experienced opponents who have done their homework thoroughly.

Preparation means defining:

- your negotiating aim – the settlement you want
- your bargaining power compared with the other side's
- what your negotiating strategy will be

■ whether you can strengthen your power or weaken the other side's

■ what the detailed bargaining points are that will achieve your overall aim

■ whether your case is well-researched and documented

■ whether the bargaining team is fully briefed

■ whether those who will bargain on your behalf know the limits of their authority.

Prior to serious negotiations, for example, most trained trade union representatives analyse what may arise during the discussions and assess bargaining strengths. They would also determine which outcomes are essential and which are merely desirable.

It can be disconcerting to start negotiating thinking that you will talk about one set of issues only to discover that the other party has a long list of others they intend raising. So develop a clear picture of the territory over which the negotiations may range:

■ What issues will the other party be likely to raise?

■ What information do you need to deal with these issues?

■ What is your intended response to these issues?

■ What is negotiable and what is non-negotiable?

■ What will make you walk away from the negotiating table – that is, what is your bottom line?

Suppose you decide on the top limit to a proposed pay increase. This becomes your non-negotiable position. Once you know it, you can review different ways to approach the negotiations:

■ What are your highest and lowest demands?

■ What concessions are you willing to make?

■ What are the biggest and smallest concessions?

Strategy

Your bargaining strategy is how you intend to get what you want. It is your battle plan. It may consist of various bargaining tactics.

Negotiating strategy needs to alter according to each situation, so adopt a flexible approach. For example, your exact strategy depends on:

- your bargaining strength
- your relationship with the other party
- other constraints, such as conventions.

You can also have either an offensive or defensive negotiating strategy. For example, a win/lose approach is an offensive strategy, while a win/win approach is a defensive one.

Although a win/win strategy is usually an ideal outcome, it only works if the other party has a similar approach, or can be persuaded to adopt it. If the other party is using a win/lose mode, it may be harder to reach an outcome.

It is generally more effective to start negotiations using a win/win approach, since you can revert to win/lose later. If you start with the latter position, though, you cannot easily revert to a win/win strategy because by then trust may have broken down between both parties.

Since no single strategy works for all occasions, watch out for:

- opening moves
- attempts to increase bargaining power
- sanctions.

Opening moves are an important part of effective negotiations because they set the pattern for future discussions. For example, one of your opening moves might be to insist that the negotiations exclude any discussion about future redundancies. Once the other party agrees to this it may prevent them raising all kinds of issues that you want to avoid. Or the other party may ask the negotiations to occur in a location of their choice, which may not suit you.

Increasing your bargaining power

- Try to determine the agenda, for example by excluding or including certain issues.
- Recruit an ally.
- Obtain important new information.
- Gain advantage over the other party.
- Delay negotiations until you improve your position.
- Initiate action in another area, raising the costs to the other party of disagreeing with your offer.
- Link the current issue with other ones that may not initially seem significant, yet later become critical.
- Weaken the other party's position in some way.

Ideally, you should do everything possible to maximise your position. However, improving your bargaining position is not an end in itself. For example, if you are dealing with people who report to you, they are likely to feel you have quite enough power already.

Sanctions are a drastic way to alter your bargaining position. You can use them either before or during negotiations. They are a way of punishing the other party; only do this if you previously assessed the likely response and can accept the consequences.

A typical sanction is announcing during a strike that you will not negotiate unless people first return to work. A more drastic one is threatening to lock employees out unless they first return to work. A typical sanction in commercial negotiations is to warn the other party that the price will rise if a settlement cannot be agreed by a certain date, or if the order is not of a sufficient size.

Sanctions are manipulative and can quickly cause antagonism. They can therefore damage the final settlement. However, they do show that you mean business and affirm your bargaining position.

Offer

At some point you will need to put your offer on the table, unless you merely accept someone else's. This is when you state your position confidently and clearly. Explain what you want, without offering many specifics.

What should be your opening bid in a negotiating situation? Pitch it too high and you risk driving the other party from the negotiating table. Set it too low and you may find it hard to achieve a settlement above this later.

Generally, a high initial demand works better than a low one. For example, it is harder to start low and increase your demands, than to start high and reduce them.

You know that your opening bid has been set too low if the other party immediately accepts it. But this may not matter if you have decided in advance what your minimum requirements are.

At this point if you need further information, ask open questions requiring more than a yes or a no. Using a process of questions and answers, you may never need to put your full offer on the table, instead allowing it to emerge naturally as the negotiations progress.

Present your initial offer as a basis for discussion. An experienced trade union negotiator, for example, will simply respond to a 'take it or leave it' statement as merely a negotiating tactic.

Clarify the situation

Any offer will almost certainly need further clarification. This can be a crucial way of eliminating unnecessary conflicts. For example, you might seek agreement on issues such as timescale, what certain terms mean, the scale of charges, the implications of cancelling an order halfway through a contract and so on.

Having listened to the other party's aims:

■ summarise the aims of both parties
■ obtain agreement that your summary is correct.

Many negotiations fail at this stage because one or more parties makes assumptions about the nature of the offer that later prove to be wrong. For example, in some merger situations both parties claim it is a joining of equals. When later this proves incorrect, there is conflict and a possible breakdown of the arrangements.

Deutsche Bank tried to merge with its old rival Dresden Bank in early 2000. The negotiations were a classic example of failing to face up to inherent conflicts.

Both banks claimed it was to be a merger of equals, but later this proved wrong as Deutsche Bank tried to throw its weight around and ultimately antagonised senior members of the other organisation.

Failure to negotiate clear terms about what would happen to an important trading arm led to key staff leaving and finally the whole deal crumbled.

'No' may really mean:

- Give me more information.
- I cannot afford it at that price.
- How can I trust you?
- Can I justify this to my boss?
- You get on my nerves.
- I'm not signing because I don't understand it.
- How can I say yes without losing face?

Negotiate

This is when there is give and take by both parties. You each jostle for a position that ultimately may not be achievable. Although every bargaining situation is unique, the general negotiating process is similar. You are searching for:

- a consensus
- an advantage
- a settlement.

In the hunt for these you need to adopt some spoken or sometimes unspoken acceptable ground rules:

- We previously bargained about an issue, so we can do so now.
- We stick to what we agree.
- There is a deadline for completing our negotiations.
- It is disruptive to impose sanctions before the negotiating deadline.
- There is always room for manoeuvre in both parties' position.

The last of these is a particularly important assumption, since it underpins most negotiations. There is room for manoeuvre because you have more than one position:

■ *Ideal settlement:* the negotiations achieve everything you want and maybe more.
■ *Acceptable settlement:* gives you most of what you wanted and is acceptable because the costs of trying to achieve still more would be too high.
■ *Minimum fallback position:* you must achieve this or you will leave.

Tactics

You adopt tactics as part of negotiating. Two important ones are:

■ Assume everything is negotiable.
■ Never offer a concession without receiving one in return.

No matter how strongly the other party asserts its position, assume that at some price, or with some concession, the other party can be persuaded to do what you want.

You may not know the price of the final settlement; merely take it for granted that it can be achieved. If everything can be negotiated, it encourages you to bargain with confidence and to keep looking for opportunities to reach a conclusion.

Since most negotiations consist of concessions by both parties, it is a sound tactic to only give something away if you get back something in return. For example, when negotiating with a customer who demands a discount, you might concede it in exchange for a large order.

Sometimes what you get in return may not be entirely tangible. It might for example be goodwill or renewed motivation. For example, your response to a subordinate who asks for an extra day off might be to demand that he or she completes a report before leaving.

Dos and don'ts

- Trade – don't concede.
- Ask – don't assume.
- Get what you want – not even.
- Respond – don't react.
- Build bridges – don't burn boats.
- Focus on what matters – not minor issues.
- Think long term – not short term.
- Stay calm – don't take it personally.
- Be patient – don't act in haste.
- See their side of it – not just your own.

Choose a tactic because you believe it will help you achieve a specific result. For instance, during a negotiation rather than saying 'Let's have coffee,' instead choose a moment when an adjournment buys you time to consider an issue, or take the pressure off you or your negotiating team.

Requesting an adjournment is also a useful way of encouraging your opponent to spend time considering whether to accept an offer, without losing face.

Well-tried tactics

- In the early stages, conceal as much information about your own position as you think sensible.
- Try redefining how the other party sees its own position, so encouraging a shift towards your own position.
- Undermine the arguments of the other party by:
  - challenging assumptions
  - disputing facts; attacking conclusions
  - pointing out inconsistencies.
- Reduce the other party's credibility by:
  - questioning their experience

- ■ suggesting that they are losing control
- ■ negotiating to the point of their mental exhaustion.
- ■ Strengthen your own arguments and credibility by:
  - ■ demonstrating a mastery of detail
  - ■ making an appeal to reason or emotion
  - ■ minimising your weaknesses by claiming the point has already been taken into account.
- ■ Encourage the other party to move their position by:
  - ■ summarising the negotiations so far
  - ■ suggesting it is time for mutual concessions
  - ■ offering a new position that represents a different point of departure for both parties
  - ■ linking two or more issues to help get nearer a settlement
  - ■ suggest an adjournment while indicating that during it you want the other party to pay attention to a certain issue.
- ■ Help the other party abandon a previous commitment by:
  - ■ describing all the concessions you have made so far
  - ■ suggesting that circumstances have changed
  - ■ blaming some other party or situation for the present situation – for example the Government, another union, competitive pressures
  - ■ suggesting that there has been a misunderstanding; referring the whole matter for resolution to another individual or group – for example asking ACAS, the government arbitration service, to help reach a settlement.
- ■ Attempt to move towards a settlement. Be alert for ways of concluding matters – choose a moment when events are going well.
- ■ In reaching a settlement, ask the other party to restate it in their own words.
- ■ Agree ways to monitor that the settlement is being implemented as intended.
- ■ Insist on finalising and documenting the agreement.

Never underestimate the power of a smile to move the negotiations on. If you are always frowning and looking serious, the other party may adopt the same approach and from there on it can be downhill.

It is easy to assume that the other party has all the power, but this is seldom the case. Work through your position and you will almost certainly find you have more leverage than you thought at first.

Close
Now it is time to summarise what you have discussed and ask:

■ Have we got a deal?

It may seem tough to growl, 'take it or leave it', but this is seldom good negotiating tactics. It merely encourages the other party to say, 'I'll leave it then', wasting the time spent negotiating so far. However, it can pay to be absolutely frank and explain that you have absolutely no further room for manoeuvre. For example, you might shrug and explain that 'this is all the money we have for a pay rise, there just isn't any more. So do we have a deal or not?'

When you summarise what has been agreed, be sure that the other party keeps nodding as you list the areas of agreement. If you detect any hesitation, stop and check again that you have agreement.

In closing, confirm that you will be producing your own notes of the agreement and will be circulating them.

Implementation
Successful negotiations mean some agreed action, or even inaction:

- A trade union agrees to adopt a new working practice, not to ban overtime, not to go on strike.
- A customer accepts a contract, a price, a delivery time.
- A direct report agrees to behave in a new way, write a report, complete a project.
- Another department agrees to produce a product, provide information, join a project team.
- You agree not to take legal action in return for a supplier replacing faulty equipment.

It is sometimes said that whoever writes the minutes of a meeting holds the real power, and in negotiating situations this can certainly be true. With complicated negotiations, it may be hard to remember every concession and every figure agreed.

If the other party fails to make careful notes, yours may be the ones that ultimately determine the final arrangements. Even if the other party does make careful notes and circulates them after the bargaining session, be sure that you have your own version ready to circulate. This helps retain your authority over the entire process.

When an agreement has been reached, the follow-through should involve both parties. Since many negotiations break down at this point, it is worth making a prior commitment jointly to monitor progress. This would include a further meeting shortly after implementation begins.

Joint monitoring of implementation allows a rapid response to any divergence from what both parties expect from the negotiations. It also enables you to jointly agree some action.

Top 10 principles

■ Don't bargain unless you need to. If you can achieve what you want without making a concession, don't offer one.

■ Do your research. Learn as much as possible about your bargaining power and the other party's.

■ Make the other side respond. Issuing an important demand early on and sticking to it forces the other party to work hard to obtain concessions.

■ Initially, apply power gently. Only gradually, let the message percolate through that you could do the other party harm, cause them problems, or offer benefits.

■ Make them compete. Typically in sales negotiations, force the other party to try hard to get your attention, letting them know or think that they could lose out to someone else.

■ Leave yourself room. Allow enough space to manoeuvre around the offer; initially ask for more than you expect and concede less than you would ultimately be willing to give.

■ Maintain your integrity. Do not lie; if you make a commitment, stick to it. If necessary be tough and abrasive, yet always trustworthy.

■ Listen more than talk. Encourage the other party to reveal its information and position first; the more you listen the more you will learn about how to increase your bargaining power.

■ Keep contact with their hopes. Stay in touch with the other party's reactions and expectations. Large demands need to be floated gently – there is a limit to how much you can demand without causing deadlock; watch for signs the other party is being pushed too far or too fast.

■ Let them get used to your big ideas. It may take time to come to terms with your demands; be patient and try not to settle too early.

E-mail negotiation

The Web is producing some entirely new negotiation situations that managers may find themselves facing. For example, instead of just issuing a price list of products or services, managers may face exactly the same from potential customers clubbing together. Their message is simply 'here's what we're prepared to pay, want to deal?'

Recruitment, financial deals and purchases may all require your attention. But around one-fifth of all such negotiations by e-mail tend to fail. Dealing with someone at the end of a modem is clearly different from eyeballing them across the table.

In e-mail negotiations you may find that the other party is:

- more ready to hold back information
- tougher in making demands
- wants shared rewards
- less ready to make concessions
- less willing to break a deadlock or compromise
- readier to use delaying tactics
- more likely to suddenly shift tactics or bargaining stance
- more combative.

Because there is less scope to use your body language of shrugs, smiles, grins or nods, you may find it harder to communicate easily with the other person informally.

How can you improve your chances of making your e-mail negotiation succeed? Probably the simplest step you can take is try and get to know the other party first before you try to negotiate through the computer. For example, can you talk over the phone, have a brief meeting, or a videoconference?

Next you can share some personal information before starting the serious business of bargaining. If your e-mail correspondence gets bogged down, move it on by a phone call or meeting.

Finally you can call in some honest broker to provide a neutral oiling of the wheels. In routine negotiations, for example, insurance claims can be settled via a third party this way.

Training

Negotiating is an art, not a science. Not everyone is a natural bargainer but it is surprising how much you can learn from practice and how much confidence you can gain by role-plays and simulations.

You can obtain formal training in analysis, preparation and tactics. Trade unions, for example, run extensive negotiating training sessions for their full-time officials and it is sensible for managers to receive similar help.

A typical programme may last around three days.

Further reading

FISHER R. and URY W. *Getting to Yes: Negotiating an agreement without giving way*. London, Business Books, 1991.

HODGSON J. *Thinking on Your Feet in Negotiations: Rapid response tactics*. London, Prentice Hall, 2000.

KENNEDY G. *Everything is Negotiable*. London, Hutchinson Business Books, 1982.

MADDUX R.B. *Successful Negotiation: How to create a win-win situation*. London, Kogan Page, 1999.

SERBIUS J. and LAX D. 'Interests, value and the art of the best deal'. *The Financial Times*. 2 October 2000.

STEELE P.T. and BEASOR T. *Business Negotiation: A practical workbook*. Aldershot, Gower, 1999.

REPORT-WRITING

Anybody can write a management report. The hard part is getting someone to read it. The world is awash with management reports; it is almost like a disease. Most managers and leaders spend much of their working lives reading or escaping from countless reports of some kind.

So, is your report necessary? Often you will be more effective delivering a simple verbal presentation. Communicating in person can be nerve-wracking, yet it can also have more impact than relying on written words.

Given the power of a verbal presentation, is it sensible to even bother with a written report? What are such reports for and when are they essential?

The changing report environment

E-mail and the Web have changed how managers tackle reports. Once, reports were carefully prepared in near secrecy and only released at a carefully chosen moment.

E-mail and web technology make it more appropriate to draft a few lines around an idea and ask for lots of people to critique it. From here the report evolves, maybe page-by-page, until the final version is one to which a whole host of people have contributed.

Conventions such as spelling mistakes and the like become less critical because the two essentials in this electronic hothouse are:

- speed
- involvement.

Speed

The faster pace of the business world leaves less time for the nuances of report-writing that once dominated. A terrific layout, a superb set of charts and a wonderfully argued case are often less influential now than simply getting your ideas and proposals into the system. A pressure for speed, though, does not always apply so much with finished documents where sloppiness of thought or of presentation can still undermine your ability to persuade.

Involvement

Far more people expect to be party to any report that impinges on their area. Because of the ease of sharing through e-mail, there is less excuse for not consulting and involving others in your report preparation.

Choice

Most management reports deal with a choice about what to do next. They are usually concerned with taking action – even though this might mean doing nothing for the moment.

People need written reports because these contain more information than can be conveyed verbally or because a personal presentation is impractical. For example, bringing all the interested parties together in a room to consider your arguments may be too expensive.

Successful managers:

■ know when a written report is the best solution
■ understand that adding the strategic context helps make a report powerful.

Understanding these points will almost certainly help distinguish you from other report writers: first, because so many people rush to send a written report when it is not needed; second, because placing your report in a strategic context conveys a level of awareness that senior colleagues will find both thoughtful and useful.

You may be asked by a senior person to 'prepare a report' and it is tempting to simply just get on with it. While that may seem like the right response – 'doing as you're asked' – it may eventually prove exactly the opposite.

Instead, analyse what lies behind the request. A verbal report may be just as acceptable. Also, you may uncover that the real reason for the request differs from the one you started with.

For example, digging may reveal that the person asking for the report wants to impress senior colleagues, to shake up people's thinking, to sound a warning and so on. Knowing the true purpose makes it easier to tailor material suitably.

A written report also freezes your views publicly, far more than a verbal one. Even within a quick e-mail floating a report idea, having launched it, you cannot easily retract contentious facts, uncomfortable conclusions or erroneous arguments. While people are forgiving of these in the e-mail environment, it is still important to think through:

■ Do I really want my views, observations or findings permanently out there?

The strategic context

Placing your material within a strategic context means relating it to:

■ *strategic intent* – what the organisation wants to achieve, broad aims, aspirations and vision for its future

■ *formal plans* – such as a business plan showing how its aims will be achieved.

If you do not know these, now is the time to discover them. Simply asking the questions will tend to raise your personal profile and word soon gets around.

Having decided that a written report really would be useful, your next task is to select what kind to create. For example, e-mail creates a natural pressure to put your material straight into writing. However, people can easily ignore e-mails. A physical document can often prove preferable, even though it involves more effort to print and circulate it. Its length can also prove critical, as can the structure and the overall message.

Writing a formal report
Preparation

■ identifying the issue
■ terms of reference or report requirement
■ information-gathering
■ analysis.

Production

■ structuring
■ writing, testing, revising, editing
■ summarising
■ physical production and distribution.

Follow-through

■ presentation
■ further action.

The two starting points for any management report, whether a formal hard copy document or an e-mail presentation, are:

■ defining the audience
■ using plain English.

It is essential that you understand your audience and discover what it needs. This is fundamental to any management communication and particularly so for a written report.

Short, simple words and easy-to-read brief paragraphs are the foundations for good report-writing, especially if you are relying on e-mail to get things done.

Persuasion

Your reports are all about persuasion – using the written word to make something happen that you want. The basics of persuasion appear in the 'persuasion pyramid'.

The persuasion pyramid

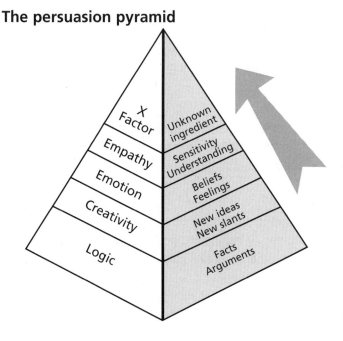

The core of most business reports is a logical argument:

- *link* – a logical link between one part of the document and another
- *connection* – clear joins between paragraphs
- *flow* – a natural sequence in which one set of facts or arguments lead obviously to another.

These features enable your readers to grasp the relationship between disparate bits of information. It helps them answer unspoken questions, such as:

- Why are you telling me this?
- What is the connection between this and that?
- How have you arrived at this conclusion?
- What evidence supports this argument
- Why is this true?

Logic

Logic alone, though, is seldom enough to persuade others to do what you want. If you are relatively new to the management role, you might imagine that common sense will prevail, so long as your report reflects sound logic. Surely, readers will see the logic and act accordingly?

Sadly, this is seldom the case. Business people are human and respond from both the heart and the head. Build that awareness into your material.

Creativity

Persuasive documents go well beyond mere logic and inject creativity into them. Simply telling people what they already know does not show that you have a grasp of the topic; instead it is a giant turn-off.

Finding that vital creative ingredient is what makes persuasive writing such a challenge. You need to find something unexpected to add value and go beyond what people expect.

Emotion
Because business colleagues are not soulless logic machines – however much some of them may appear that way – your reports need to contain an emotional element: this might be what you or others believe, or shared feelings about an issue. It is something that enables you to make contact with other human beings.

Injecting emotion does not mean flowery language or quoting poetry. It is merely important to show that you really care about the issues and convey relevant feelings such as excitement, concern, enthusiasm and so on.

Empathy
Sound management reports also convey empathy and understanding for the audience. They seldom work as just bald words on paper or a screen. Look for ways to demonstrate an appreciation for what the audience needs to make a choice or form an opinion.

The x factor
Persuasive reports and writing is an art, not a science. So there is often a unique ingredient that helps make the material impactful. This could be a:

- story
- picture
- quote
- sequence of facts
- promise.

Equally it could be your personal style, your presentation, how you deliver the material and so on. Only you, the report creator, can find and inject this unknown ingredient.

While there are now many powerful guidelines for effective management reports, the ones that persuade tend to be:

- focused
- brief
- readable
- structured
- credible
- presentable
- accountable.

Focused

Do you know exactly who will read your report? Sometimes it is not immediately obvious. Unknown people may end up with your material and they may prove ultimately the ones who influence action.

For example, you may give a report to a board of directors, all of whom you know quite well; you may even be one of them. What you may *not* know is that the chairman shows your report to a colleague not even in the organisation whose response may prove the defining one.

Invest time checking out:

- Who else might read my report?

Being highly focused also means holding a mental picture of a specific person for whom you are writing. Imagine talking to them and how you would explain what the material is all about. If you have done your focusing well, you should almost hear their reactions in your mind as you write.

It makes you more precise in your writing when you adopt a single person as your immediate focus. Even when you are directing your report at a team, a board of directors or a committee, think of at least one of them to whom you can address your message.

Brief

E-mail is reducing people's readiness to spend ages ploughing through a dozen pages to reach material that can be summarised in three lines.

It is easier to write a long report than a short one. It takes far more time to produce a short one that is not wordy and makes the point in the shortest possible space. Being concise takes time and effort.

Most management reports are overlong. Some companies insist that all reports fit on a single A4 page. This ruthless approach forces writers to be clear about what really matters. An extreme solution works.

A powerful device you can apply to your report is to:

■ eliminate every other word and see what is left.

This seemingly crazy exercise will instantly show all the words and phrases you can drop, in favour of yet more simplicity:

■ Keep your report brief enough to hold people's interest.

Brevity is a matter of judgement. As a broad guide, most management reports, as opposed to highly technical documents, need to be:

■ under half a dozen A4 pages – often much less.

To achieve brevity – stay simple! Simplicity is a hidden persuader and is often underrated, even when the subject is complex. Einstein once claimed, for example, that it should be possible to reduce any complex theory to a single page.

You can generate simplicity and brevity if you:

- use frequent summaries
- eliminate jargon and complex phrases
- write short sentences
- use visual images instead of words
- use metaphors and similes
- put detail in appendices
- use easy-to-grasp numbering systems.

Start by listing the key points you want to make. Prepare a one-page summary – the one you intend placing at the front of the finished document.

It may seem a paradox to prepare the summary before you have even written the full report, yet this forces you to answer the basic question:

- What do I need to tell them?

Most management reports fail through excess of facts, not a lack of them. Since you are not preparing an encyclopaedia, keep asking:

- Is this fact or statement really essential?

A particularly powerful method you can easily adopt is the 'must know/nice to know' formula. You merely divide your proposed report material into two categories:

- *must-know information* – material that the reader must have received by the end of the report, otherwise it has failed in its basic purpose
- *nice-to-know information* – material that it might be helpful for the reader to know, yet which is not essential for an understanding of the report.

When you use this classification, it can be surprising how much material falls by the wayside. In doing so, it also leaves room for more creative and imaginative ways of presenting the core document that must *persuade*.

Readable

If you focus your report as suggested above, you are well on the way to making it readable. Readability can be measured, and is not entirely subjective.

Many advanced word processors can assess readability. For example, MS Word uses the Flesch Reading Ease score, which rates text on a 100-point scale. The higher the score, the easier it is to understand the document. You can choose what kind of document to measure for readability: casual, standard, formal and technical.

You can also set up your custom version in which you choose whether to ignore jargon, split infinitives, colloquialisms and so on.

For most standard documents, MS Word suggests that you aim for a score of approximately 60 to 70. This chapter, for example, scores around 50 on this system.

Such techniques are only a guide. They are no substitute for understanding what happens when people actually read your report.

It may seem, for example, that when we read we allow the words to flow past us. Yet reading is not a passive activity. To make sense of information the brain constantly reorganises it. This has important implications for what makes material readable:

- Keep opening paragraphs clear, short and relevant.
- Pose issues concisely.
- Offer decisions or proposals in a neutral, thoughtful manner.
- Use short sentences of fewer than 25 words.
- Test the report on a 'guinea pig' to discover any faults.
- Avoid jargon even if readers understand it.
- To express emphasis use language rather than underlining.

Watch out for:

- jargon
- clichés
- redundancies and tautologies
- overwriting
- sexist words
- passive verbs
- hidden verbs
- misused words
- grammatical faults.

Since word processors can spot many errors, there is little excuse for not doing so. One of the most irritating aspects of having to read other people's management reports is seeing poor writing that you know could have been avoided by using the word processor properly.

- Use the technology available.

Structured

Management reports need a definite structure, although this will depend on the type of report. The following is an example of a structure for a formal report:

- management summary (one to two pages)
- introduction
- background to report

- body of report, including analysis
- conclusions
- recommendation
- appendix.

In a lengthy report these sections will be physically divided from each other by headings, separate pages, different coloured paper and so on.

Consign low priority material to appendices or even to a separate supporting document. Often no one will read these volumes, which may seem disappointing but in fact enhances your persuasiveness. Merely providing the background material shows you have done two sorts of essential homework:

- *choosing* – the 'must-know' versus the 'nice-to-know' information
- *digging* – sufficiently researching your report topic.

A sound structure means that sentences, paragraphs and sections fit logically together. For example:

- Does each new paragraph flow logically from the previous one, or does it move to a new topic without warning? (see also above)
- Is there adequate supporting information?
- Do recommendations or decisions logically follow from the analysis?

When you start a long report – that is, one over about five or six pages – explain its structure early on. This helps readers understand the flow and makes them more willing to wait for the presentation of information.

For example, you might begin by explaining that: 'This report explores a problem we hit with production last month and concludes with 25 recommendations for further action.'

For e-mail reports, the structure needs to be simple. A summary plus a background note may be enough in many cases. You may, however, need to provide additional sources of information via a dedicated webpage or some other source if people want to go deeper into your report.

Credible
A formal report is more credible if you:

■ provide sufficient factual evidence
■ show how your analysis leads to your conclusions
■ explain the reliability of the evidence
■ state the value judgements and preferences used
■ think through the likely consequences of recommendations
■ ensure consistency of approach
■ present the material in an attractive, professional format
■ avoid spoilers and errors that undermine your reliability.

Fail to do any of these and it may consign your report to the bin or that dreaded shelf from which few management reports ever return.

E-mail reports have more leeway on issues such as layout, spelling and even consistency. Speed may be more important than perfection.

Facts
Since facts are so essential to most management reports, how do you choose which ones to use? The starting point is always the realisation that:

■ there is no such thing as an objective fact.

It may seem that certain facts are 'hard data' devoid of emotion.

In practice the very act of selecting one fact and leaving out another makes each choice personal. The decision implies judgement and therefore bias. What makes your report more credible is when you explain the basis of your choice.

Numbers

Business report readers usually expect quantified information and without it some readers will simply not regard your report as credible. The danger here is trying to use numbers for the sake of it.

Why do readers want numbers in a report? First, it helps makes sense of complex data or arguments. Second, it is a fast way of conveying a convincing argument.

Numbers help people grasp the importance of issues. However, masses of figures are seldom convincing; they usually end up causing confusion. For example, will numbers taken to several decimal places really enhance the report?

It can be painful to consign many hard-won facts to an appendix, especially if you are a 'numbers' person and have worked hard to produce data, Yet, this may be the best way to help the reader.

Spoilers

You can quickly destroy your credibility around numbers if you allow even small errors to creep in – columns that do not add up, percentages that are awry and so on.

If you cannot face checking all the numbers for accuracy, ask someone else to do it – but do it. For example, columns and rows should tally and formulae need to be the right ones and free from typing errors or arithmetical slips.

Strictly limit the number of columns and rows that you include in tables. Instead, put your attention where it matters:

■ Ensure figures reveal patterns or messages that the reader cannot readily miss.

Where possible, rank numbers from highest to lowest, from most important to least important, from current to most dated and so on:

■ Rankings improve clarity and help the reader to see patterns.

Presentable

Making your report presentable covers a large territory, including:

■ general appearance
■ numbering systems
■ graphics.

Even with e-mail reports, appearances matter. People see so many documents that yours needs to stand out enough to grab their attention.

General appearance

If a formal report is worth writing, it is worth presenting with impact. Make sure there is a high standard of typing, with clear, easy-to-read printing.

Are there any spelling mistakes, typographical errors, wrong numbers or punctuation disasters?

It may seem wasteful to spend lots of time on such apparently minor issues as how to make the front cover look interesting, or what might be an attention-grabbing title. Yet these can determine people's immediate reactions to a report.

If you present numerical tables, does each have a reference number and proper explanatory title? Is the layout of tables helpful? For example, vertical lines between columns of figures tend to prevent the eyes from moving across the page and absorbing the data as a whole. Once again, a good word processor can come to your rescue on this and provide easy-to-create layouts with reader impact.

Good page layout design underpins a good report. For example, use generous margins of an inch or more. Use plenty of white space and start different sections of the report on a fresh page. Consider whether the whole report will work better with double spacing.

Even the binding can make a difference to how the document feels to each reader. Spiral binding, for example, though allowing pages to lie flat for easy reading, is seldom particularly attractive to handle. Thermal binding systems let pages lie flat while also looking neat.

Your overall aim in this area of presentation is:

■ How can I make the reader want to pick it up?

You are trying to say through the outward appearance of a document that: 'This is an interesting or important report, you'd better have a look.'

With e-mail reports, the issue is: 'what will make people want to continue reading this material?' Often recipients have to whiz through scores of e-mails and your report may soon be lost amongst the dross.

Find a way to make your e-mail report stand out, without spending hours on formatting or adding in countless graphics. Often just colour, larger headings and a few pictures will be enough to show that your report is more interesting than the average memo.

Numbering systems

Numbered paragraphs may delight the glutton for detail but in a management report, these can soon destroy readability or persuasiveness. Some organisations, though, insist on it, and certain readers feel happier seeing all of those numbers.

If you must number your paragraphs, keep the sequence simple. The decimal method of paragraph identification allows you to use many levels. For example, in the first level you label paragraphs:

1.1, 1.2, 1.3 and so on.

In the second level, you label sub-paragraphs:

1.1.1, 1.1.2, 1.1.3 and so on.

A third level makes it yet more complicated, with figures such as 1.1.1.1, 1.1.1.2. If you get to this level of complication, go for a rethink.

While decimal paragraph numbering can occasionally be useful in lengthy technical reports, for management purposes it can show you have lost sight of the plot. The purpose of your report is to provide meaning and be persuasive. You cannot do that with complicated numbering systems that merely get in the way.

Some useful guidelines are:

- use bullet points rather than numbering systems if possible
- write reports with no more than three levels, after that use a different notation.

For example, having labelled your paragraphs 1.1, 1.2, 1.3 etc, you can avoid any further complication by putting any further level of detail as bullet points.

If you must distinguish further levels – remember this is a management report, not a technical treatise – then try using a notation such as:

    1.1

        (i)
        (ii)
        (iii)

If you absolutely must further subdivide, adopt yet another notation:

    1.2

        (i)
        (ii)
        (iii)

            (a)
            (b)
            (c)

However, do you even need to label the second and third levels? Often a good desktop publishing programme or word processor has a good range of bullet points with different styles and indentations. For example:

    1.2

        ●
        ●
        ●

            ◆
            ◆
            ◆

If a two- or three-level structure does not seem detailed enough, you are almost certainly not thinking managerially. The aim is brevity, so rethink what you are saying and simplify it.

Graphics

Pictures, diagrams, charts and images can all convey your message with more impact than words alone. However, information is not automatically communicated merely because it is in graphical form.

Vary your graphics. Endless pie or bar charts, for example, do not make compelling or even convincing reading.

Make sure that all graphics are:

- properly numbered
- titled
- neat
- professional-looking.

With presentation software so readily available, there is now little excuse for presenting badly drawn graphics or amateurish looking charts.

The widespread availability of clip art – MS Word, for example, has masses of ready-to-use images – makes it tempting to crowd your reports with pictures. Be wary of overreliance on computerised drawings; they often look rather soulless. Instead, try finding some relevant photographs.

Colour is also now an important way to gain reader attention, whether within drawings, text or other layout devices. Again, be sparing in how much colour you adopt. Often it makes more sense to use just one or two colours but consistently.

Accountable

You will often be producing reports to persuade senior management or others to part with some of their budget. So, your reports need to show that you fully understand their needs in agreeing to do what you want.

One of the advantages of a written report, against a verbal presentation, is that you can often more fully anticipate their reactions. To gain their commitment to your proposals:

- show why the issue is important
- initially request resources for a short period
- accept variations in the implementation of your proposals
- show why they will achieve a desired outcome
- explain why the proposals are an improvement
- present the proposals' superiority over others
- justify the costs
- demonstrate that it is possible to easily evaluate the proposals.

As indicated earlier, it is seldom enough to present a management report with only facts and information. You need to make sense of the implications and give the data meaning. Just offering raw information is abdicating responsibility.

Inexperienced managers often feel uncomfortable about being accountable for more than just presenting facts. Yet a management report without your conclusions or recommendations is only half written. It runs the risk of evoking the response from readers: 'so what?'

By implication, you know more about the issue than someone who has not written the report. No matter how many people contribute to a management report, you need to show accountability by suggesting the next steps and their implications.

Through inexperience, it can be tempting to pack a report full of recommendations. Unless you can really support and argue for each recommendation, keep proposals short and simple. Break complicated ones into smaller 'suggestions' that can be separated from formal 'recommendations'.

Recipients of management reports want guidance on what to

do; they want to hear what you think and what you believe should happen next.

Further reading

LEIGH A. *Persuasive Reports and Proposals*. London, CIPD, 1999.

LEIGH A. *and* MAYNARD M. *'Getting it Down' in Perfect Communications*. London, Century Business, 1993.

MORRIS R. *The Right Way to Write: How to write effective business letters, reports, memos and e-mails*. London, Piatkus 1998.

MEETINGS

Chapter 7

Visit the restaurant at Egg, the Internet bank based in Derby, and there are people chatting, studying papers, making calls on their mobiles and generally looking as if they are having a good time. This is where many of the company's meetings occur.

The Egg managers have had to learn to trust their staff to work in a setting that does not look like a working environment in the conventional sense. In the 24-hour wired world, people are apt to be at work any time of the day or night. Meetings for them often turn out to be casual encounters, happening just about anywhere.

There are over 70 million boardroom meetings around the world every day. And research from BT indicates that the average senior executive spends three and half hours a day in meetings. An organisation of 100 people could save £250,000 a year by reducing the amount of time spent in meetings by one hour per person each week. How many of your meetings could be cancelled or reduced in size?

MLA consultants, for example, were invited to work with a major supermarket chain on a development programme for a new store concept. Apart from the actual store manager, another 12 people crammed into the room. Half of these people, though, turned up merely because they did not want to miss anything. By the end of the meeting, most had drifted away leaving the hard core that really needed to be there. Ironically, one wall of the room displayed a large poster explaining how to hold good meetings!

Making meetings matter

- *Stand-up meeting* – hold it in a place without chairs; it will be over surprisingly quickly
- *Topsy-turvy meeting* – start with the decision and work backwards; this cuts out waffle and focuses attention on consensus
- *Label-it meeting* – call the meeting something that explains what is expected from people, for example 'Problem-solving', 'Ideas generating', 'Updating' and so on
- *Far-from-the-madding-crowd meeting* – take people off-site in pleasant surroundings to talk about crucial matters for a prolonged period, not just an hour or so
- *Tell-me-more meeting* – a departmental or company-wide meeting that gives information only; there is no time to argue or debate, this has to occur elsewhere. It is efficient and on a regular basis kills rumours and keeps everyone updated
- *Make-or-break meeting* – the only choices at these meetings are 'yes or no'; it forces everyone to concentrate on the issue and avoids rambling debates
- *One-subject-only meeting* – instead of a raft of regular agenda items, focus entirely on one issue.

Partly adapted from 'Briefing encounter', in *Director*. June 2000.

As a manager, you have an important role in ensuring that meetings are focused on important organisational issues that relate to the future, not just the past. When you call meetings, keep asking:

- How will this help the company to thrive in the future?

Meetings can:

- focus attention and feelings on what the organisation is all about
- involve people in decisions so that they are more likely to support them
- make people more accountable
- encourage analysing and creativity
- help unfreeze fixed ways of thinking and generate options
- sell proposals, justify decisions and stop unwanted actions
- help you gain power.

What is it for?

Unproductive meetings usually happen because people attending are unclear about how to contribute. Make a conscious effort to clarify the reasons for getting together by asking:

- Why are we here – what is the aim of this meeting?

It is surprising how powerful this simple question can be, even in the most high-powered setting. It tends to focus everyone's minds. This is sensible particularly if there is no formal agenda and the gathering is at short notice.

Make it a habit at the start of each meeting to restate its purpose. Even if you are not chairing it, you will gain impact by suggesting that the chairperson does so.

Who is minding the store?

With the amount of meetings happening every day it is hardly surprising that a common experience is being told the person is 'in a meeting right now'. When managers are in meetings, it means they are not available for other work colleagues, for customers or for anything urgent that may need their attention.

In a small company it is also worthwhile checking that there are enough people who are not attending the meeting who can deal with the day-to-day business. For example, if the whole office team decides to meet, who looks after the phones or deals with a customer enquiry?

Do those left behind know how to deal with an urgent issue; are they confident enough to interrupt the meeting? What will they tell customers who call in asking to speak to someone in the meeting? Being told 'they're all in a meeting' can send a negative message to new clients and antagonise existing ones.

Plant and equipment maker Caterpillar holds morning briefings for management, office and shop floor staff that focus on just three questions:

- ■ What is going well?
- ■ What are today's concerns?
- ■ What action will we take to try to put things right?

These meetings never last longer than 15 minutes.

Who is attending?

Meetings seem to have a life of their own, escalating to include far more people than may be needed to deal with an issue. Fear of offending certain people, or not having the right information, tends to prompt more invitations to attend than the situation warrants. Others invite themselves in case they miss something.

Less is definitely more and the aim should be to identify only those who 'must' be at the meeting for it to succeed.

Who is leading it?

Meetings need chairing. It is fine to be democratic, to encourage self-led teams, and generally reduce the impact of hierarchies.

Yet, effective meetings need people who take care of:

- the process – is this meeting being effective
- the pacing – are we keeping to time
- the agenda – what we are going to talk about
- the venue – where we meet and its facilities.

As a manager, ensure that your meetings consider these issues. For example, you can insist that someone always chairs a meeting. Chairing might be shared across several people; the important point is that somebody takes responsibility for helping the group focus its energies and monitors whether the session is being effective.

Will people look forward to your meetings? It pays to gain a reputation for holding enjoyable meetings because:

- the right people are more likely to attend
- attendees feel more willing to contribute
- the right atmosphere encourages ideas and creativity.

What will make your meeting rewarding often depends on the effort you have put into it. It is not enough to just call people together giving them a time, place and topic. People need more than that if they are to fully participate.

So first get clear in your mind exactly what you want from each meeting and what are the essentials to cover. Be ready to use other people's experience and their views on what information they require to make a useful contribution.

What questions might people want answered? Prepare the information in a form they can rapidly absorb – for example, would it make sense to devise some charts or flipchart pages to summarise key facts? Also, how will you deal with people's reactions to a controversial subject? For example, will there be plenty of time for people to express their feelings?

Preparation

Well-organised meetings

■ someone leads, chairs or supports
■ prompt starts
■ focused discussion – people stick to the subject
■ clear purpose or agenda
■ agreed procedures
■ time-limited – usually a maximum of 90 minutes
■ good preparation
■ effort to reach conclusions via consensus
■ discussion of relevant matters
■ few interruptions
■ everyone can contribute
■ regular summarising
■ good listening
■ end on time
■ rapid publication of results and further action
■ each person's contribution is respected
■ each person is actively invited to contribute
■ there is high-quality listening by everyone
■ new ideas and suggestions are welcomed.

The agenda

It is said, 'whoever controls the agenda controls the meeting'. You will certainly find it worth investing time getting your agenda right.

SOME OF THE BASICS OF AGENDA PLANNING ARE SHOWN IN THE CHART ON PAGE 115

.

Hundreds, possibly thousands, of hours can be saved by taking a tough line on agendas by insisting:

■ Let's have it in writing.

If a meeting you attend does not have a written agenda, then model sound behaviour by insisting on creating one as the first item of the meeting. Put it perfectly tactfully, but the message should be clear:

■ Before we start can we agree the agenda and when we're going to finish?

Ideally, the agenda represents a target for what the meeting will cover. It has to be a manageable list that can be adequately dealt with in the time available.

Be prepared to break with tradition and get rid of long-serving items like 'any other business'. This is a perfect excuse for people to drone on about their pet ideas. If they have something important to say, ask them to put it on the next agenda.

Circulated papers

If you circulate papers in advance of the meeting, make it clear on a covering note and on the agenda that people are expected to have read them by the time they attend.

Reward those who have studied the papers in advance by thanking them and inviting them to speak first. If someone says that they have not read the papers, ask them to listen to the discussion rather than comment.

If many people say they have not read the papers, suggest either that the item be delayed until another time or that the meeting adjourns for coffee so people can read the material.

Get real

A powerful contribution to an effective meeting may prove to be the initial tough observation that:

■ We can't deal with all these items. Which ones shall we leave out?

You may need to make this point more tactfully if someone has laboured hard to create an elaborate and perhaps well-presented written agenda. Yet the reality is that meetings with excessive agenda items can leave everyone feeling dissatisfied.

One reason why the agenda may be overlong is that it contains carried forward items from previously ineffective meetings. Take a hard look at any item that has survived several carry forwards. Why is this item being avoided repeatedly? Is it someone's pet issue and can it be dealt with somewhere else?

If you chair a regular meeting, adopt the simple idea that any item carried forward to more than two meetings must be dealt with as the first item on its third appearance.

Good agenda habits

■ always aim for a written agenda
■ distribute agendas well in advance
■ explain location, date, start and end times
■ make agenda creation a participative experience
■ agenda items should reach chairperson at least three-quarters of the way between one meeting and the next
■ put easy items at the beginning, the harder items in the middle and end on an 'up' note.

Will the agenda create interest, even excitement? Constructing an effective agenda is a definite art. Put the items in the wrong order and the meeting can waste everyone's time. Write the topics in a boring way and people will come resigned to 'yet another meeting'.

Start and finish with an item that involves everyone. People's energies will be higher in the middle or towards the start of the meeting than at the end. The bell-shaped agenda curve shown in the chart below is a useful guide for devising an effective agenda.

The bell-shaped agenda structure

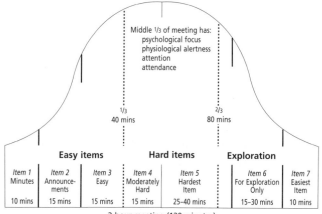

Middle 1/3 of meeting has:
psychological focus
physiological alertness
attention
attendance

1/3
40 mins

2/3
80 mins

	Easy items		Hard items			Exploration	
Item 1 Minutes	Item 2 Announce- ments	Item 3 Easy	Item 4 Moderately Hard	Item 5 Hardest Item		Item 6 For Exploration Only	Item 7 Easiest Item
10 mins	15 mins	15 mins	15 mins	25–40 mins		15–30 mins	10 mins

2-hour meeting (120 minutes)

Also, what does the actual agenda look like? A boring version that will get people wondering whether they really must attend will trundle through a litany of stark headings from apologies for absence to date and time of the next meeting – all guaranteed to get people yawning before they arrive, let alone at the meeting.

A well-written agenda does not need to look bureaucratic and heavy. It is an opportunity to start steering the meeting towards an effective outcome. Use it to explain why items are there in the first place – just a couple of lines should be enough – and the expected outcome from the discussion:

■ for information only
■ for discussion
■ for decision.

Giving people a clear picture of what they will be talking about and what is expected of them encourages them to prepare for the item. If you offer only a stark topic heading, you tend to close off any pre-meeting thinking.

Similarly, by explaining how long each item will take, you show that the meeting is going to be properly handled with a concern for people's time.

Interruptions

Interruptions can seriously damage your meetings. The two main types you face are internal and external.

Internal interruptions

Internal interruptions occur within the meeting itself. They are rather easier to anticipate, although not always easy to resolve.

Notice and develop a strategy for people who:

- break off to make a phone call
- leave their mobile phone on
- shuffle papers noisily
- talk during someone else's delivery
- play with gadgets: pocket organisers, laptops, mobiles etc
- wander around the room and cause diversions, such as opening or closing windows
- arrive late or leave early.

Tackle disruptive behaviour before it becomes entrenched. The other participants will be grateful that you are leading the way and insisting their time is used well.

The following techniques can be used to handle particular distractions.

Phones

Unplug room phones or neutralise them in some way. Ask in advance whether people have switched off their mobiles. To the person who says: 'But I'm expecting an urgent call from (who-ever)', ask:

■ So we're likely to be interrupted during the meeting?

If that does not sort the problem, ask them to leave the phone with someone outside the room who is authorised either to take a message or interrupt the meeting in the least distracting manner.

Papers

When the meeting starts, ask people to handle papers quietly. Catch the eye of a noisy offender and press a forefinger to your lips while pointing at your own papers. If they still fail to get the message, say directly that you would appreciate it if people would keep the noise of paper movement to a minimum. You do not need to name the guilty person.

Talking

If people start speaking to each other rather than to everyone, act swiftly to end this. Otherwise, your meeting may spiral rapidly out of control. At the very least it will greatly irritate those not party to the discussion.

Three tactics you can try are:

■ Invite the chatterers to share what they are discussing with the rest of the meeting.
■ Stop the meeting by saying, 'There appears to be a separate meeting going on over there,' and wait for a reaction. In most cases the chatterers look embarrassed and stop; they may even apologise.
■ Say something like: 'I think we should all give John [the person addressing the meeting] our full attention.'

Gadgets

Some people love playing with something distracting during a meeting and will continue doing so until you or someone stops them. Before you become too concerned about their anti-social behaviours, ask yourself:

■ Is the behaviour actually affecting others adversely?
■ What is such behaviour saying about this meeting?

In many cases the gadget fiddler is sending a clear message that the meeting is either becoming boring or the item under discussion is not one to which he or she can readily contribute.

Tactics to deal with gadget fiddling include:

■ Ask the meeting to agree a ground rule that fiddling with gadgets is distracting.
■ Offer the persistent gadget fiddler something else to do, for example take over the minute-taking, become the time manager for the meeting, making sure items are completed to schedule.
■ Make a playful gesture as if about to slap the person's wrist – do it with a rueful smile.
■ Invite the person to comment on the item in some way.

Wandering

This is a difficult interruption to counter, as some people need to release their creative energies. Constructive wanderers, though, stay in touch with the meeting, nodding and looking interested. Destructive wanderers get up and sit down with little energy, move around aimlessly, opening windows, fiddling with objects. However, their behaviour is telling you clearly that the meeting is not holding their attention.

Tactics you can use to deal with destructive wanders include:

■ Invite them to stay seated for the benefit of everyone else.
■ Ask if they find the meeting boring – if the answer is 'yes', invite them to say what is wrong, or suggest that perhaps they leave; if the answer is 'no', suggest that wandering around implies otherwise, so could they please stay seated for the moment.
■ Give them a definite task to do, such as keep the minutes.

Late arrivals and early leavers

Some people seem to enjoy taking a meeting off track. If you hold a regular meeting with the same group of people, everyone can join forces to keep the meeting on course. For example, you could establish a group visual 'signal' that warns the discussion is veering off course.

Late arrivals are a common form of disruption. Tackle it early in the life of your regular meetings. Explain clearly that you want people to arrive on time since this shows respect for everyone else's time. Be sure, though, to set a good example by always being a good timekeeper yourself.

If someone persistently arrives late, avoid trying to confront him or her in public. Instead, ask privately if he or she has problems with the time the meeting is happening. It may be resolved by moving the meeting to a different time.

Tackling lateness

Do you actively confront people who arrive late for your meetings? It is all too easy to slip into a culture of tolerance around this issue and, once established, it can then be hard to reverse. One newly appointed chief executive, for example, threw a tantrum the first time people turned up late for one of his meetings. From then on all his meetings ran to time.

Two basic managerial responses to lateness are:

- reward
- punishment.

Rewarding

By offering late arrivals a full summary of the discussion so far, you merely reward anti-social behaviour. Likewise, if you always start meetings late to accommodate late arrivals, you punish those who have arrived on time.

Allow a strict margin of five minutes over the starting time and no more. Try asking people to arrive 10 minutes early and giving them something amusing or creative to do that they will enjoy, such as a puzzle or a problem to solve.

Positive reward actions include:

- To those who previously arrived late and who begin to arrive less late or on time, offer a public acknowledgement that there has been an improvement.
- Send a written note thanking them for the improvement.
- Give the person some new role in the meeting to demonstrate that you have a renewed confidence in them.

Punishment

Actions include:

- Ask the person to make no comment on the item under discussion.
- Invite the person arriving late to apologise, not to you but to the entire meeting, for being late.
- Ask person not to attend if they cannot arrive on time.
- Try a closed-door policy – once the meeting starts no one else is allowed to enter.

External interruptions

External interruptions are those imposed on your meeting from outside, not by those attending it. These distractions include urgent phone calls from top management, messages to be distributed to someone at the meeting, unexpected visitors, fire drills, noisy building work and the arrival of refreshments.

For unexpected messages and visitors, try posting a 'please do not disturb' notice on the door and indicate what the person should do meanwhile, such as go to another contact point.

You probably cannot avoid random fire drills, but it is always worth checking whether there is likely to be one scheduled during your meeting.

There is nothing more distracting than someone barging into a meeting with a tray of drinks and setting them down noisily and proceeding to serve them. It is your meeting and you can decide on the domestic arrangements. Organise things so that refreshments arrive at a known time.

Contributions

You almost certainly want people in your meetings to contribute. Yet a common complaint by those who chair meetings is the difficulty of getting others to speak up.

Large meetings, though, can be daunting and people may be reluctant to speak, even if they feel quite strongly about something. Small meetings, too, can make certain individuals feel that every word they say will be put under the microscope.

Try breaking the participants temporarily into smaller groups to discuss an issue for a few minutes, and then invite a response from each one. Alternatively, you can ask the group to summarise its views, rather than putting any one member on the spot.

Another approach is to ask people to arrive at the meeting with a considered response to an issue. You then go systematically around the table seeking their comments.

Encourage people to contribute by giving total attention to their contributions. People notice if the manager is bored or distracted, so stay fully alert.

You also encourage more participation by inviting people to express their objections and criticisms in a positive rather than a negative way. Coach everyone to watch out for that familiar negative phrase, 'Yes but...'

Building on contributions

A particularly powerful method worth using is to encourage people to summarise a previous person's contribution before making their own. This promotes listening, and people learn to build on each other's ideas.

Summarising and rephrasing also helps participation, since it shows contributions are being taken into account. However, do not overdo this technique, as too frequent a summary can prove oppressive. In a meeting of say 90 minutes, a summary every 20 minutes should be adequate.

Decisions

Business meetings are mainly about some form of action. It is therefore important that you check out at the end of the meeting exactly what has been agreed.

No matter how long a meeting, it is normally possible to have a quick recap before everyone leaves to summarise the agreed actions. It is important, though, to present this task as a help to participants, rather than you the manager wanting to satisfy yourself that everyone knows what they have to do. This can be achieved, for example, by using a comment such as: 'Before we all leave let's just go over what has been agreed today so we're all sure what is supposed to happen next.' This can also be a task allocated to a participant, as part of keeping that person involved.

Minutes

Minutes are an underrated aspect of well-run meetings. They do not need to be elaborate or verbatim reports on what occurred. Resist allowing them to become a sort of newsletter about the previous meeting for those who did not attend.

The whole point of attending a meeting is to take part in it. If you miss it, you cannot expect to gain the benefits of attending.

Instead, issue minutes that focus mainly on:

■ action.

That is, produce a list of what was decided at the meeting. Poorly led meetings leave people wondering what is supposed to happen next.

The action minute method merely records:

■ topic
■ action
■ by whom
■ when.

Sticking closely to action minutes, rather than a description of what was discussed, saves someone the chore of writing up the meeting. It is perfectly possible, for example, to complete the entire action minute by the time everyone leaves the meeting.

A useful technique is to record the action minute in full view of everyone by writing the decisions as they happen onto a flipchart. The page is torn off at the end and the results issued in written form.

In some cases you might even adopt an electronic whiteboard that produces an A4 printout of the written material, which can be instantly e-mailed to everyone. They may even receive the completed minutes by the time they return to their desks!

The attenders

The kinds of people who can create difficulties in your meetings include:

- obstructer
- bore
- comic
- aspiring leader
- bully
- observer.

The obstructer

This person keeps shoving blocks in the way of progress. These might include constantly asking questions, challenging the veracity of information or demanding more facts.

Obstructers are usually adept at the 'Yes but...' technique. They often behave in this way because they fear that they have nothing of value to offer, so they end up attacking other people. They find plenty of negative reasons why things cannot be done or will go wrong.

Action

Turn these people to your advantage by directing their critical skills, asking them to follow up on detail, prepare a report and so on.

The bore

The bore likes the sound of his or her own voice and leaves little room for anyone else's. Bores inflict their views on the rest of the meeting, regardless of relevance. They talk a lot, repeat themselves and abuse valuable meeting time.

Action
Deal with the bore by limiting the person's airtime. Intervene firmly after they have had their share. Try asking directly the relevance of their point – although this may precipitate yet more verbiage.

Ask pointedly, 'How does this move us forward?' or 'What solution are you proposing then?'

A technique for undermining both bores and obstructers is to write key decisions already made during a meeting on a flipchart. This stops them continuously returning to old territory, since others will soon say that the matter has already been dealt with.

The comic
Comics make jokes all the time, often very funny and frequently at other people's expense. People initially enjoy their humour, until it starts to damage the meeting. Comics often use jokes as a form of defence to avoid being vulnerable to attack.

Meetings without humour are dreary, but excessive humour stops serious ideas surfacing and prevents people expressing strong feelings in case they are ridiculed.

Action
Comics are particularly hard to handle because whatever you do can seem wrong. Failing to confront them may leave the meeting at their mercy; tackling them can make you appear humourless and intolerant.

Make it clear to your comic that while you welcome humour it becomes wearing for everyone if it happens too often.

Sometimes it works to play tough and set a different tone, for example:

- 'This is a rather a serious issue and making jokes about it won't really help us tackle it.'
- 'Peter, I love your humour, but not right now!'

The aspiring leader

The aspiring leader, without your agreement, keeps trying to do your job of chairing the meeting, directing conversations and generally seeking to take control. For example, the aspiring leader may persistently try to sum up and attempt to close down discussion prematurely.

Although leadership in meetings often moves around the table, aspiring leaders are seldom happy when other people start doing it too. If there are two or more aspiring leaders in attendance, competition and in-fighting may start to distort the meeting and make it less effective.

Action

Like comics, aspiring leaders are hard to deal with, since ideally you want people to take responsibility and act assertively. A sound tactic is to welcome their intervention but state clearly where you stand on an issue.

Be prepared to act tough on premature summing up. This can be destructive and frustrating for others who do not welcome the aspiring leader's self-appointed role.

When the aspiring leader attempts a premature summing up thank the person for the effort and continue along the lines:

- 'I think there are still people who want to explore this issue further. Let's leave the summing up until later.'

The bully

Bullies make others feel unsafe or humiliated. They are poor listeners and bulldoze their way in meetings. They are insensitive to feelings and are usually excessively task-centred.

Bullying can range from constantly interrupting people to hustling everyone to agree when they do not.

Action

Bullies rely on people not challenging them and if you do so, you will usually gain support from the rest of the meeting. As a manager and leader, it is important that you make it clear that people in your meetings are entitled to respect. If you do not act on bullying, why should anyone else?

The observer

The observer never really participates and stays on the edge of the meeting the whole time. The classic observer ploy is to take extensive notes so that they appear busy and thus avoid a contribution.

Because the observer says so little, other people begin to feel that their silence is oppressive. Yet, when they do speak they often refuse to commit themselves or say what they really think about an issue.

Action

Appreciate their willingness to listen but ask them to leave their extensive note-taking until later. Point out that you will issue minutes anyway. Perhaps even ask what the notes are about. You may discover to their embarrassment that the notes are unconnected with the actual meeting.

Another useful tactic is to invite each person to comment on an issue and refuse to let the observer off the hook. For example, you might say, 'I'd really appreciate knowing how you personally feel about this issue?'

In these situations, the observer often gives strong body language such as no eye contact or silently shaking their head that says:

■ Leave me alone.

Do not take this as an answer. Ask again, for example, 'where exactly do you stand on this issue?' Wait out the silence until you get a reaction.

If the observer persists in such withdrawn behaviour, it may be sensible to tackle it outside the meeting. For example, you might hold a one-to-one coaching session in which you tackle the lack of contribution and your need for the person to give more input.

Signs of failure

Be constantly alert for signs that your meeting might be failing and be ready to take remedial action.

Danger signs include:

■ discussion drags on interminably with no conclusions
■ poor participation
■ many late arrivals
■ wrong people attend
■ meeting goes too fast or too slowly
■ excessive conflict
■ bad interpersonal relations
■ meeting goes astray, such as ignoring current organisational strategy
■ no minutes recorded
■ chairperson overinvolved and ceases to be neutral.

If you are chairing the meeting people will expect you to take care of these matters.

Handling conflict

It can be scary chairing meetings because you are expected to handle conflict. Many managers react to this by trying to suppress it, hoping that this will produce peace and constructive results. Often it achieves exactly the opposite.

Meetings need to be safe places, where conflict can be handled appropriately, not eliminated. For instance, if your reaction is to become aggressive, you are unlikely to deal with it to the benefit of everyone else.

The basic principle is:

■ allow conflict to surface.

Having spotted a potential conflict situation, be positive and insist on the pros and cons being fully aired. Use a flipchart or white board divided down the centre and ask someone to list the arguments for and against. This focuses attention on facts rather than feelings.

Handling conflict also means dealing with the feelings, not just the facts. Try asking yourself these three questions:

■ What does the speaker mean as opposed to what they are saying?
■ What is the speaker feeling?
■ What are the other people in the meeting feeling?

These questions can help you diagnose what is happening and decide what to do next. For example, if someone is looking agitated or fuming with anger, indicate openly that you can see they are upset or concerned. Encourage them to share their feelings by suggesting that they state what exactly is worrying them.

Steer the discussion away from attacking individuals in terms of personalities. Instead, encourage people to clarify their disagreement with examples.

■ Many conflicts vanish once you have detailed cases.

An excellent method of resolving conflict between two parties is to ask each to:

■ summarise the other's person's arguments to their satisfaction.

There is sometimes a choice between dealing with the conflict and completing the group task. Unless the conflict is making the group task harder, it may be better to leave resolving it until later.

The alternative of smoothing ruffled feathers and giving people support and encouragement, may win friends yet ignore the importance of the task.

Culture consciousness

For meetings with people from different organisations or national cultures, consider:

■ How formal should relations be?
■ What are people's attitudes towards time and scheduling?
■ How many different professional groups are there?
■ Is there likely to be much jargon involved?
■ Do all participants have authority to act?
■ Is the chosen language acceptable?
■ Are people from very different sorts of organisation?

A useful solution is to ask someone else in the meeting to be responsible for oiling the wheels – seeing that the process is working. This could mean taking a special interest on your behalf, watching for people who are feeling strongly about an issue and encouraging them to speak up.

Technology-based meetings

The average business traveller makes 21 trips a year and spends 37 nights in hotels. Many business meetings are at quite a high personal cost in terms of stress and effect on family life and high in terms of the organisational overheads involved.

Video and audio conferencing are tending to grow as the technology for these improves. These have certain benefits in reduced travel and lower costs, yet they also create their own particular range of problems.

In 1998 BP Amoco Exploration began an R&D project called 'Moving Work to People' by using virtual teams across language, cultural and geographical borders.

The company used an integrated audio and data conferencing tool for dispersed teams. 'We have improved team productivity and interaction without the need to be in the same place,' explains BP Amoco's manager leading the project.

Help people attending these 'virtual' meetings by coaching them in some of the essentials:

- Talking over someone does not work – it is essential to take turns speaking and listening.
- State explicitly what you are doing and why.
- Avoid jokes.
- A formal approach tends to maximise time and focus.
- Warn people that they could be 'on camera' at any time.

■ Good and informed chairing is essential – for example, allow more time for each new speaker to come into view.
■ Confirm any decisions and action agreed.
■ Follow up rapidly with good documentation.

Meetings that inspire

As a manager and leader, people look to you to hold inspiring meetings, not merely pedestrian gatherings where routine triumphs over involvement. You need to develop ways to lift a meeting, energising people and tapping into their natural creativity so that they wish to contribute. How do you do that?

Encouraging participation as outlined above is certainly one way. Another is to keep trying new ways to get people's interest and attention. For example, why does the meeting always have to be held in the same place? Could it be held in some unusual and imaginative places, such as another company site, a local theme park, a theatre foyer, an art gallery?

Rather than stick to exactly the same format for each meeting, try experimenting with an entirely new one occasionally. For example, you could:

■ restrict the meeting to just one item for which everyone is asked to prepare in depth
■ introduce a 'fast and furious' agenda one day, in which no item is allowed more than 10 minutes' airtime
■ invite someone unusual to address the meeting
■ invite people to raise concerns by 'painting' a picture of it with coloured pens or even paints.

Further reading

DOBSON A. *Managing Meetings*. Oxford, How To Books, 1999.

FORSYTH P. *Making Meetings Work*. London, CIPD, 1998.

INSTITUTE OF DIRECTORS. *Effective Business Meetings: Managing time, mastering technology.* London, IOD, 2000.

LEIGH A. *and* MAYNARD M. *Leading Your Team.* London, Nicholas Brealey, 1995.

TYLER K. 'The gang's all here'. *HR Magazine.* Vol. 45, No. 5, May 2000. pp104–13.

WILLCOCKS G. *and* MORRIS S. *Making Meetings Work in a Week.* London, Hodder and Stoughton, 2000.

DECISION-MAKING

Chapter 8

Martin Williams was a rat catcher with Doncaster Council. He lived in an average semi-detached house in the small town of Thorne, and seemed to lead an unremarkable life. Then he was sacked for taking time off work without permission, which he strongly denied. That decision has come to haunt Doncaster managers. Williams won a High Court order against the council to prevent it closing an old people's home in a legal action paid for by Williams, who in his anger at what had happened got elected as a councillor.

The once inoffensive rat catcher who loved his job turned out be independently wealthy, part-heir to a family fortune worth over £11 million. Williams went on to set up his own pest control business and began taking customers off the local council. In another dubious decision, the council sacked its environmental health officer on similar grounds and the two men teamed up to make the life of managers at Doncaster Council a misery.

Ultimately 13 Doncaster councillors were found guilty of fraud and five subsequently jailed, with more perhaps to come. And it all began with that decision to sack their rat catcher.

That is the trouble with decision-making. You often never know what the consequences of a particular choice will be. Sometimes you only discover the result when, like the Doncaster managers and councillors, it hits you where you least expect it.

'Often you have to rely on your intuition,' remarked Bill Gates of Microsoft. Most managers think they make decisions rather well, while the evidence is not so favourable. As a training director of C&P Telephone Company put it more brutally: 'Most of our executives make very sound decisions. The trouble is many have then not turned out to be right.'

A study of management decision-making approaches found that in over a third of the cases managers still preferred to issue edicts enforcing the adoption of decisions. Yet the top-down method worked less well when compared to persuasion and participation, mainly because the implementation rate was so poor. The top-down brigade, though, failed to take this factor into account.

When companies are facing rapid and constant change, top-down methods and narrow choices made by a few managers often mean poor choices. Sound business decisions depend on knowledge and judgement and managers can no longer claim to have a stranglehold on either.

The Internet, too, is fundamentally altering decision-making, from purchasing to hiring, from outsourcing to pricing. New

> When the UK lottery came up for grabs in 2000, the decision on who would run it was the responsibility of the National Lottery Commission. The Commission considered bids from Camelot, the existing licence-holder, and Sir Richard Branson's People's Lottery. After looking at the bids, the Commission announced that it was only prepared to look at the bid from the newcomer. Camelot went to court and in the highly publicised case the judge called the Commission's decision 'conspicuously unfair'.
>
> Shortly afterward, the Commission's chairman Dame Helena Shovelton resigned.
>
> Decisions behind closed doors often have a habit of going public, put under close scrutiny when you least expect it. People expect decisions to be 'fair', 'understandable' and 'realistic.'

arrangements encourage companies to share some kinds of decision-making with allies and even competitors.

For example, where once a single procurement officer could make a sound decision about the best buy for a company's raw materials, now it may take a collaborative effort through the Internet between many companies to nail down the best deal.

They are unavoidable

'Make every decision as if you owned the whole company,' suggested a once-renowned head of Avis Car Rentals. 'Wherever you are in the organisation, decisions are unavoidable and an essential part of the job. Treat each as if it affected the entire enterprise and you will be acting strategically.' This will soon get you noticed in the right quarters.

You will constantly face choices – who to hire, how much to invest, what price to charge, which new commercial to use, whether to launch a new product. Not every choice justifies detailed analysis, and as the Bill Gates' comment above suggests, some simply come down to intuition.

A decision is necessary only if:

- there are two or more possible outcomes
- the outcomes have value or importance
- the outcomes differ in some way.

Without choice there is no need to make a decision. Similarly, if there is no real difference between final outcomes, choosing hardly matters either.

As with so much of management, you often learn more from things going wrong than when everything goes smoothly.

Decision disasters

■ **Doing it too fast** – deterring buy-in from those who must implement the decision

■ **Doing it to death** – too many choices or reducing them to oversimple either/or options

■ **Doing it with numbers** – too many statistics, glossing over calculations and not handling the complexity

■ **Doing it with consultants** – consultants are more likely to design a system based on a customer's wants rather than needs

■ **Doing it alone** – not involving enough or the right people

■ **Doing it with solutions** – people presented with a solution tend to be attracted to it so that the debate centres on whether to support it or not, rather than looking for alternatives

■ **Doing it by copying** – seeing similar decisions taken by other organisations and adopting them unthinkingly

■ **Doing it by anchoring** – overreliance on experience, using past cases to guide choices rather than viewing the situation afresh

■ **Doing it by satisficing** – searching for an acceptable rather than the best solution, only generating alternatives if the first possibility is rejected.

The decision process

You could think of a decision as the 'moment of making a final choice'. Yet this is one part of the task of choosing. Rather than treat decision-making as a single point in time, treat it as a process, not an event.

Improve your own decision-making by using a systematic approach to:

- generating choices
- evaluating the alternatives.

Though you still use your intuition and judgement, you base these first on a formal analysis that throws more light on the likely outcomes.

> In a study of the decision process in large US and Canadian firms: in nearly 60 cases there was little attempt to explore options; managers found it hard to cope with uncertainty, leading them to make premature choices.

Start by adopting a framework for handling the decision process. For example:

- define the issue or problem
- gather information
- identify and evaluate alternatives
- choose and then act.

This is a rather simple framework and is only a way of guiding your thinking as you tackle a decision task. While it will not guarantee that you take effective decisions, it can prompt you to tackle the task thoroughly, generating more knowledge about the possible consequences and risks.

> **Decision frameworks:**
>
> - ensure that you include all important steps in making a choice
> - provide a way of judging the choices
> - help explain your choices to other people
> - inspire confidence in your decision-making
> - counter the tendency to rush to judgement.

The chart below provides a nine-stage decision framework that includes monitoring all the stages. This has been tested on several thousand managers who reportedly found it helpful in making important choices.

The nine-stage decision process

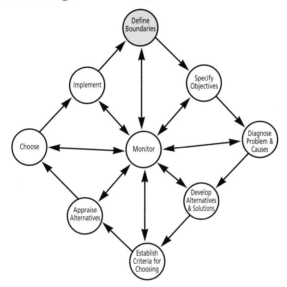

You would not use the framework to decide what phone call to make or which meeting to attend. But it can be a powerful tool for dealing with challenging choices where the stakes are high.

It may take several tries to make this particular approach work for you and you may want to simplify it further. You will soon find it gives your more important decision-making a definite logical structure.

Decision analysis
Decision analysis is the number-crunching end of decision-making, with intuition being at the other end. There are a host of tools that keep evolving as we become more sophisticated at understanding complex choices.

Most decision analysis tools try to quantify some aspect of the decision process, for example by systematically weighing and evaluating alternatives. Yet no matter how elaborate the method, ultimately it complements rather than replaces judgement.

Handing over the management task of decision-making entirely to computers is fine for certain routine actions, but for anything important it is a sure way to head for a disaster. For example, it is one thing to instruct a computer to warn that shares in an investment portfolio have reached a 'sell' price, and quite another to blindly permit the computer to complete the sale without any human assessment of the suitability of this action.

Decision components

Decision-making deals with the impact of events in the future, which is never absolutely predictable. So two basic components of all decisions are:

- uncertainty
- risk.

Both of these are usually incorporated into formal methods of decision analysis.

Uncertainty implies unknown outcomes. We cannot know all the possible results of a potential decision, as the managers in Doncaster Council found out when they dismissed Martin Williams the rat catcher.

Uncertainty over the outcome is why some people find decision-making so stressful. You can try to minimise the uncertainty by:

- identifying as many possible outcomes as possible
- analysing consequences
- maximising the amount of information available at the point of choice

■ avoiding decisions where the degree of uncertainty is simply unacceptable.

Risk analysis

In formal decision-making, 'risk' has a more precise meaning than 'uncertainty'. It is about the *degree of uncertainty*. Rather than saying the outcome is uncertain, we quantify the nature of this uncertainty.

Risk estimates are based on measurements such as guesses about the chances of something happening. These may be based on all kinds of probability calculations, yet ultimately they come down to guessing.

You adopt risk analysis so as to use a structured approach to making choices. For example, when a company accepts a quality standard of one faulty component in 10,000, this is usually determined from detailed information of past failures and any new systems installed to prevent them occurring.

Risk analysis is a highly numerate discipline, involving applied mathematics and statistical techniques. Using these, risk analysts try to reduce the level of uncertainty attached to the final choice.

Most busy managers do not have time to become experts in risk analysis. However, be aware that such a discipline exists, that there are people trained in methods of calculating risk, and when it might be worth using such specialised support when the stakes are high.

Tools

The key to being an effective manager is learning which tool to select, when to apply it and how to interpret the results. Often it is best to seek expert help, although increasingly managers – and even those on the shop floor – are required to use the simpler tools such as basic statistical methods. These help unravel cause and effect and predict trends.

Tools you may find useful include:

Pros and cons
The best-known decision analysis tool is a sheet of paper divided down the middle. You list the alternatives and below each add the pros and cons on either side of the page.

Having listed all the arguments for and against, you decide if a pro cancels out a con. This is usually more a matter of judgement than mathematical calculation.

As you gradually eliminate the various pros and cons you may be left with alternatives where all the pros and cons cancel each other out. You drop these alternatives and consider the rest. Finally you are reduced to alternatives where the pros and cons are not equal and use this clearer picture to make the final choice.

This simple idea dates back to the eighteenth century and has blossomed into elaborate and often arcane methods, often using computer modelling. Even so, it comes down to naming and weighing up pros and cons.

Outcome table
You may be able to improve your decision-making by listing systematically the likely outcomes from a potential decision. You create a table showing the various outcomes under different circumstances.

Suppose you want to decide whether or not to raise the prices of your product. You may consider two important possibilities: increasing the prices by different amounts and the reaction of competitors. The payoff table on page 143 summarises some potential outcomes:

Own price rises

		Small	Medium	Large
	No response	Result 1	Result 2	Result 3
Competitor reaction	Matched response	Result 4	Result 5	Result 6
	Reduction	Result 7	Result 8	Result 9

Potentially, all decisions could be fitted into a table along these lines. In practice, only certain ones justify the effort. Some choices, for example, are too simple to make it worthwhile, others are too complex to handle in this way.

SWOT
A popular and useful version of the outcome table is SWOT analysis. This requires you to analyse the decision in terms of:

Strengths
Weaknesses
Opportunities
Threats

You look at a potential decision in terms of various aspects and whether it represents an opportunity or a threat. Similarly you assess whether it represents a strength or weakness in the situation. Likewise you examine threats to see how far they could be a strength or a weakness. Alternatively you can start with an issue that you regard as a strength and explore how far it could be an opportunity or a threat.

Here is a real SWOT analysis conducted at Maynard Leigh Associates when we were reviewing the possible decision to buy our office building, Marvic House:

Marvic

	OPPORTUNITIES	THREATS
STRENGTHS	■ Being a landlord is usually profitable ■ Property is a respectable asset ■ Can adapt space to suit business needs ■ No longer have to be a tenant	■ High rents in Central London make Fulham more attractive, but increases the competition
WEAKNESSES	■ Existing tenants' leases run out soon ■ Being a landlord – the impact on the core business ■ What state is the building in now? ■ May have to relocate instead	■ Property overvalued? ■ Risk of negative equity ■ Cost of getting new tenants ■ Heavy debt+personal risk=pressure on business

The advantage of SWOT analysis is that it is intuitively easy to do and others will rapidly grasp the issues when you hand over the table. The drawback is that it can create a 'So what?' reaction. You cannot do a SWOT analysis and just leave it there; it merely provides a powerful way to look at the underlying issues.

Decision tree

The decision tree helps you compare options and uses probabilities to make sense of the choices.

Even without a computer to work out the consequences of alternative decisions on the tree, the act of putting the choices down in this way can help clarify what is at stake.

The chart on page 145 shows a typical decision tree, examining choices around launching Product M997.

Decision tree

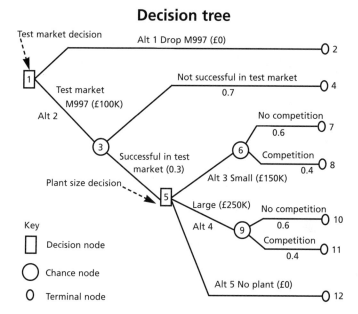

Test market decision

Alt 1 Drop M997 (£0) ————————————— O 2

Test market
M997 (£100K)
Alt 2

Not successful in test market
0.7 ————— O 4

Successful in test market (0.3)

No competition
0.6 ————— O 7

Competition
0.4 ————— O 8

Alt 3 Small (£150K)

Plant size decision

Large (£250K)
Alt 4

No competition
0.6 ————— O 10

Competition
0.4 ————— O 11

Alt 5 No plant (£0) ————————————— O 12

Key

☐ Decision node

O Chance node

O Terminal node

Value tree

This aims to clarify and quantify objectives. It makes the decision-maker articulate initially vague wish-list criteria and presents a hierarchy of implications.

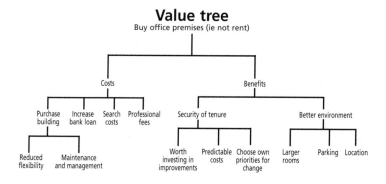

Value tree
Buy office premises (ie not rent)

Costs				Benefits		
Purchase building	Increase bank loan	Search costs	Professional fees	Security of tenure		Better environment
Reduced flexibility	Maintenance and management			Worth investing in improvements	Predictable costs	Choose own priorities for change	Larger rooms	Parking	Location

To make the tree work well, be sure that it is comprehensive – that is, you are sure that you have included everything of concern. Also, to evaluate the various implications they need to be in enough detail to make that possible.

Fishbone diagram

This tool looks rather like the backbone of a fish and is also called the Ishikawa diagram. It aims to identify root causes in a logical sequence.

It shows the relationship between causes and their relative importance. Using these, the decision-maker gains a better picture of the possible consequences of actions.

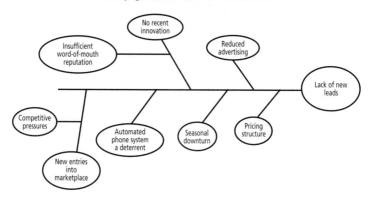

Fishbone diagram
Identifying causes of lack of new business leads

Clarity

All of these tools bring more clarity to issues such as:

- who the decision-makers are
- the importance each person will have in making the final choice
- defining the alternatives
- solving complex problems
- making predictions
- specifying the criteria for judging the choices
- quantifying the risk of making different choices
- pinpointing obstacles likely to achieve desired outcomes.

While formal decision analysis can improve the decision process, it is usually time-consuming and costly. For instance, to analyse the environmental impact of a major investment decision, such as where to build an oil refinery, may take many months or even years.

Quantification often lends the whole procedure a spurious sense of scientific reliability. For example, assessing the chance of something happening may ultimately rest not on hard facts but on subjective assessments. On the other hand, decision analysis makes you define the problem more explicitly into logical steps. It also forces you to document the whole process.

The decision kitbag

Experienced decision-makers gradually acquire their own kitbag of methods for making better decisions. Sometimes these include the formal decision analysis tools, used at the appropriate time.

You do not need to learn all the many decision tools to be an effective manager. You do, however, need to be aware of what is available and be able to apply some of the simpler ones yourself.

Apart from the decision tools described already, you should at least become familiar with the capabilities of:

- **statistical methods** – averages, dispersion, indices, time series, sampling, regression, probability distributions
- **information systems** – obtaining, analysing and evaluating relevant data
- **decision models** – methods to simulate the different decision situations
- **linear programming** – a statistical technique that takes into account the constraints in making important choices
- **Monte Carlo simulations** – use computers to generate a large number of possible combinations of circumstances

- **SMART (Simple Multi-Attribute Rating Technique)** – for simple analysis; it helps spot options and measures and weighs them using a value tree.

While some of these tools are simple to use, even quite large companies do not use them because they mistakenly believe that they are difficult or inappropriate. For example, you hardly need to be a statistical genius to realise that some types of averages are more appropriate than others. A grounding in basic statistics is a minimum management competency these days.

Models

We use mathematical models every day without even realising it. For example, calculating how long it will take to drive from one place to another requires an estimate of both distance and likely travelling speed to produce an expected arrival time.

Models help replace rule-of-thumb decisions with a programme that identifies the best or optimal decision. Even without understanding the mathematics of a model, you need to know the assumptions underpinning it when they relate to your decisions. You may need to play a major part in determining which variables to include or exclude. You may even need to offer a subjective estimate of the probability of certain events occurring.

Models you may come across include the following:

- **Quantitative models** involve rigorous logic and precision, usually at the expense of realism. They leave little room for any ambiguity since there are stated givens.
- **Qualitative models** are based on formulae, which produce a simple, often elegant solution. Here the givens are less explicit.

Model it

- **Strategic models** are used for: planning company objectives; planning policy; selecting locations for new factories; environmental impact planning; non-routine capital budgeting.
- **Tactical models** are used for: financial planning; manpower planning; designing plant layout; routine capital budgeting.
- **Operational models** are used for: credit ratings; media selection; production scheduling; inventory control; time and motion analysis; quality control.

New models are being produced all the time. These may simulate a market situation or solve a stock control problem. The mathematical techniques are also constantly being improved. There are some powerful low cost software packages that enable non-statisticians to do complex analysis without learning the actual mathematical techniques.

There are many other techniques – such as marginal analysis, utility theory and heuristics – that also have highly specific uses in decision-making. It would be useful to gain a general understanding of what these can do, without necessarily learning how to apply them in practice.

Group decision-making

The fiasco over the UK's Millennium Dome is almost a case study in how groups can keep on making bad decisions, even when the evidence that they are heading into trouble is blatantly obvious. No one person can really be blamed for the Dome disaster, a black financial hole into which millions of pounds disappeared.

Likewise the London Stock Exchange lost millions on its notorious Taurus computer system and the result cost the chief executive his job. In fact he had been in post only less than a year. Again, no one person could really be blamed, as many of the Exchange managers went along with the scenario that the IT experts presented – that a few more months and yet more money would bring the project to fruition.

Groups play an important part of most managers' decision-making. The often-convoluted stages of a major decision may involve many different interests within an organisation.

Groups or teams can improve your decision-making because they handle variety well and often save time in undertaking analysis. They reduce your own bias by bringing a wider perspective to the decision arena. They may also overcome resistance to getting a particular decision made or implemented. For example, the members will often have far more influence collectively than a single manager working unaided.

The danger of groups is that they sometimes reject diversity in the decision arena, and demand a damaging conformity. This is called group think and happens when the members become overcommitted to a course of action and cease to be willing to look at the alternatives.

Group think occurs, for example, when a board of directors manages to convince itself, despite strong evidence to the contrary, that an investment is worthwhile. In the worst days of IBM's decline, for instance, group think gripped senior policy-makers who seemed unable to accept overwhelming evidence that policies that had previously worked no longer did.

Much the same happened in General Motors, which took years to come to terms with the reality of Japanese quality.

Stress
It can be stressful making important choices, especially if the consequences of a wrong judgement may be personally damaging.

SEE ALSO CHAPTER 16

Too much stress damages your decision-making. For example, it stops you thinking coherently and in some situations may cause you to act irrationally. An extreme example of this happening is panic.

Another adverse result of stress is a 'paralysis of analysis'. People delay making a decision while demanding yet more information. To counter this tendency:

■ Set firm deadlines by which a decision will be made.

Sometimes any decision is better than no decision at all.

Creativity

Effective decision-making requires creativity. We often tend to think of creativity as only being about inventing products or see it in the purely artistic sense. Sometimes it is seen as merely generating lists of ideas.

However, creativity contributes to all nine stages in the decision process described on page 139.

Creative conflict

Recent research suggests that when people differ in opinion and thinking styles, this can improve decision-making. High conflict teams, for example, have more:

■ distinct points of view
■ thorough creative discussion of decisions
■ understanding of the strategic issues facing the company.

In low conflict teams the understanding of strategic issues is often superficial and managers tend to miss important considerations.

Decision-making is concerned with the future and we need to use many of the essentials of creativity to handle forward-thinking: curiosity, looking beyond the obvious, taking risks, wondering if there is a better way.

Creativity makes an important contribution when we must generate alternatives from which to choose. Generally the more well-researched the available choices are, the better the chance of reaching a sound decision. Use your creativity to promote:

- different courses of action
- likely causes
- possible solutions
- a variety of outcomes.

Implementation

Busy managers often rush into a decision without properly working through how they will implement it. For example, literally hundreds of companies have plunged into total quality programmes, downsizing and e-commerce based on hasty decisions with inadequate follow-through.

Ideally you want to feel good about your decisions. Managers often suffer from decisional regret, though, and start undermining the implementation stage by attempting to reverse the decision in some way. For example, previously rejected alternatives are resurrected; previously unattractive choices seem more acceptable now that the decision has been made.

Frequent changes of mind after a decision has been made shows that some part of the decision process was handled badly.

- Act as if the choice cannot be reversed.

This does not mean being blind to new information but having confidence in the choice that was originally made.

Better decision-making through creativity

■ **Brainstorming** – generating as many alternatives as possible. Evaluation only occurs after completing the idea-generating stage.

■ **Free association** – the mind roams over broad territory by linking one word, idea or a concept with another in a chain. It can be a highly focused way of exploring alternatives.

■ **Mind mapping** – a visual way of drawing links between disparate ideas in a non-linear way.

■ **Checklists** – ensure that we look at the problem or situation more systematically. They work best for straightforward situations.

■ **Role-playing** – works well when trying to identify new alternatives to existing situations, gains people's commitment to decisions and triggers new thinking about an old problem.

■ **Drawing** – helps us contact a part of our brain that may not usually have a chance to contribute to a decision.

■ **Metaphors, analogies and images** – can redefine the problem or decision. For example, seeing a company acquisition as a 'marriage', an 'act of war' or a 'soap opera' may provide powerful new insights into the choices.

Contingencies

Contingency planning makes you prepare for unexpected consequences of your decision. You can rank these according to:

■ how likely the outcome is
■ how serious it would be.

The more serious the outcome, the more you need to consider:

■ How will you know that the problem has arisen?
■ What actions might stop it happening?

■ Can you eliminate the causes?
■ What might minimise their impact?

Commitment

Getting a decision implemented can be even harder than taking the decision in the first place. It happens when you have not spent enough time getting people's commitment to what you want to do.

Most decisions go wrong, not from careless analysis, insufficient alternatives or poor information. The commonest reason is failing to gain enough support to see the decision through. Whenever you face a decision situation, try asking:

■ Whose help do I need to get to make it happen?
■ What do I need to do to gain their commitment?

Further reading

ADAIR J. *Decision Making and Problem Solving*. London, CIPD, 1999.

BLAKELEY K. 'Decision style, stress and managing change'. *Organisations and People*. Vol. 6, No. 2, May 1999. pp13–18.

HAMMOND J., KEENEY R. *and* RAIFFA H. *Smart Choices: A practical guide to making better decisions*. Boston, Harvard Business School Press, 1999.

LEIGH A. *Perfect Decisions*. London, Random House, 1995.

POKRAS S. *Successful Problem-Solving and Decision-Making: Finding realistic solutions to the problems you encounter everyday*. London, Kogan Page, 1999.

NETWORKING

Who would you call if you were fired? Where do you go when you have a problem that no one nearby can solve? Who do you know who knows someone, who knows the person you need to know?

Nowadays it is no longer the possession of knowledge that ensures your success as a manager. Instead, the people who know where to look for information are fast becoming the valued members of an organisation.

The Internet has turned networking into a worldwide phenomenon. You can pose a question to strangers and in minutes receive amazing answers that really work. E-mail has turned networking within a company into a completely new way of working and webpages on intranets make it even easier to contact those with the information you need.

Networking is now an essential life skill that no manager can do without. It is no longer enough to know who is directly above and below you, or even on a par with you. This may matter less than being part of a group that regularly corresponds on an issue and finds answers collectively.

To be an effective networker you need to be able to draw on contacts from a wide spectrum, across an entire organisation and beyond it. As organisations have de-layered, re-engineered, flattened and in many cases disintegrated into individual business units, getting things done is no longer just a case of issuing orders.

To make things happen you have to know the right people.

Traditional organisations relied on self-contained units, a pyramid structure of known communication channels and a hierarchy of decision-making. These worked for routine and stable enterprises and government agencies. In today's fast-moving business environment, you have to operate rather differently.

Despite the fast changes, the principles of effective networking have not changed that much. You cannot expect to build contacts and get the best from them if it is all give and take – you take, they give. Successful networking depends on a shared willingness to do the unasked, to help when you do not have to, to share when there is not apparently much in it for you – short term.

In an age of brain working, the importance of contacts in business has become a critical measure of an effective manager. If you cannot or will not network, it will soon be obvious to everyone that you have limited resources at your disposal.

A sure sign that networking has come of age is the amount of software now aimed at helping people keep track of their contacts. Some, like Microsoft's Outlook, give you a basic contact system that is not much more than a sophisticated form of an address book. Specialist programmes like Act or Goldmine allow you to sort, sift and rearrange your contacts so that you can find details of anyone you want the moment they call.

On an even larger scale, client relationship management systems keep track of contacts. They create sophisticated databases so that companies can network in the broadest sense with their customers.

Networking therefore needs to be seen in the wider context of the organisation's strategic intent. It is hard enough trying to design the future, but doing it alone is almost impossible. Networking is an important way of gaining a collective view of what the future might look like, drawing on resources for implementing change.

> *Networks of companies help build successful economic regions. A person's own network helps build a career* – Daniel Muzyka in 'Thriving on chaos of the future', in Mastering Management section, *The Financial Times.* 2 October 2000.

The management role

Most managers now spend much of their time in lateral rather than vertical relationships. Interpersonal skills are therefore important, and networking in particular demands these skills.

Talk to effective managers and you will almost certainly find they work to build contacts in other departments or elsewhere. They have long ago discovered that seniority alone does not guarantee the help they need to succeed. It takes a network of personal relationships.

The point about networking is that it is personal. It involves you relating to other individuals rather than to an institution. The people you know make up your network.

Networks are loosely constructed arrangements that bypass the hierarchy. If you work in an organisation that relies heavily on projects or temporary teams, you will need an anchor as you move from one group to another. A network provides that support.

Networks facilitate direct person-to-person connections. This might be through phone calls, meetings, faxes, videoconferences, e-mail and so on. Instead of having around you one specific team, as a networking manager you build a 'virtual' team you can call on at any time.

It is important to learn the art of networking because organisations are increasingly:

- decentralised
- heavily interdependent on links between people of different knowledge and skills
- based on common and demanding standards of performance
- willing to allow leadership to be exercised by informal leaders
- ready to accept challenges to traditional boundaries.

Why network?
You get:

- more contacts leading to more business
- wider knowledge and service you can offer others
- more exposure, a higher profile
- opportunities to learn
- improved cover for periods of illness
- formal and informal support for projects/problems
- variety of information
- to offload worries and be listened to
- career enhancement
- constructive feedback
- celebration of success
- help in confronting senior people
- assistance in deciding priorities.

Others get:

- better service
- more business
- the chance to share your knowledge and expertise
- promotion of the organisation
- speedy problem-solving.

Networkers may be unacquainted with each other yet willing to help when contacted. There may be few fixed relationships and many diverse skills. Those who are appointed to run various kinds of teams may not be the most senior people, but are able to call on important resources. There is therefore a high degree of sharing and trust amongst network members. Different opinions are valued and there is considerable openness and information sharing.

Anyone can form a network. All you need is people who are flexible, willing to take responsibility and understand how their work dovetails into other people's.

You may never know the full benefits of your network, since it can help you without you even realising if. People come your way, contacts emerge, and knowledge somehow arrives, things happen. Good networkers trust that it will work for them and they put in as much as they take out.

The network is everywhere

An executive making a career change on his return from a long overseas assignment reported an exciting week because he had been to two funerals. 'You won't believe the people I met there,' he told a colleague. 'I met two headhunters, a company director and one of my cousins who is personal assistant to the chief executive of a major company.'

This manager knew few people in town and embarked on a determined networking effort. He organised a party of old school friends, many of whom had become successful since leaving school. He kept scrupulous notes of meetings, contacts and other interactions. He was polite and courteous to people who spent time with him. He maintained the contacts he had made and eventually he was offered a job.

You never know when the network will come in handy. So keep up the contacts, for months, even years, and eventually it will pay off. The connections may be so extraordinary that looking back on them it scarcely seems credible that such tenuous links led to a solution.

Dedicated networkers know that the links are never entirely clear or predictable. They just trust that these links will somehow deliver. In my own company, for example, we regularly 'put out a call' to the network, asking for help. Does anyone know a brilliant administrator? Has anyone heard of an inexpensive odd-job person? Has anyone a contact at a particular company? Each time we are surprised at the convoluted route the answer has taken to reach us.

Parcel to Saskatchewan

It is said that it takes just seven people to get a parcel taken by hand to Saskatchewan in the USA. If you contact seven people and ask each of them if they know of anyone going to the required destination, someone is bound to know someone, who knows someone, who knows someone, who . . .

In other words, networks can make just about anything happen.

Sundridge Park Management Centre asked over 300 professional women in Britain and the USA about their networking. British women found networks valuable for the social contacts they gave, whereas the American women had a much more focused approach and viewed them as business arenas. While British women saw networks as ways to meet people with similar interests, their US counterparts tended to leave a network if it did not lead to business and job opportunities.

Only a few years ago many women seemed to feel that networking was something only men do in their golf clubs and through the 'old school tie'. Such reluctance is rapidly disappearing, if not gone already. There are now scores of women's networks, including City Women's Network, Forum, Focus and Women in Business. There is even one that creates a web of contacts amongst women who attended certain private schools.

Networks enable organisations to compete in a highly volatile climate. No traditional corporate structure, regardless of how de-layered and uncluttered it becomes, can match the speed, flexibility and focus that business success demands. Networks, though, are fast, smart and fluid. They are reshaping how business decisions are made, allowing the right people to converge faster, in a more focused way.

Building your network

In the best network relationships, you do someone a favour, asking nothing in return. It is the small things that count, returning calls, e-mails, passing on a lead. Some time later, maybe weeks, months or even years, you receive a favour back from someone else in the network. Nobody keeps a score – the network lives because people want it to.

Networks focus on getting things done, rather than on procedures. They upset some managers because there is no one in charge. The Internet, of course, is the ultimate example of an uncontrolled network.

The advantage of networking is that through them you can make things happen, often bypassing traditional systems and structures. One of the unwritten principles of successful networking is the Law of Hidden Returns. This says that whatever you put into a network will eventually come back to you, perhaps multiplied several times over. You may never really know how, when or even why this happens. Often the return is invisible, yet it happens. You just assume that the system works in your favour – you trust that it does.

There is nothing metaphysical about the Law of Hidden Returns. The network succeeds because like teamwork the sum is greater than the parts.

Making contacts

Making contacts for your network can be a passive or an active process.

Passive contact building is slow, occurring naturally as you do your daily work. You extend the web by raising your awareness of how people might fit into your network and discussing with them ways of co-operating. The more you know about the people you meet, the better placed you are to see how they can fit into your network. What are their skills and experience? Who do they know? What are their goals and how might you help them achieve them?

People network by joining clubs, going to lunch with friends, attending conferences, joining industry associations, going to reunion dinners and staying in touch. They network with church members, school friends and community organisations.

The key to networking is spending significant time developing new contacts and managing the old ones. People need calling, meeting, lunching, contacting. A network is more than just a list of people or a little black book, although you can make notes of the people in it.

You cannot make networking succeed for you by arriving two minutes before a meeting starts, never contributing, making little or no time to get to know people.

Active contact building means building lists and constantly refining them. It includes everything from Christmas cards to phone calls, from lunches to sending someone the odd article about some topic you know they are interested in. You should look for excuses to call, to write, to meet. It can be time-consuming and, if you pick the wrong people, incredibly wasteful. But with the right people, your efforts will be amply justified.

Networking basics

You already have a network! The people you met at school, on your first day at a job, the supplier you work with regularly on some project. As you start to deliberately build your network, make the first move and avoid making requests. Sending out your promotional literature is not networking, it is selling.

Be prepared to help other people. Start listing the members of your network on index cards or a computer. Note down:

- when you hear information of use to them
- details of their interests, facts they have shared with you – keep it personal.

You may have to experiment to find the right approach. For example, which member should you approach with your request and how do you make it? When making a request, do not always seek the obvious. Instead try to get different answers or perspectives on an issue.

Avoid pressure when you are networking. People like to be approached gradually, not hustled into helping you. Carefully assess the ability of the person you plan to ask.

Use people's time wisely. Decide what you want before you ask for it and try to think things through before picking up the phone or dashing off an e-mail. People are forgiving of e-mail requests since they are so easy to ignore. But no one will thank you for bombarding them with requests for help that are ill thought out or unrealistic.

Check for reasonableness. Are you asking someone to take a big risk? Will it require much time and money? If the tables were turned, would you do it for the other person?

Respect people's priorities. Even though your request is impor-tant to you, the other person may be too busy to help. Accept this with good grace.

Be specific. If you are vague, you may not even get a reply. Calling half a dozen people may be useless if they are the wrong ones. Explain what you need and why. Ask them how they would approach the same problem.

Think about the phrasing and how you convey your requests. Putting a request as if it is sales patter may be less effective than presenting it as an opportunity.

Reciprocate. If someone asks you for help, give it generously. If you cannot provide it, recommend someone else to contact. Show a real interest in their problem. If you think of a way of helping after you have ended a recent verbal contact, follow it up with an e-mail explaining that you have been giving their problem some thought.

Give value. Offer value rather than trying to make a sale. In our company, for example, we often send clients articles, extracts from research papers, even whole books if we think it might help them. If you speak at conferences, write articles, or join associations only to make a sale, people soon get the message and stay out of the way. Give value without expecting anything in return.

More network principles

If someone gives you the name of someone to call, do not just thank them. Keep them informed about how you got on. That way the person feels the effort has been worthwhile and you protect your contact.

Always thank people for their help. Never take someone's good nature for granted. In networking, you really do get out what you put in.

It is never too early to start building your network. The time you need help from the network is always when you least expect it. Suddenly you are looking for a job, suddenly you hit a problem and cannot see how to solve it, and suddenly you want something from someone

Networks are based on trust, respect and personal chemistry. It can takes years to create a strong network. Paradoxically it can also happen in days when lots of people are facing the same issue and want to work together to solve it.

Networking means staying in touch. It needs nurturing. So be creative about keeping in touch; often all it takes is a quick e-mail to ask how someone is getting on or if they still need help with some issue.

Maintain a balance between asking for and giving help. Too much giving is as bad as excessive taking. When you give without ever accepting something in return, you end up making recipients hesitant to ask for more. It implies that they have nothing to offer.

When you are part of a network, people expect to be able to rely on you. Good networkers therefore deliver on promises and do not make promises they cannot honour.

It can be tempting to keep using someone in the network because they keep coming up with answers or further leads for you to follow. Refrain from exploiting a few people as this can destroy the best relationships. Instead, spread the load.

Be human. If someone asks for your help about a problem they have been wrestling with for weeks, the last thing they want is for you to solve it in seconds. This implies that they have over-looked the obvious and are stupid. Try being a good coach. Ask questions that lead them to the solution by themselves.

Although networks can be great gossip channels, people expect their issues to be treated in confidence. Do not share sensitive or confidential information with anyone else. If your sources realise you are unreliable, they will cease trusting you.

No matter how crazy or irrelevant the requests for help you receive from the network, take them at face value. Avoid pass-ing judgements on someone's situation. Even if it seems foolish to you, they may have important reasons that they cannot reveal.

Draw your network

What does your network of relationships look like? Try drawing it and you will probably find it is larger than you think. Use a large A3 sheet of paper to develop a framework like the one on page 167.

It is usually easier to start with internal relationships. Identify people you feel free to contact above and below you in the ver-tical chain. Only show those in your network where you have a direct one-to-one relationship with them. If you never speak to the boss's boss, that person is not really on your network.

If you work in a large organisation, try dividing the relationships into divisions, groups and so on. Also, avoid listing people who just happen to have the same job title. You are trying to chart genuine connections, not formal organisational arrange-ments.

Drawing your personal network

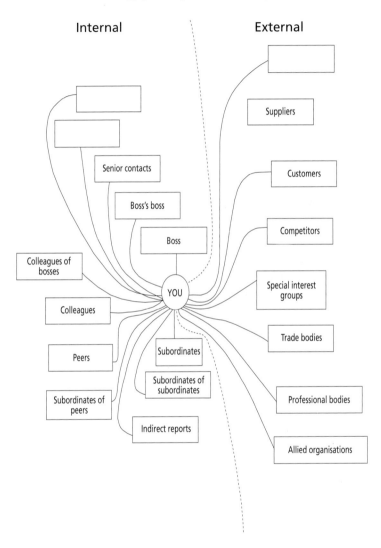

Internal   External

Suppliers

Senior contacts

Boss's boss

Boss

Customers

Competitors

Colleagues of bosses

YOU

Special interest groups

Colleagues

Trade bodies

Peers

Subordinates

Subordinates of subordinates

Subordinates of peers

Professional bodies

Indirect reports

Allied organisations

The resulting chart may open your eyes to how many people you already know. It can prompt you to start exploring ways of widening the network, or strengthening your links with key individuals.

> **Analysing network relationships**
>
> ■ What do they want from me?
> ■ What do I want from them?
> ■ How do they tell me what they want?
> ■ How do I tell them what I want?
> ■ What are the main issues or things involved in the exchanges I have with them?
> ■ How do I know if my or their performance is satisfactory?
> ■ How do the relationships vary in type, importance, and degree of interdependence, strength, political closeness, nurturing, intensity, formality, and effectiveness? Are they upwards or downwards in the hierarchy, giving or taking, static or dynamic, comfortable or difficult, social or business?
> ■ What can I do to strengthen the relationship?
> ■ Is enough time being invested in a particular relationship?
> ■ Is the networking helping me to be more effective?
> ■ How could the network serve me better and what action must I take to ensure that it does?

Look for gaps in your network and try to plug them. Similarly, be willing to weaken or sever relationships that have no hope of being productive in the long term.

It is no use cluttering your contact list with hundreds of names if you either cannot devote time to them or if they are unlikely to be of practical use. In building and maintaining your network you will always be:

■ initiating contacts
■ testing and reviewing relationships
■ developing key contacts.

Network meetings

The smooth running of a network that meets regularly depends on the effectiveness of its meetings. It is sensible to have one person chairing it, another managing time-keeping and another looking after the documentation.

Someone may need to take responsibility for running the network, for example by sending out information or calling meetings.

The meetings might be of several kinds, for example educational, networking and training events. Educational meetings might involve outside speakers and group members contributing their experience. Networking meetings would have as their main aim the achievement of every member's individual goals.

Maintaining your network

Keep seeking ways to build your network, even if you keep it as a small one. The quality of the contacts is usually more important than the quantity. Also, try discussing your network with your boss. He or she may be able to contribute to building yours.

Networks have a life of their own and need handling like any other change process. When moving into a new managerial position, effective managers spend considerable time reforming their network of co-operative relationships. They work hard at identifying and building links with those that they think will help them make a successful impact in the new role.

Your management job involves being sensitive to what is happening around you. No matter how much power you acquire, you always need to have this awareness. In fact, the more senior you become the more important it is to refine your antennae.

You need to understand the various political factions, formal and personal alliances and the leaders who may help you succeed in your job. For example, is your boss's secretary on your network? This may be a key relationship for gaining inside information and seeding ideas.

Networks are highly effective ways to tap into what is occurring above, below and around you in an organisation. If you are outside an organisation, good networking can help you obtain an excellent picture of what is happening within it. Sometimes one phone call or quick e-mail is all it takes.

The blocks

Are you a reluctant networker? Perhaps you find the whole process distasteful or messy? Often such reluctance reflects a defensiveness that ultimately damages personal effectiveness.

Shyness is certainly one reason why people avoid active networking. It takes a certain amount of confidence to call someone you hardly know and ask for help.

One of the commonest reasons why people fail to make networking succeed is that they simply forget people's names, lose their phone numbers, or fail to keep proper records.

If you are reluctant to network it is time to explore the barriers and begin to overcome them. Maybe you could benefit from some personal development programme to build your confidence. If you keep losing names, use a computer-based contact system such as a personal assistant device, or more simply use a business card holder book.

If you are unsure who might be useful as a network contact, try discussing with people how you might co-operate.

Although networks are powerful ways of getting practical help, they are not therapy groups. While networking may be therapeutic, it is not usually meant for that purpose. The exhilaration of talking to others who are active, concerned listeners should not be allowed to crowd out other activities and aims.

Networks are a recipe for personal and organisational success. Nurture yours and it will repay you many times over.

Further reading

CATT H. and SCUDAMORE P. *The Power of Networking: The power of using your contacts to advance your career.* London, Kogan Page, 1999.

FISHER D. and VILAS S. *The Power of Networking: 55 simple steps to professional and personal success.* London, HarperCollins, 1999.

LOCKETT J. *Powerful Networking.* London, Orion Business, 1999.

FORCE-FIELD ANALYSIS

Chapter 10

'The figure of 150 seems to represent the maximum number of individuals with whom we can have a genuinely social relationship,' claims anthropologist Robin Dunbar. '...it's the number of people you would not feel embarrassed about joining uninvited for a drink, if you happened to bump into them in a bar.'

If you are interested in making things happen, creating an epidemic as some experts call it, the rule of 150 is a good starting point. It is also a handy guide for influencing even the largest organisation that may employ hundreds or thousands of people.

Critical mass is a sort of contagion, a mini epidemic all of its own. It is one of the most useful secrets of making things happen in organisations. You do not need to get everyone on your side, or even half or a quarter of the people around you. All you require is enough people to start a contagion. Get this critical mass moving and any change acquires an irresistible momentum.

What is so impressive about critical mass is that it can be as few as two people, or it could be a dozen. It is seldom more than a handful, and rarely as many as the 'rule of 150', as defined by Dunbar.

Once you build critical mass thinking into your management approach, it can make life a lot easier in getting things done. However, you need to identify who has the power – the ability to say no, say yes or block progress. Some of these people may be low in the formal pecking order yet possess considerable influence.

Critical mass is therefore a lever for creating change, using the minimum amount of force. It is also at the root of the widely used force-field analysis (FFA).

FFA has been around a long time and has outlasted many high-profile management fads that have since vanished into obscurity. It survives because generations of practising managers have found that it works and helps them do their jobs more effectively. Strangely, not much is written about FFA, despite its proven effectiveness.

Assumptions
FFA assumes that:

■ at any given moment in any situation an organisation is in a brief state of equilibrium
■ the equilibrium state can be upset.

The first of these is a large assumption, yet not entirely an unreasonable one. If you studied science at school, you will recognise it as being similar to Newton's law that a body will be at rest when all the forces acting on it cancel each other out.

With organisations it is not that simple. Organisations are more likely to conform, not to Newton's idea of physics, but to those of quantum mechanics. In the latter nothing is ever in equilibrium.

In quantum mechanics you cannot even be sure of describing how things are, since certainty in one area implies uncertainty elsewhere. Likewise, organisations are complex adaptive systems. Assuming that they are stable is comforting yet wrong. In fact, they are in a continuous state of movement, although this is not always immediately obvious.

The assumption that the equilibrium can be upset is important because unless this is true then change would not really be possible.

If a company is an example of a complex adaptive system, we need to be aware of:

- **the butterfly effect** – an established part of chaos theory that shows that a small change in one place can set in motion large-scale events elsewhere
- **speed of change** – in complex adaptive systems, when change comes it can happen fast.

Both of these features feed the power of force-field analysis.

Any equilibrium is consequently notional, or at least short-lived. Instead of an indefinite status quo there is a dynamic tension between the various counteracting forces:

- restraining forces
- driving forces.

The dynamic equilibrium state

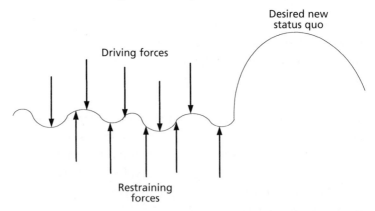

The chart above shows the situation in an organisation that is facing continuous change. The restraining and driving forces mainly cancel each other so that there is no major shift in what is happening.

But when you disturb the checks and alter the balance, something new begins to happen. With the butterfly effect in operation you never really know what will happen, as the ramifications may be unexpectedly large. In the chart something has altered and there is a new desired status quo that returns the company to another new dynamic equilibrium.

Since no organisation is ever entirely in absolute equilibrium but a constant state of flux, any status quo seldom lasts long. Yet FFA works just as well even in a fast-changing environment, so long as you use it as a way to diagnose how to influence change.

FFA in action

Suppose some people in an organisation decide that it is time to launch a new product. They may have clear ideas about this product, how much it should cost and who will buy it. They can point to strong driving forces:

- The company badly needs a new product range.
- Profit margins of existing lines have fallen sharply.
- The company has good cash reserves.
- The new marketing director wants to identify profitable new opportunities.

However, the natural checks and balances in the organisation mean that although the proposers of the new product have allies, there are restraining forces:

- Some people are not yet convinced.
- Financial managers feel the time is not right for such expenditure.
- The actual cost of development will be high.

■ The product development manager is retiring soon and is anxious not to leave on a failure.

■ The sales force has no experience of the new product area.

Right now these factors just about cancel each other out. Some work is taking place on new products but in practice there is an impasse. Even though many people see the urgency of launching a new product line, nothing much is changing. The company is stuck with the status quo, albeit a dynamic one in which minor shifts are constantly occurring.

What can the new product developers do? They need to create sufficient critical mass to make it impossible to obstruct serious work on new product design. Yet how do they do that? Using FFA language, they can either:

■ strengthen the driving forces for change
■ weaken the restraining forces for change.

In critical mass, you do not need to convince everyone to go along with what you want. Applying this to FFA you do not need to alter all the driving and restraining forces. Just changing one or two may be enough to break the impasse and precipitate change.

In our new product example, the enthusiasts for the new venture decide to strengthen the driving forces by forming a new product committee chaired by the new marketing director. This increases his commitment and is enough to get things moving.

They also decide to weaken the restraining forces by gaining the support of the head of personnel, who encourages the existing product development manager to take early retirement.

Once the equilibrium of driving and restraining forces is disturbed the change begins.

But once you set change in motion it may not turn out as expected. Altering the driving and restraining forces that currently maintain a particular situation therefore has its risks. It could lead to the achievement of the new goal and creation of a new equilibrium. On the other hand it might result in:

- a return to the previous equilibrium
- the establishment of a new, unexpected equilibrium
- long-term destabilisation.

In our example, the new product enthusiasts get their way, and a new sales line is launched in a test market. But it does not immediately achieve outstanding success. This leads to loss of confidence and insufficient investment, leading to the new line being withdrawn after a year and the company returning broadly to the way it was previously. This actually happened to the Disney Corporation shortly after its founder died. Nothing seemed to offer the same spectacular returns as Mickey Mouse. So the company kept killing off new ideas and entering new markets half-heartedly or not at all.

Using FFA

FFA focuses attention on the power of driving and restraining forces. Using it involves a mixture of defining the problem or situation, then reviewing the various forces to see how best to affect them. FFA involves the following stages:

Step 1: state the problem area

What do you want to achieve or change?

First define the broad topic area. You might be concerned for instance about affecting personnel, marketing, production or administration. The problem must be a real one and sufficiently important to be worth trying to resolve.

State the exact problem area that represents the present equilibrium, for example:

- sales of a particular product
- personal remuneration
- rejects in manufacturing
- the quality of our service.

These define the boundaries of what you want to alter.

Step 2: define the situation
Next describe the situation by stating what you want to alter, for example:

- We need to sell much more product.
- I should receive a big pay increase.
- We require fewer rejects in our manufacturing.
- The quality of our service needs to radically improve

Try to state the exact nature of the change you want, expressed for instance in how much more product should be sold, how large a pay rise you want and so on.

A problem defined is often a problem half solved, so it pays to produce a tight specification of the shift in the status quo that you want. If you are going to upset the equilibrium, be clear about what you are trying to achieve.

Step 3: specify the new equilibrium
Nail down a tight description of the new equilibrium. This is a goal statement of how the situation will look once the restraining or driving forces have been altered and new ones have come into operation.

Express the goal in quantified form, or at least provide some measurable way of deciding whether the new equilibrium has actually been reached. For example:

■ Sales of product are at a new norm of 20,000 a month.
■ My new salary is 30 per cent more than my present one.
■ We have a maximum reject rate of one part per million.
■ Our services are the most comprehensive in the industry.

Step 4: analyse the forces
Now you create two separate lists to identify the:

■ restraining forces
■ driving forces.

These lists may emerge from a brainstorming session or detailed organisational research. You need to know the forces currently at work, not ones that might arise in the future or have recently ceased to exist.

You might also choose to classify these two sorts of forces further into whether they are strong, medium or weak. This helps to decide where you are going to apply leverage. You could use a chart similar to the one on page 180.

A complicated force may need to be broken down further to make it easier to decide what might be done about it. For example, suppose that one of the restraining forces is identified as:

■ the sales force has no experience of the new product area.

This might be further broken down into:

■ The sales director is worried that he will be blamed for any failure of a new product.
■ The cost of retraining the sales force is high.

Analysing the forces

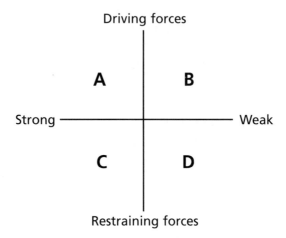

Driving forces

A	**B**

Strong ———————————— Weak

C	**D**

Restraining forces

Having analysed the forces into these four segments, you may conclude that it is better to affect those falling into segment A rather than those in segment B.

Similarly, after further analysis, you may conclude that the restraining forces in the C segment are too hard to influence and it is better to spend time trying to further weaken the restraining forces in segment D.

- The cost of retraining the sales force is high.
- The new product line requires the sales force to operate complex new software on their portable laptops and many sales staff resist this technology.

It may also be worth further dividing these into:

- ☐ **personal forces** – ones that deal with attitudes, feelings, weaknesses, relationships, education, income etc
- ☐ **relationship forces** – ones that deal with how different individuals and groups relate to one another, such as the

organisation and government, the department and a customer, the team and other teams etc

☐ **systems forces** – ones that form the organisation's environment, including political, social, legal, environmental and local conditions.

Categorising forces this way gives an added perspective to what you might do about them.

It can be helpful to draw a chart showing the forces for and against the change you want to make, as shown in the chart below.

Force-field analysis in action

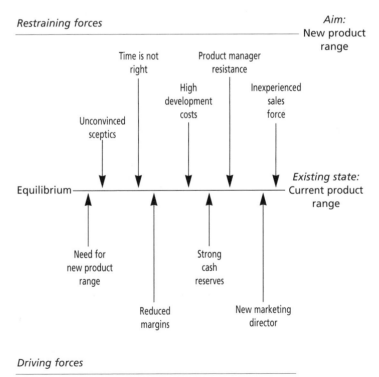

Step 5: devise a strategy

Having identified and visually portrayed the various driving and restraining forces, you now need a strategy for altering the status quo.

You cannot know all the driving and restraining forces. There just is not enough time to uncover and analyse these. As we saw earlier, this is not necessary. With the situation in dynamic equilibrium you only have to locate one force susceptible to your influence.

Selecting the right force to influence is like an army commander probing for the enemy's weak spot – you may only need one. The trick is to exploit it to the full. In reality, of course, you may not know precisely how strong the various forces are, nor what impact changing them will produce.

You can choose to:

- strengthen driving forces that do not increase resistance to change
- weaken restraining forces that do not create an excessive reaction with unpredictable consequences.

In our earlier example, one possibility would be to try to influence the early retirement of the product development manager. This action, though, would be highly political and might unleash all kinds of consequences. If the product manager is a powerful figure, he might resent such an attempt and retaliate against whoever tried to engineer it.

If you are unsure about the relative importance of the various forces, the best strategy may be a mixture of weakening a restraining force and strengthening a driving force.

Step 6: develop an action plan

Having decided on a strategy for affecting one or more of the forces, you need a detailed plan of action. This should consist of practical tasks in which you are clear about what is to be attempted and by whom.

Keep the various steps of your action plan simple. Affecting the equilibrium may take several actions. Go for a number of small successes rather than one large one. To have a real effect on a driving force, you need to be determined and able to decide whether or not your strategy is working.

Step 7: establish a new equilibrium

Having precipitated change you face two distinct reactions:

■ the change gets out of control
■ everything returns to how it was before.

Revolutionaries are often consumed by their own creation and if you are not careful this may happen to you too. For example, suppose in their enthusiasm for weakening one of the restraining forces the new product enthusiasts persuade the head of personnel to consider the early retirement option. This might lead to an unexpected top management decision to introduce much wider compulsory redundancies.

Once an equilibrium has been disturbed, there is always the chance that the original goal will be left behind. A new, undesirable situation may be created instead. For example, when the London Stock Exchange decided in 2000 that it wanted to merge with its German equivalent, it set in motion a whole raft of unexpected consequences, including a hostile takeover bid from a Swedish technology company.

While the Exchange fought off the Swedish bid it became clear that the merger with the German exchange was now dead in the water and unlikely to be revived.

Most organisations have a natural inertia. Even if the equilibrium is successfully altered and a new situation created, there is always the risk of a gradual return to the previous status quo. To institutionalise change the new equilibrium must become essential to the organisation. For example, there must be powerful restraining forces preventing any return to the previous position.

FFA offers a simple framework to help you decide what action to take. It reduces problems to a manageable size, stimulates informed discussion and encourages thinking about new courses of action.

When situations look set in concrete, FFA can often reveal that a careful alteration of the driving and restraining forces is both possible and relatively easy.

It also tends to encourage an optimistic view about making things happen and is attractive because it can be used by a single person or a large group. Using FFA with your own team, you will also discover that it promotes a common understanding of a situation and encourages better teamwork. Once people have worked their way through the analysis they are also usually more committed to affecting the change.

FFA depends for its success on the quality and completeness of the analytical work. If you do not properly identify the main driving or restraining forces you may choose one that is too weak to make much difference.

Further reading
LEIGH A. and WALTERS M. *Effective Change: 20 ways to make it happen*. London, CIPD, 1998.

PROBLEM PEOPLE

You cannot avoid the problem people. They pop up constantly, sometimes going all the way to an expensive employment tribunal to make their mark. Yet what seems a problem person may be only someone making your life as a manager difficult, for example by challenging your judgements, questioning your decisions, constantly asking for explanations.

The danger is branding such people as troublemakers when perhaps they are merely different. All organisations need mavericks. As Anita Roddick of The Body Shop has argued, find the mavericks and you will find those who can help you define the future.

It is always worth considering:

■ How much of this person's behaviour is a serious problem?

For example, when someone is 95 per cent brilliant and 5 per cent disaster, it may not be worth investing management time trying to effect change. Only when the ratios are more balanced may the effort be sensible.

No one is perfect and demanding too much from people is a sign of management weakness. It is important to show a tolerance for personality differences and individual strengths and development needs.

Not every problem person is someone to get rid of. For example a star performer, bringing in more sales than anyone else in the team, may also argue with others, be aggressive or make other people's life at work unpleasant. Managing this person may be a tough yet ultimately manageable job.

It is important how you handle so-called problem people because that may be partly how you are judged as a manager. After all, anyone can handle easy-to-manage people!

Self-destructive people

■ **the hero** – pushes himself and subordinates too hard for too long
■ **the meritocrat** – thinks the best ideas are objectively determined and ignores the political dimension in any situation
■ **the bulldozer** – runs roughshod over others in a quest for power
■ **the pessimist** – shows constant victim behaviour, seeing the downside of every change, always sees what could go wrong, not how to improve things
■ **the rebel** – automatically fights against authority and convention
■ **the goalscorer** – tries to do too much too soon.

Adapted from WALDROOP J. *and* BUTLER T. 'Managing away bad habits'. *Harvard Business Review.* Sept-Oct 2000.

Defining problem behaviour

Problem people are the ones you complain about. They may be brilliant, yet also require more of your time than anyone else, causing you headaches in countless ways.

The most obvious sort of problem person is someone who does poor work, is a bad time-keeper, resists change, constantly upsets other people, fails to speak enough, misses deadlines, annoys clients and so on.

Even experienced managers sometimes say, 'I've run out of ideas on how to deal with him' or 'She could do so much better, but

I just can't seem to make any progress' or 'He simply never does what I ask.'

Since problem people can be effective under different circumstances, such as a different manager or job, try viewing their behaviour as a symptom rather than a problem. You want to alter their behaviour, not their personality.

When asked to describe some of their problem employees, managers often use words like: 'lazy', 'poorly motivated', 'negative', 'devious', 'vague', 'living in a world of their own' and so on.

When you talk of someone in this way it assumes that you know what is going on in the other person's mind. It is useful to adopt the simple guide that:

■ Nobody comes to work to screw up.

To manage adverse behaviour you need to be specific about it:

■ Does 'lazy' mean that the person arrives late every morning, or only on Tuesdays and Fridays? And how late is late – 10 minutes, 20 minutes or just five past the hour?
■ Are there examples of what you mean by 'being negative?' Were there disparaging remarks about other employees, about the company, about themselves? What sort of remarks, to whom and about whom?
■ Are there observable consequences? Pay less attention to attitudes, feelings or intangible motivations. These are not easily altered. Instead, focus on what precisely the effect is of this person's behaviour. For example, other people are upset, frightened, frustrated, angered by what this person does.

Describing adverse behaviour using practical examples helps you to become clearer what to do about it. For example, is the cause due to internal or external factors?

Internal factors	External factors
has poor motivation	meets boyfriend who finishes early
dislikes meetings	meetings last too long
is a poor time-keeper	has a faulty watch
has low morale	is exhausted from overwork
is bored	has just been paid
has a low drive	contributions usually ignored
lacks ideas	is seldom asked for an opinion
is impatient	has an excessive workload
has poor concentration	is unwell

Even when it is possible to alter someone's behaviour, it matters who attempts to do this. Are you the right person to try to help the employee change? For example, once you raise your concerns with the individual concerned it is important to:

- describe the issue in concrete terms with examples
- show you are determined to tackle the issue
- devote enough time and energy to altering the situation.

Unless you can do all three you probably will not succeed in changing someone's behaviour. For example, simply telling someone that you are unhappy with their behaviour at work may shift some people's behaviour immediately. Problem people may take more effort.

Managing the creatives

SEE ALSO PAGES 32–3 IN CHAPTER 2

Everyone at work can potentially be creative. The danger is that we start seeing one person or a particular group as 'creatives', which conveniently relieves us of acknowledging the universal nature of creativity.

The danger is that you will treat the creatives as 'problem people' when they are simply different, because they spend more of their time honing and using their creativity. You need these people because of their exceptional ability to use their curiosity and imagination. They see things that others do not and have unusual thought processes.

Because they are also sometimes tense, neurotic and even self-pitying with brittle egos, they can end up being pushed out of the organisation simply because they are difficult to manage.

Real creatives are excited by the act of being creative, which can often mean that they have little interest in conforming or building relationships with those who they see as not contributing to the creative task at hand. So they can easily come across as cold, manipulative and uncaring, with an aversion to working in teams. For them a team may indeed be unrewarding if not entirely focused on the current creative obsession. For them teamwork may be just a distraction.

Despite the negative aspects of working with creatives, many are clearly worth the trouble and you need to find your own creative way of managing them.

Modifying behaviours

Your job as a manager and leader is to inspire and influence people to do what you want. Command and control tactics work only in situations where you have huge power over other people and increasingly this is not the case.

So how do you get someone to alter behaviour at work? Is it even possible?

An important ground rule is:

■ Do not try to be a therapist.

You are not there to offer psychological counselling and unravel deep-seated causes for why someone is behaving in an unacceptable manner. Behind inappropriate behaviour may lie family history and personality flaws that you cannot expect to resolve. These may include:

- not understanding the world from other people's perspective
- failing to recognise when and how to use power
- unwillingness to accept authority
- negative self-image
- a personality damaged by life experiences.

It is seldom a sound use of your time to attempt to resolve these problems.

Ways to tackle flawed behaviour at work include:

- coaching

| SEE CHAPTER 4 |

- counselling
- appraisal interviews

| SEE CHAPTER 3 |

- behaviour modification
- training
- confrontation
- job restructuring
- neutralising
- transferring
- punishment
- dismissal.

Informal ways to tackle problem behaviour

■ ignore it
■ delay your reaction and play for time
■ stand firm and declare your boundaries and limits
■ yield and accept it
■ acknowledge and tolerate it, then move on
■ change or adapt your own behaviour
■ influence the other person to change
■ pull rank and get the system to exert pressure
■ call it a shared problem and seek a contract to resolve it
■ seek help in relating to the difficult person.

Behaviour modification

■ It is easier to change the situation than the behaviour.
■ It is easier to change the behaviour than the attitude.
■ It is easier to change the attitude than the person.

Behaviour modification (BM) has nothing to do with brainwashing or other dubious procedures. It merely uses some basic ways to affect other people's behaviour. These stem from a mixture of psychological research and practical experience. You do not need to be a psychologist to use them.

The essence of BM is that you ignore the many possible causes behind someone's behaviour. Instead of exploring motivations, feelings or even attitudes, you focus on:

■ actions.

As a manager you are affecting people's performance all the time, without necessarily giving it a fancy name like behaviour modification. For example, you devise new work schedules, ask people to write reports, initiate projects, meet customers and so on. The question is not whether you will influence behaviour, but how.

BM influences a person's behaviour by:

- affecting the triggers or cues preceding someone's behaviour
- rewarding the results of behaviour.

Triggers

A trigger is any event generating adverse behaviour. Once you know the trigger it becomes possible to either alter or perhaps eliminate it.

For example, suppose each time you ask someone to submit a report on time it arrives late. This person's response may be due to one of several unknown triggers:

- resentment at being distrusted to deliver on time
- a dislike of imposed deadlines
- fear of report-writing.

Unravelling the root cause is unlikely to be particularly productive. What you do know is that a request for a report accompanied by a warning not to deliver it late seems to trigger lateness.

You might try altering the trigger by:

- using skilful conversation to encourage the person to offer a report without being asked
- mention when the report is needed without saying anything about late delivery.

Instead of looking at detailed causes you concentrate only on external events – the fact that every time you ask for a report it is late. You avoid guessing what is happening inside the person's head and tackle the trigger itself.

Rewarding

The second way of affecting someone's behaviour is based on

the idea that people learn from the consequences of their behaviour. That is, they obtain a 'reward' for particular forms of behaviour. If they did not do so, they would act differently.

So for example, someone may be rude because they have learned through experience that this usually gets them what they want, or enables them to avoid something they do not want to do.

■ Change the reward and you begin to affect the behaviour.

If you can uncover what reward a person might receive for adverse behaviour, you start to unlock the key to influencing them.

If each time your sales force reaches its monthly target you respond by setting an even higher target, people soon learn that it does not pay to hit targets. That is, their 'reward' for not hitting the monthly figure is that you do not raise it again.

Reinforcement

Another important part of using BM is the dual nature of rewards. Behaviour can be:

■ strengthened (reinforced)
■ weakened (discouraged).

Strengthening behaviour

When you strengthen someone's behaviour you reward him or her for doing something that you want. For instance, if you smile every time one of your direct reports says 'Good morning', you are positively rewarding their behaviour and they are likely to repeat it.

Likewise, if every time a direct report makes a suggestion you smile and then ignore it, you are in effect discouraging that behaviour and they are unlikely to repeat it for long.

Reinforcement is a powerful management tool because it is relatively easy to use. You are looking for behaviours to encourage and then find ways to 'reinforce' these so that people do more of them. Even a relatively small amount of the 'right' behaviour can lead to a larger shift if you actively encourage it early on.

So, the principle of reinforcement is:

■ Catch someone doing something right and celebrate it.

The steps for using reinforcement effectively are:

Step 1   Decide what you want the new behaviour to be.
Step 2   Identify the stages needed to get there.
Step 3   Watch for any sign of behaviour moving towards the first stage.
Step 4   At the first sign of behaviour in the desired direction, describe to the person concerned what he or she did, and offer encouragement and recognition. Explain how this behaviour helps you or the team.
Step 5   Continue reinforcing whenever the desired behaviour occurs, until it seems permanent.
Step 6   Watch for signs that behaviour is moving in the desired direction of the next stage and reinforce.

For example, suppose you want someone to be more responsible and take decisions. When they ring you and tell you they have done just that, you give a notional cheer! You reinforce what they have done along lines such as:

■ 'I'm really glad you made a decision. When you take responsibility like that it really helps me.'

■ 'I see you took a decision. I completely trust your judgement on these issues.'

Weakening behaviour

Similarly, in weakening someone's behaviour your 'reward' takes the form of a negative response – in effect a form of punishment. For example, suppose someone says detrimental things about other team members. If you smile and look really interested they are likely to carry on. But if you frown and immediately change the subject you are 'punishing' their behaviour by not rewarding it.

The trouble with punishment, though, is that it is easily misunderstood. You will often discover that you are inadvertently either rewarding undesirable behaviour, and thus encouraging it, or mistakenly punishing good behaviour.

Suppose someone keeps phoning you for approval every time they want to make even a minor decision. The constant calls interrupt your work and yet you always listen sympathetically, offer advice and ask pertinent questions until the person rings off. By asking, 'What is this person's reward (pay off) for calling me?' you may begin to identify how to change the person's actions. For instance, rewards might be:

■ gains detailed advice
■ shares the decision load
■ avoids making a decision unaided
■ feels important for being able to interrupt the boss.

It may be sensible to reverse your approach. Next time the person rings asking for help you might withhold the reward. Instead of offering advice and prolonged listening, you might listen in a totally non-committal way and indicate you have limited time available. Soon the employee learns that calls about minor decisions no longer gain the desired response.

The 12 dos of behaviour modification

- Choose an appropriate reward or punishment.
- Supply ample feedback.
- Recognise that different people need different rewards.
- Reinforce constructive behaviour.
- Schedule rewards intermittently.
- Ensure that rewards/punishments quickly follow observed behaviour.
- Remember that ignoring certain sorts of behaviour may eliminate it.
- Tell people what they must do to be rewarded.
- Punish people in private, not in front of others.
- Make rewards or punishments fit the behaviour.
- Change the rewards periodically.
- Reward only real changes in behaviour.

The essence of behaviour modification is:

- Find the trigger for behaviour and use it to influence change.
- Catch people doing something right and encourage them to do more of it.
- Uncover the 'reward' a person gets for adverse behaviour and then stop rewarding it.

Confrontation

Fear of an unpleasant scene makes some managers carefully avoid any form of confrontation. This could be for many reasons, including a fear of being unable to handle their own emotions in dealing with difficult people.

Yet, confrontation need not be a miserable experience. It can even be satisfying and inspiring. Direct confrontation means tackling adverse behaviour as it occurs, or shortly afterwards. For example, in our own team the rule is to confront someone within two weeks if they behave unacceptably. Otherwise, the issue is considered dead. This prevents resentment smouldering and gnawing away at our mutual respect and trust.

Another method we employ is regular development sessions in which team members sit opposite each other in pairs and communicate directly on two issues:

■ 'What I really appreciate about you is . . .'
■ 'What I want less of from you is . . .'

Invariably the experience is both challenging and satisfying. Many potentially 'difficult people' problems are dealt with by this simple method.

■ You can confront telling the truth, in a kind or loving way.

Effective confrontation starts with an 'I' statement about what you want, expressed in a positive form. For example, 'I want you to get your next three reports in on time', rather than 'Your next three reports must not be late.' For other examples, see the box on page 198.

Avoid indirect statements such as:

■ 'The team feels . . .'
■ 'The company would like . . .'
■ 'One just does not do that sort of thing.'

Positive confrontation is saying what you want, rather than what you do not want. Plan when and where this will happen:

■ For instance, before a meeting, think about what the person does well, such as making good sales presentations, developing leads, attending to detail.

Confrontation

Negative	Positive
I think you're obstructive.	I want constructive criticism.
I dislike you always being late.	I need you to arrive on time.
I consider you talk too much.	I want you to listen more.
I find your reports too long.	I need shorter reports.

Step 1 Say clearly what you want:
'I'd like you to listen more and be more constructive.'

Step 2 Explain clearly what effect the behaviour has on you or others:
'I find it insensitive when you keep interrupting.'

Step 3 Give a specific example:
'When John made his proposal you rushed in and rubbished it.'

Step 4 Ask for change:
'In our next meeting I'd like you to listen more and say how you can improve things, rather than producing negative comments.'

- Find recent examples to show these in action. Even if you never use them, it reminds you that the person makes positive contributions too.
- Similarly, be ready to offer specific examples of the behaviour you find unacceptable.
- It often makes sense to take the person aside, rather than confront him or her in public.

If you intend to confront the person in your office, greet the person pleasantly when he or she arrives and step from behind your desk. Smile and say something friendly like 'Thanks for coming.

Let's both sit over here.' You will probably do this anyway if you are an outgoing person.

Give thought to the seating arrangements. Desks or tables create a communication barrier between people. Sitting next to someone, side-by-side, makes it harder for them to be aggressive and confrontational back. However, be careful to allow the person sufficient physical space from you.

Often a person already knows that their behaviour is causing problems. At least give them the chance to acknowledge that there is a problem. So, for instance, in your own words ask:

- 'Do you feel there is anything that needs to change in how you are currently performing?'
- 'I am concerned about your performance and wonder if you know why that might be?'

If someone mentions their problem behaviour, start discussing the changes you want. If the person does not mention it, say directly what you want. Maintain eye contact, without glaring. Wait for a reaction, then if necessary ask for a response.

Use fact-seeking questions to discover whether the person sees any problems in achieving what you want, for example: 'What do you need to do to do it differently next time?'

Use open-ended questions to encourage the person to talk about the issue. For example, 'What do you think of your tendency to keep interrupting other team members?'

At the end, ask the person to summarise the conversation. Check that they have heard and interpreted it correctly, including the agreed action.

Dismissal

Unless you are an extremely unfeeling person, dismissing someone is seldom a pleasant experience, even when the person has been causing problems for a considerable time.

There are increasingly tough employment laws making it harder to simply exercise managerial power and dismiss someone. For example, legal action is possible based on wrongful dismissal, racism and so on.

Nor can you continue dismissing people without damaging your reputation as an effective manager of people. At some point, you will be stuck with someone whose problem behaviour must be managed.

The case for dismissal

Organisations differ widely in what justifies dismissal. Usually it includes:

- dishonesty – lying or derogatory remarks about you or the company
- excessive absenteeism
- substance abuse
- lack of co-operation – in carrying out instructions, not checking acceptability of methods, constantly complaining to the senior management without first confronting line management
- lack of productivity.

Managers are often surprisingly reluctant to take the final step of dismissal. It can certainly be emotionally difficult through:

- guilt – what did I do wrong?
- reluctance to tell the bad news

■ fear of legal ramifications
■ concern about finding a replacement
■ worry that the decision will reflect on their ability to manage.

While these are understandable feelings, they prevent one from making a rational decision on behalf of the organisation. It is therefore important to be able to discuss the potential dismissal decision with either a senior colleague or an employment expert. Sometimes it even pays to spend time with a coach who can help put the choices into a better perspective.

Is it necessary?
An actual dismissal may not be necessary. By exploring the situation, the person concerned may come to see the options for themselves. For example, a person may even suggest that it is mutually beneficial to part company.

If you decide to go for dismissal:

■ Seek professional advice – there may be specific organisational rules about issuing written and verbal warnings before you are empowered to take this course of action.
■ Explore termination options with the employee.
■ Reduce the possibility of legal action with sound documentation; for example, up-to-date record of warnings, failures to perform or other adverse behaviour. Keep the person's appraisal record up to date.
■ Be willing to stick to your guns; dismissal in large organisations and public agencies can take quite a time.
■ Watch out for the 'reverse sympathy' phenomenon. While you are dealing with the problem behaviour, you may attract sympathy. Once you begin the dismissal process, however, you may be viewed as the villain.
■ Do not take the whole process too much to heart. While it is not a light-hearted matter to dismiss someone, it does not have to be a personally destructive matter either. The unpleasantness will pass.

References

If you think you can offload troublesome employees quickly by giving them a glowing reference, think again. It may cost your company dear. It may be tempting to exaggerate to help a friend or to encourage someone to leave. But court action has shown that all references must be true, accurate and fair to everyone, including prospective employers.

If a new employer can show it has suffered a loss, the former employer risks being sued for negligence and could end up paying for all the new company's recruitment, training and legal costs. What is worse, the problem employee could even use the argument that an over-favourable reference is proof that he or she is competent and was wrongly dismissed.

One way to avoid trouble is to avoid giving any reference at all. Even this can be seen as victimisation. Or you could add a disclaimer along the lines of 'no responsibility can be accepted for any error, loss or damage by relying on this reference'.

The best solution is:

- stick to the facts
- do not volunteer too much
- leave out any emotion.

Finally do not be tempted to expand the reference over the phone, you could still find yourself in legal difficulties.

Handling a collision

Even if you feel confident about dealing with a problem person, others may be less sure of what to do. As a practising manager, therefore, one role you may find yourself playing is facilitating an improved relationship between a problem person and someone else. Sometimes it may even be sorting out a collision between problem people.

You may be asked to act as a mediator, or to merely chair the discussion where you can be an objective party without taking sides. When you have to sort out a collision, what actions do you need to take? Here are the main ones:

- *Prepare* – ensure that you have a comfortable room, rather than a confrontational setting.
- *Arrange* – rather than place the two chairs directly opposite each other, put them almost side-by-side and pointing towards the third chair where you will sit. It is harder for people to argue when they sit next to each other rather than opposite.
- *No interruptions* – make sure that you will not be disturbed. It can be galling to just get two people communicating well with each other only to be interrupted in some way.
- *Set boundaries* – create the right atmosphere by explaining what outcome you want and getting both parties to agree to this. Be wary of trying to get both parties to debate the desired outcome as this may merely precipitate more disagreement. Get both people to agree that they will first give a definition of what they think the problem is. Even if one says they see no problem, ask this person to make a guess at what the issue is. *Then ask each to summarise the other person's position to that person's satisfaction*. This forces much greater clarity about what the issues are, rather than merely expressing dissatisfaction.
- *Let go of content* – your job is to facilitate the process, not worry about steering the conversation in any particular direction. By not becoming involved in the detail and focusing on how the two people are communicating with each other, you avoid getting drawn in too deep.
- *Focus on process* – pay attention to what is going on, rather than content. What is not being said? Are they being authentic and expressing themselves honestly or are they holding back? Simply commenting on what is happening can be a powerful way of moving the interchange on.

- *Be more than do* – it is more important that you bring energy and your personality to the situation than use lots of facilitation techniques. By being calm, smiling and empathic you can create a safe environment where people can be open and honest. If you are truly present, every aspect of your body language will convey that you are neutral and interested in helping to resolve their mutual problems.
- *Intervene when appropriate* – by carefully observing what is happening you will detect when it makes sense to intervene. In these situations less is more. You may intervene to:
    - tell people what to do
    - make suggestions
    - ask for agreement
    - leave both parties to decide how to proceed.
- *Tackle the tough situations* – do not avoid dealing with issues that seem difficult or conflict-ridden. You cannot be effective if you are fearful of making a mistake or being unpopular. If the situation gets sticky, suggest a coffee break. If someone is being aggressive or disruptive speak to the person privately, giving them feedback on what they are doing.
- *Close* – often both parties will make it clear that they have gone as far as they want to solve their mutual problem. So you sum up and gain agreement on what each will do next. Check that both parties agree with your interpretation of what will happen next. Alternatively you may need to bring the proceedings to a close by first indicating that there are five minutes left and then to formally end it. Sometimes both parties may seem reluctant to leave. This can be a good sign, for example that they want to continue working on communicating. Quietly get up and leave, thanking them for their efforts.
- *Congratulate* – if both parties have reached a consensus or some resolution of their dissatisfaction with each other, show how pleased you are with this result. Wish them luck in the

next stage of their relationship with each other. If necessary, suggest a follow-up date to review progress.

Further reading

HONEY P. *Improve Your People Skills*. London, CIPD, 2001.

HONEY P. *Problem People: And how to manage them*. London, CIPD, 1992.

LLOYD K. *Jerks at Work: How to deal with people problems and problem people*. Franklin Lakes, Career Press, 1999.

PALMER S. *and* BURTON T. *Dealing with People Problems at Work*. Maidenhead, McGraw-Hill, 1996.

SALTER B. *and* LANGFORD-WOOD N. *Successfully Dealing with Difficult People*. London, Hodder and Stoughton, 1998.

TEAM BRIEFINGS

Chapter 12

It took only a few hours for a message from a Roman general to reach every centurion. Team briefings have been happening for millennia and are essential for running any effective organisation.

Teams are now a pervasive way of organising work so it is essential to be an effective briefer. However, the difference between the days when Roman generals used team briefings and today is that modern briefings tend to be two-way affairs. They are not merely about cascading information downwards, like tablets from the mountain. They are also concerned with funnelling information upwards, so that decision and policy-makers are better informed about what they are doing.

Good briefings are a valuable management tool and when they are well run everyone has an opportunity to contribute.

Research has shown that managers usually rate team briefings as one of the best ways of communicating with their workforce and hearing staff views.

Purpose of briefings

Briefings do not just disseminate information; they also affect how an organisation manages its future. Feedback from these events enables the organisation to plan its long-term future.

For example, what do those taking part in such briefings think customers want? What ideas do they have for maintaining and enhancing the organisation's competitive edge? Often the answers seem highly parochial because people only know about their team, their own jobs and their local situation. By giving the team a wider context, you help people contribute to making the organisation adaptable and more able to redefine its future.

Team briefings

- encourage co-operation
- shape individuals into a team
- promote standard-setting
- increase commitment
- enhance your leadership role
- counteract the grapevine
- reduce misunderstandings
- encourage sharing.

Team briefings in many organisations are not an optional extra. They are how the enterprise gets many things done quickly. It is a way of bringing everyone together to share information.

Increasingly e-mail and webpages are being used to keep a team in touch with events and to provide rapid feedback on what people are thinking. Telephone and video conferencing are other ways of holding a team briefing. The best briefings, though, happen face to face.

For managers the briefing is an opportunity to convey important messages, either of their own, or ones coming from more senior management. This is not an occasion for chastising people or a disciplinary session. You do not use the briefing to get revenge or to put people in their place.

If people leave feeling blamed, then the session has been a failure. Briefings are really just an extension of regular team meetings, and if you do not already have these, it is certainly time to start them.

How often?
The briefing session you call helps build your team, strengthening relationships and enhancing collaborative working. Some

organisations, like Federal Express, make these gatherings mandatory and regular. Everyone comes to expect a team briefing at known intervals.

Briefings at Federal Express
The company's in-house guide explains that a team briefing is:

- a half-hour meeting
- to allow two-way communication
- held monthly and in company time
- with dates displayed in advance
- led by the work group leader
- monitored by the work group's manager.

Content:
- core brief
- contract information
- work group information
- performance measures.

A Premier League football team that only met once a season with its coach would not stay at the top for long. Teams need to meet regularly and briefings need to happen with reasonable frequency. Regularity makes the briefing system work for you. It gives everyone plenty of opportunity to learn how to use the time constructively.

Choose appropriate events to trigger a briefing session. Ask people to reserve specific dates in their diaries for the regular briefings. This allows them to plan their own time well and underpins the principle of regularity.

Most teams require a formal briefing at least once a month and many meet weekly or even daily. The nature of the issue and the sort of team dictates how often to call briefings. There needs to be a significant issue that is worth sharing. Avoid calling one when you have nothing worthwhile to say.

A well-run team briefing should normally last no more than an hour and often much less. Beyond an hour, people start losing concentration. Also, most people's memories can only hold about half a dozen key points, so it is not particularly helpful simply extending the time devoted to the briefing.

■ Keep briefings short and involving, rather than long and passive.

Preparation

Briefings put you centre stage. People expect and want you to shine. So there are plenty of reasons for preparing carefully.

Even talented actors need to rehearse their lines, so give yourself space to prepare properly. You may be able to just improvise, especially if you feel particularly passionate about some issue and are fully on top of it.

In the UK government's Home Office department, a group of managers wanted to introduce a large number of colleagues to the new corporate identity and other allied information.

The briefing team took the job seriously, meeting with two expert coaches who helped them devise a creative way of conducting the briefing.

Not only was the briefing unusually powerful, everyone attending paid close attention and enjoyed the commitment of the briefing group to getting its message across.

Not preparing is risky, and while it can work occasionally, it is not the best way to become an effective team briefer. Preparation for gaining everyone's attention is similar to what you would do for any verbal presentation (see Chapter 15). You need to be clear about the purpose and the messages you want to get across.

An effective way of making briefings work is to ask yourself:

■ What is the main headline I want them to remember?

Sum up the briefing message in a single sentence, perhaps a few key words:

■ tighter budgets
■ fewer jobs
■ a product breakthrough
■ the deadline has changed
■ handling the new contract
■ we are going global.

When you are unclear about your message, people notice your lack of confidence and respond accordingly. You cannot give a good briefing if you are full of 'ums' and 'ers' and wander erratically from one point to another.

Making an impact

Beyond sound preparation and being clear about the main message, there are certain basic principles worth following. The first is:

■ Be specific.

People want the core message, not waffle surrounding a kernel of information buried inside. Give specific information with examples and facts, rather than generalisations. For example, if the purpose of the briefing is to tackle a newly imposed deadline, say so. Avoid a lengthy explanation about market forces, management pressures, technical considerations and so on.

Avoid blaming outside influences for events you are talking about; this makes you look powerless and sound like a victim. People want a picture of what has changed, what is going to happen and what they can do next.

The second principle is:

■ Explain the purpose of your briefing.

If necessary, give people the headline, the one-liner that sums up everything. It may seem too direct, but most people welcome openness.

Thirdly:

■ Break the information into manageable chunks.

If you give them a headline story, move quickly to breaking it down into its component parts. This allows people to absorb it more easily. Since people can only remember a few key points from any lecture or talk, there is little point in cramming the time with endless facts and detail. Give them digestible amounts.

Fourthly:

■ Spell out the implications.

Answer the question that everyone is silently asking: 'What does this mean for me?' This may mean covering the implications for the team, individual team members, the team leader, the organisation and other affected parties such as clients, trade unions or shareholders.

Finally:

■ Say what will happen next.

Be prepared to explain where the headline message is leading, such as changes in work schedules, a programme of redundancies starting next month, a switch in priorities from one area to another and so on.

If you do not know what the implications are, say so. People will react more favourably to someone who explains the limits of their present knowledge.

However, be careful about dumping your own anxieties on the rest of the team. For example, if you are giving people bad news, try to avoid appearing as if you are blaming other people or feeling helpless.

Breaking the bad news

■ be honest – lies will only return to haunt you
■ minimise surprise – avoid last minute news
■ do not apologise – saying sorry is nice but weakens any explanation
■ separate business from personal
■ listen carefully to any response – react but pick up important information
■ if you make a promise, keep it – put it at the top of your 'to do' list.

Involvement
Well-run team briefings involve everyone who attends, not just the manager in the spotlight. Make them two-way affairs, with people asking questions and discussing the new situation.

Inexperienced managers are often upset if there is little or no response from the team to apparently important information. People may sit there looking blank, with nobody commenting and without even any questions.

Silence does not mean the briefing has failed. People may still be trying to make sense of the news. Also, if there are more than three or four people in the room, some people may be shy and unwilling to start asking questions. Also, in some multicultural teams, the members may come from a culture where it is unacceptable for subordinates to question managers.

Spend about half to two-thirds of the time giving information. Leave the remainder for people to start processing the information and offer their reactions.

Consider calling a short break after you have delivered your most important information. Invite people to discuss what they think about what they have heard, with a colleague or in small groups. This gets people talking and breaks the stilted silence that may have arisen. After a while, ask the pairs or small groups to sum up their thoughts in a few sentences and to choose someone to convey them to the rest of the meeting. This will almost certainly raise plenty of questions or issues.

A prompt start

Because they know that briefings are important, most team members will arrive on time. Encourage them to do so by asking people to come 10 minutes early in order to socialise and have refreshments.

If people arrive late, do not reward them by starting your briefing from the beginning. Make a point of welcoming their arrival and suggest that they talk to a colleague afterwards to catch up on what they have missed.

Materials

Since some people absorb information better if they have something in writing, consider supplying a one-page summary of the contents of the briefing. Only occasionally is the information too sensitive to handle in this way. For example, it might be politically unwise to release written details of the exact timing of a new marketing campaign, or precise numbers of planned redundancies.

Take careful notes of any questions since these may be useful to share with other decision-makers. They may also remind you that certain issues need to be followed up with giving people more information.

Being briefed

Sometimes you will receive a briefing that you use to inform your own team. On behalf of the team think of questions people might want answered, challenge assumptions or explore the implications of decisions. Go to your own briefings as an ambassador or representative of your team. Take notes if the issue is complex and find out exactly what you can tell your team. For example, how much of your own briefing is confidential and how much may be shared?

If you have to hold back information, explain that nothing will remain confidential for long. Keeping secrets in most organisations is almost impossible. Most team briefings leak, so treat all of your team briefing as if it is being widely broadcast.

E-mail briefings

Many managers now run virtual teams that may be spread halfway around the world. Such teams may only have a chance to meet in a single room once or twice a year. The rest of the time the team stays in touch electronically.

E-mail briefings are essential for these virtual teams and may be the only way you can keep people up to date with what is happening. Since team members may be inundated with other e-mails, it is important that your briefing gets the attention it deserves.

Consider giving your e-mail a heading that creates a sense of flow, for example you might number each briefing sequentially, so that the topic appears as part of the message subject. Another way is to build in a regular question and answer section in which people can pose issues and get replies, which other team members also see.

Consider also creating your own team briefing webpage, either on the company intranet or on a server to which everyone can gain easy access. This webpage is like an interactive newsletter, which the team uses to find out what is happening and to share common issues.

Further reading

CLARK C. *How to Give Effective Business Briefings: Effective techniques for relaying information to and obtaining feedback from employees*. London, Kogan Page, 1999.

FORSYTH P. *Making Meetings Work*. London, CIPD, 1996.

LEIGH A. *and* MAYNARD M. 'How to run an inspired team briefing,' in *Leading Your Team*. London, Nicholas Brealey, 1995.

MCGEOUGH P. *Team Briefing: A practical handbook*. London, Kogan Page, 1995.

PROJECT MANAGEMENT

At the base of the London Eye sits an impressive plaque declaring that the giant wheel was officially opened by Robert Ayling, BA's chief executive. The inscription might well have added: 'overdue and over budget'.

Despite careful planning and the king's own close interest, plus plenty of resources, the Great Pyramid was at least a year behind schedule.

Not much seems to have changed in several thousand years.

At some point in your career as a manager you are likely to lead a project and will be expected to demonstrate basic project management skills. Hopefully you will do rather better than the project managers of the Channel Tunnel and the Jubilee Line, both of which escalated way beyond the original estimates and were finished much later than intended.

Nowadays, unlike Egypt's pharaoh, you can call on some important new techniques. However, as the Channel Tunnel shows, for example, having them available is not quite the same as making them work for you.

Project work is an alternative to getting things done on a functional basis. Instead of the finance, people undertaking an activity and the production people doing something else, a project brings them together and they work, in effect, as a team. The team, though, may be a virtual one that hardly meets, being based all around the world. The project manager ties all the activity together.

What is a project?

It is a programme of work expected to produce change. What makes projects special is that they are usually governed by:

- time – the work has a beginning and an end
- cost – the work can be planned, controlled and contained within a budget
- quality – the work can be to an agreed standard and brought to a successful conclusion.

Once project management was used to steer one-off schemes like installing a computer system or planning an office move. Now organisations are moving to team-based and often cross-functional project-based activity. Just about any manager these days is expected to know how to lead a project; it is no longer just an area for a specialist.

The idea of a project applies to an enormous range of industries, circumstances and business situations. Behind the diversity is a common thread – a set of common principles that most managers can learn and use when necessary.

Businesses are increasingly turning to project management to tackle difficult tasks. Traditional structures are often unsuited for bringing new products to market quickly or solving complex technical problems.

Although there are probably many potential projects that can help an organisation, the ones to focus on are those with important strategic ramifications – ones that help the enterprise redefine its future. However, there is a limit to how many can be run simultaneously. The limitations are available resources and time. Originally, project management meant using methods rather like a military campaign, using:

- planning
- scheduling
- implementing
- monitoring
- control.

Supporting these were techniques such as Gantt and Pert Charts, which identified and managed the 'critical path'. Alter something anywhere in the whole scheme and these systems highlighted how it affected the critical path, that is, when and how the result was reached.

Nowadays these methods are still used but are less relevant when so much changes at Internet speed. What is worse, they take little account of the key resource for most successful projects: people.

Increasingly we are seeing team-based aims in which participation in reaching a shared goal constitutes 'the project'. The task is still tightly defined, it still involves issues of time, cost and quality, but now the project manager is less a controller than a facilitator.

In today's and tomorrow's organisation, tasks are often difficult, controversial, cross-functional, risky, volatile and have uncertain outcomes. Project management in such an environment is rather different to the traditional version that used a specialist technician.

As a project manager, you are more like an entrepreneur than progress chaser, more like a catalyst than an analyst. Anyone these days can be a project manager and often is.

Since so many issues can turn into a project, it is important that you choose carefully which ones you lead and which you hand on to others to bring to fruition. Choosing to adopt a project management approach has various benefits, such as:

---

10 Commandments of Project Management

1 *Purpose* – projects are for a specific reason. Unlike a committee or permanent team, they focus on a highly specific goal and exist in response to a particular organisational need.

2 *Customer* – every project needs a customer who gains from the successful outcome; this is the owner or sponsor.

3 *Accountability* – one person is in charge. The project leader is responsible for results and needs the right to deploy the necessary resources to ensure success.

4 *Explicit* – the scope, responsibilities and policies behind the project are clarified from the start – everything is clear, from the brief to the reporting system.

5 *Planned* – you first identify the detailed project activities, and second who is responsible for what.

6 *Control* – there is an agreed method for controlling the work. Whether computer-based or a simple 'to do' list, activities are tightly monitored and controlled.

7 *Membership* – the project team is chosen with care. They represent the range of needed skills and have access to resources.

8 *Reporting* – there is a formalised way of reporting progress. It does not need to be elaborate; it needs to be regular and understandable.

9 *Deadlines* – completion times are realistic with plenty of built in slippage; there are defined beginnings and ends and everyone understands the constraints.

10 *Motivation* – concern and effort goes into generating and maintaining enthusiasm, energy and momentum.

- ■ draws on wide-ranging skills
- ■ shifts focus to linked objectives
- ■ tackles complexity and other pressures
- ■ increases the focus on business aims
- ■ is driven by a clearly identified person

- recognises the human and technical aspects
- is proactive and forward-looking
- recognises uncertainty and risk
- is a useful learning arena.

You as a project manager

What do you need to be a successful project manager? Once it meant mainly being able to analyse and control a complex piece of work. Now you might also become involved in:

- shaping and setting goals
- identifying and fighting for resources
- gaining support and sponsors
- generating motivation and commitment.

In particular, to successfully lead projects you need to be able to:

- *manage the group* – lead a proactive, creative unit, not a committee
- *manage up* – influence senior management or heads of units
- *manage across* – impact on colleagues in other departments
- *manage outwards* – interact with consultants, suppliers and constrictors
- *manage the rest* – affect those taking the project to the next stage.

Start-up

Since project management is expensive, it needs to be used selectively. Adopt it when:

- the task has a wide scope
- the work involves mainly unfamiliar territory
- the issues are complex
- the outcome depends on using disparate disciplines and skills
- the cost of failure or benefits from success are high.

What do you look for if you have to choose a project manager? The secret lies in selecting someone able to lead people well and with a knack of getting the best from them. This is far more important than sheer brilliance at the technical aspects of project control.

Someone who keeps wonderful progress charts, documents everything meticulously and has a passion for order may seem to be the ideal person. Yet, without strong people skills you only have half a project manager.

The '10 Commandments' listed above are a useful guide in establishing a project, and number 3 – having one person in charge – is particularly important. Whenever you create a project team be sure there is one designated person with the authority to lead it.

The project manager must be able to challenge assumptions and targets affecting individuals, teams, departments, customers and so on. In a multidisciplinary team drawn from across or beyond the organisation, there may be mixed loyalties. In this situation, the project manager needs to find ways to hold people's interest and maintain their commitment to the work. You can help the project leader do this through the initial arrangements. For example:

■ accountability – give the team responsibility for doing the total job
■ reporting – all project team members should look to the project leader for direction; if the project work runs parallel with their normal work, clarify how people's priorities will be decided
■ membership – where possible allow the project leader to select the team; ensure that anyone joining it clearly understands the task and the team's responsibilities; it may be necessary for you to meet team members personally and brief them on their expected contribution

- stability – do not allow project team members to be drafted to other work that undermines their project responsibilities
- feedback – find ways to give the team regular feedback on how you see its efforts and progress.

Keeping track

Projects consist of a set of activities or tasks to be completed. These can usually be broken into sub-activities. Complex projects such as building a new airliner can consist of thousands of separate activities that start as broad brush ones: build the fuselage, design the wings, create the cabin interior. Each is then divided into hundreds of other tasks.

Most people can only comprehend about 10 or 20 activities before excess detail blurs any sense of what is happening. Keep the number of main activities to a manageable number, usually around six to 15. These may then be further subdivided as separate sub-projects.

Networks

Networks are a computer-based graphical way of showing the entire project, while also revealing how one activity relates to others. With this network tool, you can explore all parts of the project and analyse its various elements. It helps you decide what needs to be done and in what order.

There are many possible ways to sequence the work. You could for example start one activity before another, but what difference will this make to the outcome? Other activities can run in parallel rather than in sequence. For example, while you are boiling the kettle for tea you can also get the cup and tea bag ready. Parallel activities are often the way to complete a project with seemingly impossible deadlines.

Certain project activities depend on the start or finish of others. By unravelling and altering 'the dependencies', a team can often find ways to speed up whole sections of the project. Network systems help you identify and explore the dependencies.

When you sequence all the activities effectively, a critical path may emerge that determines the least time it will take to complete the project. Project managers who use networks well use the critical path to control and influence the outcome.

Various inexpensive computer-based network systems do not require specialist project management skills. Many packages also offer a 'what if' facility. You can therefore explore the possible consequences of different actions on the final timing of the project. For example, you can calculate the impact of an overtime ban or a series of machine breakdowns.

Responsibilities chart

This helpful tool provides a visible record of who holds responsibilities for different aspects of a project. This is useful when you are trying to co-ordinate the inputs from different departments, suppliers or other outsiders.

The responsibility chart establishes commitments and it is usually prepared by showing activities or tasks against named individuals. It should define who would:

- carry out the work
- take decisions alone
- take decisions jointly
- manage progress
- have to be consulted before a decision or action
- have to be informed before a decision or action
- be available for advice and tuition
- provide detailed help with a task.

Once the main responsibilities have been allocated, an effective project manager ensures everyone understands what to do.

Individual tasks are broken down into sufficiently small divisions to enable people to have a weekly set of activities. With inexperienced project members, it is sensible to ensure that they only have one thing to complete at a time.

Sims Portex, a thriving UK manufacturer of medical devices, wanted to increase the proportion of its sales coming from new products to 15 per cent against less than 2 per cent. Many new products were overdue by up to a year. The only way to get things moving was to use everyone's expertise and the company introduced a project management system. Anyone could apply to become a project manager.

The criteria for potential project managers were:

- leadership
- planning ability
- commercial awareness
- a flair for finance
- the ability to assess risks.

'We wanted to change the company from being responsive to being more proactive,' explains the company's training manager. The company's project charter 'helps us think of all aspects of a project: the people available, the resources required, the scope of the project.'

Project management now permeates Sims Portex, and project software previously only used in R&D has been extended to all departments. The corporate shift has changed the company's culture. People now take more responsibility and are held accountable. Equally important, new products will represent nearly a fifth of sales by 2002.

Adapted from MacLeod M. 'Instrumental change'. *People Management*. 8 June 2000.

Reporting

Most projects have a sponsor who:

- ensures there are enough resources
- gets a benefit from the outcome
- expects to be kept informed about progress.

The project team also needs information on how it is doing. Ideally, there should be a report sufficiently frequently for the group to be able to use this information to adjust work rates.

One common danger is producing reports with far too much detail. If you are someone who revels in detail, then let someone else produce the progress report! It needs to be short and clear, rather than long and complex. Useful ones focus on general progress, with the differences highlighted between actual and expected progress.

If the end date of the project is under threat, this needs to be made clear. Good reports go further than just a list of what is on or off schedule. They also identify any actions needed to correct variances and show what the cost will be in terms of time and money.

The project manager

Systems do not manage projects – people do. They do it by making decisions and initiating action. Good project managers can handle complex, costly projects, working to tight deadlines. Major projects, such as ensuring that all the computers in Lloyds TSB avoided the impact of the millennium bug, required a full-time experienced project leader who spent nearly five years preparing the organisation's facilities for the critical moment.

Such a scheme needs someone with special qualities of technical expertise, decisiveness, calmness under pressure and diplomacy.

What do project managers do?

- complete a feasibility study
- prepare the project plan
- define the work, time and cost forecasts
- manage the project's progress
- deal with the team relationships
- report back to the project sponsor
- manage the sponsor's expectations
- produce, through the team, the project results.

Because the project may cut across many organisational, geographical and even cultural boundaries, the project manager may need to handle situations where personal authority is uncertain or ambiguous. This means being able to handle conflict. The main sources of conflict are:

- project priorities
- schedules
- administrative procedures
- technical issues
- deployment of human resources
- relationships
- cost.

Usually the best way of dealing with these is not pushing them out of site, but forcing them out into the open. However, it takes a strong, confident personality to bring such matters to the surface and ensure that they are addressed. Conflict situations are vigorously debated in a spirited, reasoned way, usually led by the project manager. The latter will stress the need to examine the evidence and resolve the issue quickly. Effective project managers also know the three Cs:

- consultation
- co-operation
- compromise.

Being appointed a project manager is usually a great compliment, even if it is a bed of nails. Once in the role you may not receive the sort of management support you expect and your relations with previously friendly colleagues may deteriorate as you drive forward to completion.

Many managers have successfully brought their project in on time yet still found themselves out of a job at the end. The pace is demanding, and once you have fulfilled the role, it may be hard to slow down again, or revert to a more leisurely style.

Wrap-up

All projects end. People may have been working together intensively for months or even years. Part of your role as project manager is to ensure that the ending is satisfying for everyone involved.

People on a project often have a strong emotional investment in the work and when it is over it can leave them drained and suffering from an anticlimax.

Start planning for the end well before it arrives.

- What will each person go on to do next?
- How can you help each person to prepare for the future?
- How can you let bosses, sponsors and colleagues know the team has done well?
- How can the learning from the project be integrated into the company?
- What will happen to all the documentation and resources the project has accumulated?
- How will the group celebrate its ending?

Further reading

BARTRAM P. *The Perfect Project Manager: All you need to get it right first time.* London, Random House, 1999.

BEE R. *and* BEE F. *Project Management: The people challenge.* London, CIPD, 1997.

MACLEOD M. 'Instrumental change'. *People Management.* Vol. 6, No. 12, 8 June 2000. pp40–42.

SMITH S. *Make Things Happen: Ready-made tools for project management.* London, Kogan Page, 1997.

WEBSTER G. *Managing Projects at Work.* Aldershot, Gower, 1999.

LEADERSHIP

What is the difference between a manager and a leader? It is not always easy to decide what separates one from the other. Yet seeing yourself as a leader could be an important way to continue distinguishing yourself from other managers with whom inevitably you are competing.

Leaders go beyond 'managing', coping or merely responding to events. Instead, they try to shape them. While managers follow procedures and do what is expected of them, leaders create or redesign the rules. They do the unexpected.

When you act as a leader, you take responsibility for the future by trying to define how it will look. Put it another way: while managers 'do it right', leaders 'do what is right'. This is not splitting hairs. Successful leaders deliberately challenge procedures. They question what is being done and how. They are willing to act on what they think will best serve a chosen goal, support a particular vision or reinforce a cherished value.

While managers can be leaders and vice versa, the best managers actually think of themselves as leaders – and behave accordingly.

Leadership is therefore as much a state of mind as a formal role. If you consider yourself a leader you are more likely to act like one. Right now as a manager, you may be confined to mainly steering day-to-day operations, making sure that they are efficient. Like a maintenance engineer you diligently keep checking that everything works smoothly. Your job is about ironing out faults, rather than anticipating them.

Thinking strategy

You are starting to be a leader when you think strategically. Even in the earliest management position that you hold, this is a key to long-term success.

Thinking and acting strategically means being in touch with the organisation's aspirations and its strategic intention. If you do not know what these are, take an opportunity to find out! Asking questions such as the following can make you stand out from others who think more narrowly:

■ Where is this organisation going?
■ What are we ultimately trying to achieve?
■ What is our corporate vision for the future?

The danger of thinking strategically, which overtakes many leaders, is that it becomes an obsession. Equally important is the ability to link this form of thinking with:

■ execution
■ decisiveness
■ speed.

> *The most dangerous leadership myth is that leaders are born – that there is a genetic factor to leadership. This myth asserts that people simply have certain charismatic qualities or not. That's nonsense; in fact the opposite is true. Leaders are made rather than born* – Warren Bennis, world expert and author on leadership

Leadership styles

Gone are the days of simplistic checklists for leadership characteristics. Today's leaders have to be multiskilled, and surveys on what makes good leaders are remarkably consistent. Two of the most common abilities are:

■ turns vision into reality
■ motivates people for whom he or she is accountable.

What has changed about the leadership role is the whole approach to style. Leading used to mean giving orders, delegating and supervising people's work. It was highly directive – those on the receiving end were expected to follow instructions and do as they were told.

This approach was disempowering because it assumed that people would not do what was best without being steered strongly in the right direction. It was also autocratic and almost entirely task orientated, focused mainly on results.

This 'command and control' style hardly works when an organisation is heavily dependent on:

■ brainpower
■ creative contributions
■ shared information and intellectual capital
■ multidisciplinary working
■ strategic alliances.

So if managers tend towards controlling, leaders tend towards trust.

Brainpower
'Today's high performers are like frogs in a wheelbarrow; they can jump out at any time,' is how a professor of human resources at INSEAD sums up the company situation for talent.

Organisations are increasingly reliant on technical and professional knowledge. Keeping them is a problem and these people will not readily be pushed around or bullied.

SEE CHAPTER 2

Once, a corporate leader was expected to possess more knowledge than anyone else in the organisation. Famously, Harold Geneen of the US giant ITT took home whole suitcases full of detailed reports and returned the next day having read them all. He knew more about what was going on in the company than anybody else.

Today that kind of leadership would soon hit a dead end. It would be impossible, and not even desirable, to be on top of all the detail.

Brainpower is more than just knowledge; it is the ability of people to exercise their thinking in the interests of the company. They may do so in many ways, and organisations increasingly depend on brains rather than brawn. Leadership in these circumstances acquires an entirely new perspective.

Now you are expected to nurture people's willingness to think and this demands a shift towards facilitating rather than directing, towards listening as much as talking.

> *Leaders can't succeed if they care more about how people feel than how they perform* – Jack Kahl, CEO and chairman of Manco Inc.

Creative contributions

The complexity and speed of change facing the average company is altering the contribution expected from everyone in it. The pace of competition means that the only long-term competitive advantage lies in mobilising the creativity of the entire organisation.

3M Corporation, for example, long ago realised this and now sets itself increasingly tough goals around creativity. A relatively small proportion of its turnover each year used to stem from new products; now it is heading towards 40 or 50 per cent.

To be an effective leader, therefore, now demands that you truly value people's ideas and suggestions, doing more than just collecting them. And because there are likely to be more ideas than you can handle or supervise yourself, successful leadership consists of a willingness to trust people to pursue their ideas without the handicap of tight supervision.

Leading in this era means balancing control and ways to stay informed, intervening and allowing people to learn by doing

Shared information and intellectual capital

Knowledge management is emerging as a discipline in its own right. Companies need ways to capture information and learning, and then share this across the entire enterprise. This is where smaller companies have a distinct advantage. It is far harder, for example, to run a car factory in a dozen different countries and ensure that the learning in one place permeates through to the rest.

Computer systems can help, yet they are a distraction from the essential issue of people being willing to share their precious knowledge. Only leaders can create the climate in which this really happens seamlessly.

Too often, the competitive culture of an organisation actually deters people from giving each other vital facts about customers, suppliers or competitors.

As a leader, develop your interest in how the company captures its core knowledge and shares it around. Set a good example in how you network and seek ways to demonstrate that intellectual capital – the lifeblood of the enterprise – is:

- **Identified** – how is key information, often held in people's heads, captured so it can be handed on to successors?
- **Respected** – how does the organisation convey that it values people's know-how and expertise?
- **Exploited** – how is knowledge turned from passive data into powerful ways to affect the organisation?
- **Rewarded** – how does the organisation express recognition and reward for people's knowledge and learning?

> *Leaders get out in front and stay there by raising the standards by which they judge themselves – and by which they are willing to be judged* – Frederick Smith, founder and CEO, Federal Express

Multidisciplinary working

In many management situations, you are no longer 'in charge' of everyone you manage. Instead, you may lead teams drawn from disparate disciplines and functions. One day, for example, you may be working with a group consisting amongst others of people from production, finance and distribution. Another day it might be a group drawn from a creative agency, the marketing department and two outsourcing companies.

Here what counts is how you inspire and motivate the group to work together. If those concerned find your meeting boring or inefficient, they may fail to turn up. If they feel disrespected or misunderstood, they may refuse to participate fully.

SEE CHAPTER 7

Strategic alliances

The ability to recognise the need for strategic alliances is a relatively new leadership demand. It has emerged because of forces such as:

- speed of change
- competition
- complexity
- interconnectedness.

All of these have driven companies from a once proud isolation in which they prided themselves on their independence, to situations where they can often only succeed in partnership with others. This is particularly so in the high-tech industries such as telecoms and IT.

Where once leadership meant attacking the competition in a ruthless parody of survival of the fittest, now it can mean urging your colleagues to work with competitors and share vital information. Where once leadership meant regarding suppliers as mere servants, lucky to be allowed to sell their products or services, now it can mean embracing them as partners.

Even large organisations have found that strategic alliances may be the only way to work. For smaller organisations it can be their whole *raison d'être*, as they leverage their limited means to act bigger than they really are.

In the early days of being a manager you may have limited opportunities to create or even propose strategic alliances. What matters, though, is that you act in an informed way, showing that you understand the importance of such arrangements.

Democratic v command

When the building is on fire, nobody wants a leader who tries to make evacuation a democratic discussion. Leadership style is situation-based. That is, the situation determines what kind of leadership you need to offer people.

Rather than worrying about something as vague as your personal leadership style, though, try focusing on specific leadership behaviour. The latter tends to be broadly directive or supportive. When you are being directive you:

- set goals and objectives
- organise people's work
- assign priorities and decide the deadlines
- clarify roles
- show or tell people exactly how to do a job
- constantly check whether people have performed.

In real life, effective leaders achieve a personal balance between being directive and supportive. Having a choice of how to lead greatly expands your leadership impact. Instead of always responding predictably to issues, you can be more flexible, choosing behaviour that matches the current need.

Systematic leaders	Intuitive leaders
<ul><li>make choices using a logical sequence of steps</li><li>justify decisions by evidence</li><li>identify constraints</li><li>emphasise the need for information</li><li>hate relying on guesses or gut reaction</li></ul>	<ul><li>jump from one logical step to another, then back again</li><li>avoid specifics while visualising the total situation</li><li>continuously redefine problems</li><li>justify decisions by results</li><li>rapidly explore and drop alternatives</li><li>follow instinct, and often act impulsively</li></ul>

Adaptability may well determine your team's or project's success. For example, if you are someone who always approaches situations systematically, there may be occasions when you would get a better result by relying more on intuition. The differences between these two approaches can be seen in the chart on page 236. Achieving the right balance between being systematic and intuitive is another example of how leaders adjust their personal behaviour.

Core leadership behaviour

To move from being a manager to a leader you need to be in touch with:

- *who you are as a leader* – this includes self-awareness, a sensitivity to how you affect others and therefore a willingness to modify your own character and how you come across
- *what your followers need* – this includes responding to individuals differently, depending on their readiness to perform a task; it is a case of understanding 'where they are at'
- *reading the environment* – this includes tapping into what is happening around you and where your input would be most productive and needed.

How can you learn to be more adaptable?

The main route is through:

- practising seeing what is required.

'Seeing' is an essential leadership skill that is surprisingly little talked about. There is, however, plenty of attention on leaders who fail to see what is needed.

'Seeing' enables you to expand your repertoire of responses and improvising. You do this by constantly reviewing what is happening in your environment and demanding feedback.

The ability to see what the particular situation demands sets leaders apart from managers, distinguishes inspiring leaders from pedestrian ones and contributes to that ill-defined factor, charisma. Charismatic leaders convince you that they really understand what is needed.

Support

People vary in how much support they require from their leader. A recently formed team, for example, with inexperienced members, may need far more help focusing on direction than an experienced one.

The maturity of those you are leading is a useful guide to how much support and direction they may need. Maturity in this sense does not depend on chronological age, but on the person's stage of development. You can broadly summarise the choice of leadership behaviour as shown in the chart below.

Leadership behaviour

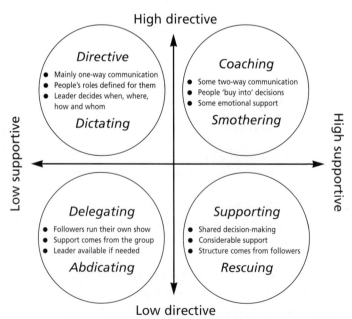

High directive

Low supportive

Directive
- Mainly one-way communication
- People's roles defined for them
- Leader decides when, where, how and whom

Dictating

Coaching
- Some two-way communication
- People 'buy into' decisions
- Some emotional support

Smothering

High supportive

Delegating
- Followers run their own show
- Support comes from the group
- Leader available if needed

Abdicating

Supporting
- Shared decision-making
- Considerable support
- Structure comes from followers

Rescuing

Low directive

Motivation

Most people want to do a good job. Or to put it more graphically, they do not come to work in order to screw up. The leadership challenge is helping them do well. Yet people will only commit to important goals when convinced about them. You cannot achieve that kind of commitment through issuing orders, delegation or close supervision.

Instead you must rely on tapping into people's natural wish to do something well. We tend to think that motivating people is something one does to them. In fact, the essence of motivation is discovering what people need in order to release their inner wishes.

As part of 'seeing', leaders try to learn what 'turns people on'. How do you do that? Mainly by asking them! It really is that simple. Spend time learning what excites people, what makes them tick, dig down to uncover what they need to perform well. Invariably, people will tell you when you show enough interest in the answers.

As managers, we are often so busy that we forget the value of spending time with people to establish what they require to perform well. We often take it for granted that simply paying them to appear at work is the same as motivating them. It is not. There are some well-established principles from psychological research for unlocking people's motivation. They include:

- goal-setting
- meeting expectations
- offering rewards.

Goal-setting

People generally enjoy reaching for goals. The harder the goal, the more it tends to provoke better performance. Managing by objectives is one practical application of using goals to tap into people's motivation.

SEE CHAPTER 1

Setting goals has its limitations, though, particularly if you are handing them out like tablets from the mountain. It is generally better, for example, to encourage people to establish their own goals with your help, rather than imposing them without discussion.

People also need to know regularly how they are doing in relation to the goals. How you offer feedback is as important as the feedback itself. Effective feedback is:

- *descriptive* – non-judgemental, objectively describing what is happening
- *specific* – avoiding generalities
- *relevant* – providing what the receiver needs at that moment
- *timely* – arrives when it is needed
- *usable* – concerned with things or events over which the receiver has some control.

Feedback can be positive – encouraging – or negative – discouraging. Use negative feedback sparingly.

Expectations and rewards
Another important way of tapping into people's enthusiasm and commitment is to understand and use their expectations. When you ask a person to do something, their response may depend on how they expect these questions to be answered:

- If I try doing what you want, will I succeed in doing it?
- If I do it correctly, will it actually lead to a reward?
- Is the reward worth having?

To learn the answers be willing to listen carefully to what people seem to want.

Most managers and leaders know that part of their job is to reward people. But rewards are a complex area of human motivation. To some people they mean a pay rise. To others it is time off, simple encouragement or a more stimulating work assignment.

Effective leaders learn to 'see' what people need and then provide it. Two main types of reward you can usefully consider are:

- intrinsic
- extrinsic.

Intrinsic rewards make people feel good inside when they achieve a goal, excel or please you in some way. They are positive feelings such as pleasure, satisfaction, pride, contentment, feeling wanted and so on.

Extrinsic rewards come from outside the person, and include pay, bonuses, a company car, longer holidays, enhanced pensions, trips abroad and promotion. Poor leaders tend to rely excessively on extrinsic rewards, often ignoring the power that intrinsic rewards have in gaining people's commitment.

Inspiration

In our leadership work at Maynard Leigh Associates we have found it useful to focus on two types of leader:

- facilitative leaders
- inspirational leaders.

While these are not entirely mutually exclusive, they broadly define the types of leader that companies seem to want. The facilitative leader is closer to what traditional managers do, but is far more inclusive and involving in style of behaviour.

In contrast, the inspirational leader uses what we call the seven 'I's of leadership:

- insight
- initiative
- inspiration
- involvement
- improvisation
- individuality
- implementation.

While it is true that some people do these naturally, it is perfectly possible to learn how to inspire others through personal development. Inspired people surpass themselves, going beyond their normal limits. They feel encouraged and stimulated to use their full potential, to give of their best.

To inspire others:

- First learn to inspire yourself.

When you connect with your own enthusiasm and vision, you give out energy and a sense of purpose. Others soon pick this up and it enables them to accept your wish to inspire them to perform in some new or challenging way.

What makes you excited, energised and enthused, willing to go that extra mile? What is it about what you and your colleagues are trying to achieve that is so worthwhile? Can you explain this to the other people?

Leaders convey excitement, making people feel part of an adventure or a worthwhile journey. You create charisma from your readiness to share what matters to you, by speaking about it from the heart.

Both research and the experiences of successful leaders show that there are three essential requirements for sharing:

- sharing your vision
- sharing your values
- sharing your understanding of goals.

Sharing your vision

Leadership vision in a company may be anything from being the world's most progressive healthcare provider to being the most innovative boat builder.

In a team, leadership vision might be anything from inventing a cure for AIDS to creating a fault-free production line for making mobile phones.

To shift from managing to leading means taking responsibility for trying to find the vision that inspires others and to help them steadily convert this into realistic programmes of action. If people are to commit themselves to trying to realise a vision, they usually need to feel that they have some choice in the matter. It makes sense to stay flexible and to be willing to respond to their wishes to modify or enhance your own vision in some way.

A team or a company without a vision is like a house without a foundation. It may stay upright for a while, but in the longer term it will start to topple. By sharing your vision you begin building strong foundations for your team or company.

Sharing your values

Values hold a team, or indeed an entire organisation, together. They are 'what matters to us around here'. Effective leaders:

- identify and articulate the values
- explain how to turn values into practical action
- demonstrate values in action by their own behaviour.

Examples of team values include:

- giving customers what they want
- honesty and integrity
- getting it right first time
- having fun
- being first
- openness
- confronting issues.

Think of a team you know well. What are its values? What seems to really matter to this team, what would the team members say really matters to them?

Model it

Leaders model the way. This is how values turn into practical action, because you are saying, 'Look at me, I'm demonstrating it right now.' People constantly look to leaders for confirmation that values are strongly held and demonstrated daily. They will only believe in a value when a leader confirms it through personal behaviour rather than merely through words.

Sharing your understanding of goals

Never assume that everyone sees goals the same way as you. Instead try this three-step approach:

1 Gain mutual agreement by explaining to people what you see as important goals.
2 Be prepared to elaborate on goals in the face of questions.
3 Allow people to refine your understanding of goals.

What is expected of you?

Given all of the above, what exactly do people expect from you? Surveys consistently show that people want from an organisational leader:

- honesty
- competence

- a forward-looking approach
- inspiration
- intelligence
- fair-mindedness.

These are both values and forms of behaviour.

So how are you doing?

To lead people well, you need occasionally to stand back from the daily pressures to review your personal effectiveness.

Old-fashioned top-down appraisals do not work when it comes to judging your leadership. Instead, you will need to be prepared to receive 360-degree feedback – information from below you, from people at your level and from above.

SEE CHAPTER 3

Leadership feedback is seldom comfortable, as it is nearly always personally challenging. However, an increasing number of companies expect their organisational leaders and senior managers to receive such sensitive information.

Do not wait to have feedback imposed on you. Seek it out. However, you can hardly expect people to say to your face or in a signed memo what they think of your leadership. Instead, you need to create some means by which they can express their experience of your leadership in anonymity.

Personal leadership feedback

To obtain 360-degree feedback about your leadership you may need to ask people to rate your abilities on issues such as the seven 'I's above.

Page 246 is a typical feedback profile chart. It shows the individual manager's perception of his or her leadership and how up to five different 'supporters' experience it.

Leadership profile

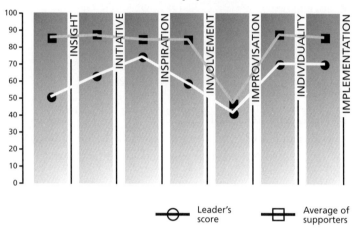

Extracting a special effort

Occasionally a leader needs to demand a special effort from people. Why do some people respond, while others refuse the challenge?

People respond to more than just facts. Facts may start the process, yet they seldom work alone. As a leader you have to learn how to appeal to people's feelings, not just to the logical, rational part of themselves.

Sharing your feelings about why a particular effort is needed may be difficult if you are a traditional manager who believes that emotions are too messy to handle. It may even feel vaguely unprofessional to resort to using emotions to get what you want.

But to convince people that they can go beyond their normal capabilities to exceed even their own view of what they can do, you need to show how much you care about achieving the goal. It is the intensity of your caring that will convince people, along with the hard facts and evidence.

Experiment to discover what will call forth and sustain a short-lived outstanding effort. Often asking people what it will take can reveal what you need to know.

Delegation

Opportunities for traditional delegation, in which you hand out tasks and others get on with them, are declining. Organisations have to achieve their goals in less hierarchical ways. So delegation acquires greater significance – since it is really about sharing your leadership power.

Managers are often happier to hand out a task than to transfer a complete role. Yet this kind of delegation is how people really learn. Delegation means accepting:

■ a longer timescale for completing some tasks
■ temporarily lower quality than you yourself could achieve
■ reduced personal enjoyment from performing certain activities
■ fewer chances to practise your skills.

Leaders, on the other hand, push for transfer of roles. This is how they bring the vision to life; it is how they create action.

There are several powerful pointers that it is time to delegate:

■ you are personally working too hard, for example you are taking work home several times a week; this is the moment to share the burden
■ a task could make a routine for others to complete
■ an opportunity to develop a person by providing them with an important challenge.

In your enthusiasm to delegate, though, you need to avoid merely dumping all of your stress and overwork on the next person in line.

Do not delegate if:

- you have no faith in people to deliver
- the task is vital and only you can deliver on time
- confidentiality or sensitivity means that it would be wrong to let anyone else do it
- the goal is so vague and ill-defined that there is little chance of someone else performing it well.

---

10 ways leaders manage the future

1 They manage the dream – creating a compelling vision, defining reality.

2 They embrace error, are not afraid of making mistakes and admit them when they do.

3 They encourage reflective talkback, welcoming personal feedback about themselves.

4 They encourage dissent, welcoming contrary views and those who can distinguish between the expected and what is happening.

5 They possess the 'Nobel factor', exuding optimism, faith and hope.

6 They understand the 'Pygmalion effect', expecting the best from people around them, stretching them without letting them fall too short too often.

7 They have, and use, instinct, a sense of where the culture is going to be, where the team must be if it is to grow.

8 They see the long view and are patient.

9 They understand the 'stakeholder symmetry' – knowing they must reconcile the competing claims of interested parties.

10 They create strategic alliances and partnerships, seeing the world globally, knowing that there is now nowhere to hide.

Adapted from Bennis W. *On Becoming a Leader*. London, Hutchinson Business Books, 1989.

Further reading

ADAIR J. *Leadership Skills*. London, CIPD, 1997.

BENNIS W. *On Becoming a Leader*. London, Hutchinson Business Books, 1989.

GOFFEE R. *and* Jones G. 'Why should anyone be led by you?'. *Harvard Business Review*. Vol. 78, No. 5, Sept/Oct 2000. pp63–70.

KOURDI J. *One-Stop Leadership*. London, ICSA Publishing, 1999.

LEIGH A. *and* MAYNARD M. *Leading Your Team*. London, Nicholas Brealey, 1995.

LEIGH A. *and* MAYNARD M. *The Perfect Leader*. London, Arrow Books, 1996.

TAFFINDER P. *The Leadership Crash Course: A 6-step fast-track self-development action list*. London, Kogan Page, 2000.

PRESENTATIONS

Chapter 15

Your heart thumps, your mouth is dry, your hands are sweaty, and there is a nasty feeling in your stomach as if butterflies are doing aerial stunts. No, you are not having a heart attack: you are about to make a presentation.

It is said to be scarier than blazing infernos or meeting a snake. Presenting has strange effects on even the sanest person. Yet it is widely agreed that being a good business presenter is a core management skill

You need good presentation skills for a myriad of reasons – for example, when you apply for a job, ask for a pay rise, seek support for a project, ask to borrow money from the bank, run a team meeting. Learning to present well can become a major asset in your life.

In a survey of 100 finance, marketing and personnel directors, three-quarters said public speaking was their most daunting task. Eighty per cent feel very, or fairly, nervous when giving TV interviews and 70 per cent feel the same way about presenting to a large audience of peers.

Slightly more than half believe that presentation skills are vital to success, more important than intelligence or getting on with the boss.

People Management, June 2000

When you tap your natural ability to present you also contact your personal power. It is a way of becoming a more effective human being, and it is not necessarily difficult. However, you do need to work at it, to gain regular feedback on your performance and to keep reaching for another level of impact. With presentations you can always do better next time.

If you are already a good speaker you may be tempted to rely too much on verbal presentations. This is risky. There are many occasions when it is wiser to rely on a written presentation. If what you have to say can be communicated adequately without you being there, send a report.

Signs that a verbal presentation is needed

- A decision is urgently required.
- You are asked to speak on a specific occasion.
- You have something to offer beyond the written word.
- The recipients need to hear from you in person.
- Your message is more likely to be accepted with you present.
- There are too many complex ideas to rely on a written document.
- Your message does not need a written document.

Being an effective presenter

Giving powerful presentations marks you out as an effective manager in most organisations. Sometimes, though, companies and individuals become obsessed with presentation to the detriment of other managerial skills.

IBM, for instance, once became so passionate about presentations that people used to spend literally weeks preparing theirs. Some managers even had overhead projectors built into their desks.

As with written reports (see Chapter 6), your presentation needs to include the wider picture of where the issue fits strategically.

That is, how does the issue you are addressing relate to where the organisation is going and how it is getting there?

Many of the topics on which you present may initially seem to have no relevance to strategic issues such as the organisation's long-term future. Yet by constantly returning to this theme and giving your presentation that extra focus, you will again set yourself apart from those with a lesser vision.

Of course, you may run the risk of being dismissed by some as having your head in the clouds, of not being pragmatic or realistic. Others who pride themselves on being down to earth may openly or covertly attack you for how your presentations always seem to include this wider context. Ignore them – making sure that your presentation includes a strategic context may be why you are eventually promoted and they are not.

Mental attitude

Apart from terror, people suffer from at least two extreme reactions to presenting. One is to the conviction that they are poor presenters. Yet, constantly telling yourself that you are a poor presenter merely sends a powerful reinforcing message to your subconscious.

In fact, everyone can present well and you are no exception. Keep reminding yourself that you can do it, and that you know it is essential for succeeding as a manager or a leader.

The other extreme reaction is believing that you are amongst the world's great presenters. Overconfidence and an inability to realise when you are not performing well can prevent you from learning from your mistakes. Instead you just plough on regardless, boring audiences or failing to grab their attention.

In both cases you need honest feedback on how you are really coming across. Those who think they are bad presenters may be perfectly sound and merely need some help and regular feedback to start delivering outstanding performances.

Similarly, those with an exaggerated view of their impact may just need a reality check so that they can focus attention on improvements.

Monitoring yourself

Try keeping an impact log – a written record showing how you performed in each presentation. Use it to review your own progress. For instance, you might score yourself on:

- how well you prepared
- how clear you were about your purpose
- whether you spoke with conviction
- whether you really used your personality
- whether you handled questions well.

You can rate yourself from 1 (=low) to 5 (=high) on each of these after each performance until you have begun to build up a reliable picture of your current strengths and weaknesses.

Try inviting some colleagues to complete the ratings on your performances too. For example, if you do a presentation to a team ask some members if they will give you some detailed feedback using the log.

Obstacles

What could get in the way of you presenting, apart from any lack of confidence? Some common barriers include:

- the use of written notes
- visual aids
- body language
- sub-text
- waffle.

Notes

Avoid a full script like the plague. Even experienced actors find it hard to sound entirely natural when reading from a script. By relying on a full, written script you will undermine your presentation in at least three ways:

- You will not sound natural or spontaneous.
- Lose your place in the script and it will be hard to find it again.
- It will prevent you from remembering your core purpose.

Poor presenters who rely on detailed notes to get their message across usually come across as stilted and boring. Notes are a security blanket. When you really know and care about what you want to say, notes soon take a back seat.

Notes are not wrong in themselves. They are a good way to start preparing for your presentation. It is the next step that counts – reducing them to just key words.

If you must write out your entire speech, make sure you go through the next two stages:

- notes
- key words.

If you practice your presentation thoroughly you will almost certainly move from a full script to a set of notes fairly quickly. It may take rather longer to move to the next stage of just having key words.

Reduce your set of notes onto small cards and this will force you to shorten how much material you actually keep with you when you present. In most business situations you will not need to learn your entire presentation by heart. Notes or key words should be perfectly adequate so long as you really know your core message.

Audiences certainly do not enjoy seeing a presenter arrive centre stage with large amounts of notes, so stick to just small ones on cards that will fit in the palm of your hand.

Visual aids

Visual aids can make or break your presentation. Carefully chosen ones can have a huge impact. You do not need that many to get your basic message across. Too many presenters in fact resort to an excess of visual aids, many of which are probably not that impactful.

Stick to a few powerful, well-designed ones. Make sure that they can be seen clearly by a short-sighted, elderly man at the back of the room, who also wears underpowered glasses. That is, make the contents large, bold and simple.

Remember that words are not visual aids. Pictures are. It is so easy now to produce professional looking aids that there is really no excuse for yours to look amateurish.

So many things can go wrong with visual aids and you need to be alert to the worst dangers. Flipcharts can appear torn, dirty or too small. Slides can be projected inverted or back to front. Film clips can break at the crucial moment. Expect the worst and be prepared for it.

Body language

Your body cannot keep a secret. Standing before an audience, it reveals hidden signs of how you are feeling and what you are thinking. Audiences pick these up automatically.

We are all experts in our own way in body language. Even highly competent presenters can undermine their impact by being unaware of what their body is doing while they are performing. The chart on page 256 shows the importance of non-verbal communication.

How we communicate

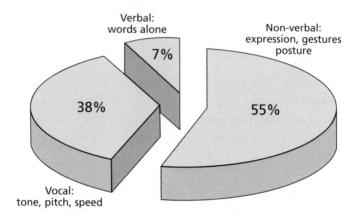

Verbal:
words alone

Non-verbal:
expression, gestures
posture

7%

38%

55%

Vocal:
tone, pitch, speed

The two main ways of improving body language are:

■ being thoroughly committed to a presentation
■ obtaining regular feedback on your performance.

Commitment is when you are totally involved with the presentation in all its aspects. This involvement communicates instantly and its sheer intensity takes care of most body language issues that would otherwise get in the way of performing well.

Obtaining regular feedback is the only viable way of discovering whether you have unwittingly acquired some distracting presentation habits. For example, you may tend to scratch your nose when you are at the most difficult part of the performance, yet you may be far too involved to notice this happening.

You can ask colleagues to watch out for negative body language such as not looking at the audience as if you wanted to make contact, coins jangling in your pockets, irritating twitches that can be controlled once you know they exist and so on.

Try using a video to take a look at yourself actually performing.

Doing it during rehearsals can be a big help, but there is nothing like an actual recording of a live performance to highlight body movements that need to change.

An audience has a sixth sense for when a presenter is feeling nervous and reads 'between the lines'. What is being communicated behind your words is as important as the actual verbal content:

■ Be clear about your purpose.
■ Have a clear commitment to saying what you mean.
■ Mean what you say.

Your purpose might seem obvious for many business presentations, but in fact this breaks down into three kinds:

■ **your core purpose** – why I am presenting and what I need to say
■ **your purpose 'in the moment'** – reactions you want at different stages of the presentation
■ **your follow-through purpose** – what you want the audience to do next after hearing the presentation.

You should be able to sum up your core purpose in a single short sentence. If you find that hard, then you probably have a way to go before your core purpose is sufficiently sharp.

At any one moment during the presentation, you may want varying reactions from the audience. For example, you might wish people to laugh, be curious, excited, worried and so on. For your next presentation, for instance, try and decide what specific reaction you want from people to:

■ the start of the presentation
■ the middle of the presentation
■ the end of the presentation.

Sub-text

The sub-text is the unspoken messages that come across during a presentation. These are not just body language; they are also within the content of the presentation itself.

For example, an audience may quickly notice what is *not* being said just as much as what is made explicit. For example, if you announce a pay rise for everyone who hits a target, the audience may read the sub-text as: 'and those who don't hit the target may get fired'.

Learning to watch for the sub-text in your presentations may take considerable practice. This is where colleagues can help. They draw your attention to hidden messages that may have crept into your performance without your realising it.

Waffle

Few business presentations last more than around 20 minutes. Any longer and you will probably risk making your audience bored, impatient or both. It is very easy to ramble while presenting.

Good presenters know if they have a tendency to waffle and rigorously try to curb it. They live by the actor's credo of leaving their audience wanting more. So, say what you have to say, and then stop.

The five Ps of presentation

While there are many systems for making managerial presentations, the so-called five Ps have stood the test of time. They are:

- purpose
- preparation
- presence
- passion
- personality.

There is a catch-22 about purpose and preparation. You cannot really decide your purpose without careful preparation. On the other hand, you cannot sensibly start on much preparation work without a clear purpose.

Purpose is really the core of the five Ps:

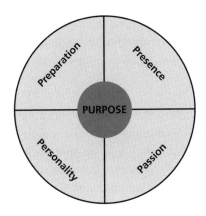

Preparation

Preparation includes everything you need to be ready for delivering your message:

- Research the audience.
- Devise the presentation.
- Organise the presentation aids.
- Check the venue.
- Rehearse.
- Ready yourself.

Researching your audience

This is certainly one of the best investments you can make. Learning about your target audience is a discipline that goes far beyond mere presentations. It is relevant to many other aspects of your work.

Five key audience research issues to resolve are:

- Who exactly is the audience?
- How many of them are there?
- What does your audience expect?
- Who might be talking before you?
- Are there any special factors that might affect your impact?

Does your audience need to be persuaded, amused, informed and challenged or what? For example, knowing that your audience will include an assertive finance director who usually demands hard evidence can help hone what you have to say to a fine edge.

There may also be some special factors to consider, such as being aware that your audience will be anxious about what you have to say. For instance, if you are announcing increased profits and plans for redundancies, your audience may not give you their full attention until you deal with the redundancy issue.

Devise the presentation
Preparation also includes the task of constructing your presentation so that it flows smoothly with a logical structure. The best-known framework is:

- Tell them what you are going to tell them.
- Tell them.
- Tell them again what you have told them.

While this is a useful guideline, it is now so well known that it may do you little good to use it. Once an audience realises what is coming you quickly lose people's focus of attention.

A particularly useful framework for devising a business presentation is:

- situation
- complication
- resolution.

The five steps to creating an instant speech

Step 1 *Get attention.* Introduce your presentation with a catchy opening.

Step 2 *Explain the relevance.* Tell your audience why the subject is important to them.

Step 3 *Present the central message.* Follow with a general statement of your purpose.

Step 4 *Give examples.* Support your message with some real illustrations.

Step 5 *Close.* End with a striking sentence that summarises your speech.

You start by explaining the situation and why you are talking about it. You move to outline the issues surrounding the situation, problems and obstacles to progress and so on. Finally you offer a way forward in which your suggestions or proposals provide a resolution of some kind.

Venue

No mater how experienced a presenter you become, it always pays to thoroughly check the presentation venue. Not only will you avoid some unpleasant surprises, such as a carefully planned fire alarm drill in the middle of your performance, you may also uncover the fact that:

- windows rattle
- floors creak
- there are no dimmer switches
- catering staff will be making noisy preparations next door
- construction workers will be busy building across the street
- your laptop leads will not fit the on-site projector machine
- the microphone lead is too short to do a walk-about
- the venue is harder to find than you were led to believe.

Rehearse

Preparation also means thorough rehearsal. People soon detect if you have skimped on this. Even those who are good at improvising know that their success is rooted in basic preparation. As author and raconteur Mark Twain once remarked: 'It takes me three weeks to write a good spontaneous speech.'

How much rehearsal time you devote to each presentation is always a matter of personal judgement. But a good guideline is at least 10 minutes for every one minute of presentation. This standard implies that you will be able to have a complete run through of your presentation at least 10 times. Many experienced presenters would argue for far more rehearsal time.

Ready yourself

Experienced actors never expect to stride straight onto the stage and start performing. They may spend a considerable time mentally and physically preparing.

This also applies to business presenting. Spend some time getting your body prepared, for example doing some relaxation and breathing exercises.

Your voice too needs readying. For instance, if you have driven to the venue you may be tenser than you realise. Get your voice in shape by practising some tongue twisters and even stretching your face muscles in various directions.

Being mentally ready is as important as physical readiness. The mind has been likened to an unruly ox and if you are someone who is anxious about presenting it can play some nasty tricks.

A good technique is to create a mental 'film' of how you intend the presentation to go. You imagine in detail how you would like the audience to look and respond. You use this image to build your confidence by constantly playing it over in your mind.

It is like watching a film in your head. The more times you play the film the more it reinforces your confidence.

You can go on playing this film up to the very moment you open your mouth to speak. You can even 'play it' in pauses during the presentation itself.

Presence

Powerful presenters establish a presence. There is nothing mysterious about this and most people can do it with enough practice. It is all about being present in the moment, when your entire attention is focused on what is happening around you.

When you are truly 'present', your senses become heightened so that you notice things that you might normally miss. For example, you see a person at the far end of the table looking glazed, you notice the room is a bit stuffy, you hear the clicking of a keyboard just outside the room. This extreme alertness enables you to respond instantly to signals from your audience.

An important opportunity to establish a presence comes right at the start of your performance. If you rush into your act the moment you are centre stage, you are not allowing yourself to 'arrive'. Nor are you leaving time for the audience to absorb your arrival.

Before you utter a word of your presentation:

- stop
- breathe
- look
- listen.

Allow a pause for five or more seconds before starting to speak. Take your time looking around, making eye contact with the audience and generally absorbing the atmosphere.

During these precious moments before you speak you may be able to sense what people are thinking through observing how they are sitting, what they are doing and how they are looking. Use this time to observe and be observed.

Passion

Passion is merely another way of saying commitment or conviction that really comes across to the audience. It is not enough to feel committed to what you are saying. What counts is sharing this feeling with your audience. Similarly, if you do not particularly care about what you are saying, why should the audience?

Your passion warms, excites, enthuses and holds your audience. When you are in touch with your passion, you hardly need any notes; the words just come naturally, and your body language, including your hands, takes care of itself.

If you tend to revel in facts, figures and analysis, you also may be someone who regards being a passionate presenter as irrelevant. Surely as long as you offer lots of hard evidence, people will be convinced?

Sadly, even business audiences are swayed by emotion and tend to vote with their hearts, not their heads. That is true even of top boards of directors or cynical investment analysts. Good presenters therefore create just the right level of involvement for their particular audience and aim to create a relationship.

Personality

It is your unique personality that will make the presentation memorable. Just what is your personality? Can you sum it up in just five words? Try it!

You can sum up my personality as:

1......................
2......................
3......................
4......................
5......................

Now how would some of your work colleagues sum up your personality? Try asking a couple of people you trust to write down five personality features that seem to represent who you are.

Now you can compare the list you have created with the ones your colleagues have devised. Are there any differences and why do they arise?

This simple exercise can yield bigger dividends than you might at first imagine. For example, others may see you as someone with a great sense of humour. Yet, for some reason you do not see it that way and so hardly use humour in your presentations.

It is critical that you present like you, not like someone else, such as someone you admire. Many people forget that they have a personality when they present, and wonder why they leave feeling that they have not done themselves justice.

It is your special personality that makes your presentation different from anyone else's. What the audience wants is you, not an imitation. So, try to let the real you come through when you present. Otherwise, you might as well just send them a report.

Practice, practice, practice
You do not learn to ride a bicycle by reading about it. Likewise, good presentations stem from actually doing it – often. Look for live presenting opportunities where you can test out different approaches and gradually find what works best for you.

Some formal presentation training or individual coaching can often help in two important ways by significantly increasing your:

■ confidence
■ effectiveness.

Presentation workshops can be fun, pointing you in the right direction. They will identify your strengths so that you can begin using them more purposefully. They will also identify areas where you need to develop more. They offer a way of practising in a safe environment.

Ask your own manager to comment on your presentations. Discover how important presentations are within the organisation and what help you might obtain to improve yours.

By choosing to improve your presentation impact, you will almost certainly impress those in positions of authority that you are serious about becoming a better manager.

Further reading

LEIGH A. *The Ultimate Business Presentation Book*. London, Random House Business Books, 1999.

LEIGH A. *and* MAYNARD M. *Perfect Presentations*. London, Random House, 1993.

McCARTHY P. *and* HATCHER C. *Speaking Persuasively: How to make the most of your presentations*. St Leonards, Allen & Unwin, 1996.

SIDDONS S. *Presentation Skills*. London, CIPD, 1999.

TIERNEY E. *101 Ways to Better Presentations*. London, Kogan Page, 1999.

STRESS

Chapter 16

'I can take about five minutes of my wife. I can stand to read only one chapter of a book. I can't get through the first act of a play. All I can think about is getting business.' Stephen Kumble describing his lifestyle was one of the lead partners in a major New York City law firm, expanding at breakneck speed.

His words sum up the world of 24/7 constant motion. Once the big ate the small, now it is supposedly the fast who eat the slow. Speed seems to be everything. Yet Kumble's pace was unsustainable. His firm collapsed amid huge debts, vicious internal conflict and legal improprieties. What happened to Kumble himself is unreported, but you can be sure he was not much healthier than his defunct firm.

According to research from the Henley Centre, the richer you are, the faster you live. You not only walk faster, you also work longer, strive harder and suffer more stress in your attempts to become even richer, or maybe just to survive in modern society.

Stressful facts about stress

Lunch is for wimps. Datamonitor, the market research company, found in late 2000 that workaholic macho Britons abandon the midday meal in favour of a sandwich eaten at their desks.

The number of men working part-time has doubled in two decades in the UK, while the number working for large companies has slumped to about one-third of the working population.

US-style practices have spread widely, such as outsourcing, de-layering, interim or stand-in management, with employees selling their services on a freelance basis, all of which generate their own kinds of stress.

In a 1999 Quality of Working Life survey, of 5,000 managers, 71 per cent said the length of their working day was having a detrimental effect on health, while a slightly larger proportion said it was affecting their family life.

Between 20 per cent and 33 per cent of managers do more than 50 hours a week, despite the European Working Time Directive designed to limit hours. A study by the Health and Safety Executive in 1999 found one in five people admitted to feeling stressed.

Ashridge Management College reported in one of its studies that three out of four managers say work causes stress. Women suffer more than men. As you climb the ladder, stress grows, rather than shrinks.

Eighty per cent of UK board-level managers regard work as stressful. For example, half the company chairs and chief executives in a survey by the University of Manchester suffered from work-related stress.

Finally, a UN survey released in late 2000 predicted that stress levels would rise dramatically with globalisation. Despair at work was common and the report by the ILO warned that the trends were 'a wake-up call to business'. The effects meant low productivity, reduced profits, high rates of turnover and increased costs of recruiting and training replacement staff.

Being accountable

'All you need is one man losing his control and you lose the entire business,' comments Professor Cary Cooper of the Institute of Science and Technology at Manchester University.

Remember Nick Leeson, the young and ambitious trader who made Barings Bank, the oldest financial institution in Britain, go bust after losing control of himself in Singapore? Too much stress and a constant pressure to perform cost Barings, where the Queen used to hold her accounts, some £800 million. The entire bank was sold for a symbolic pound to ING.

In fact stress is really a stand-in for something more fundamental – the failure of managers and leaders to organise the work environment more effectively. Once, the most stressful experiences in life were bereavement, divorce and moving house. Now it seems that work itself is the most stressful thing that anyone can do.

Unrealistic targets, fear of losing one's job, 14-hour days and toiling at the weekend all add up to being work-driven. Such environments are devoid of caring or humanity, obsessed with objectives, sales, profits and ever-longer hours. In such places, no amount of time management advice, counselling or aerobics will prevent adverse effects on employees.

Key factors behind stress are inadequate resources, lack of involvement in the decision-making process, excessive workloads and poor relationships at work. Dispirited organisations carry huge hidden costs that take their toll on productivity. More visibly, there are the obvious costs of replacing and retaining people.

Some industries, though, simply do not care. The music business, for example, is renowned for its uncaring attitude towards employees. There are simply too many people hammering on the door to get in so it breeds a management style that is as outdated as it is uncaring.

A female employee of a high street bank in the City summed it all up vividly: 'The atmosphere is so competitive you never want to tell people you are tired or can't handle the pressure.'

Only 10 per cent of employees with stress-related problems actually ask for help.

The impact of stress

Being concerned about your own and other people's stress makes sound corporate sense. Research shows that concern for employee welfare and development helps explain differences between profitability and productivity.

As a manager, you have a responsibility to:

- protect your own health and effectiveness
- check the health and effectiveness of your subordinates
- assess the impact of stress on your organisation
- avoid adverse management behaviour through stress.

Yourself

Some stress is healthy! Without it, we would laze around and achieve little. Bad stress is when we cannot cope, when the results affect our health or damage our family life. Good stress gets us going, makes our juices flow and we respond to tough challenges. Too much stress and we get sick and even die. Too little and we atrophy.

As a manager, you cannot be expected to change the entire work culture of your country or the industry. But you are not powerless. You need to master stress so that it does not master you. The Japanese even have a word for it – *karoshi*, or death from overwork. Half of them live in fear of such a death.

Heart disease is one well-known result of stress, but there are many other symptoms, including depression, headaches, aggression, alcohol or drug dependency.

We tend to ignore signs of stress as long as possible. Early warnings include tiredness, depression, inability to sleep and irritability. Next comes the inability to concentrate, job dissatisfaction, a low sense of personal achievement, high rates of smoking, cholesterol or heart rate.

Subordinates

You also need to be concerned about stress faced by your subordinates, because they are the people that you depend on for your own success as a manager. If they succumb, your own effectiveness will be reduced.

You may feel that stress is no different from tension or pressure, and that it makes people more alert, competitive and efficient. You might argue, for instance, that some jobs, such as the emergency services or transport, are inherently stressful and if people choose to work in them they have to expect to handle stress.

You depend on work colleagues for your own success as a manager. At one time, you could wait for an individual to crack, and only then respond to their distress. Now this is no longer acceptable, particularly in organisations driven by knowledge and brainpower.

Also, in many countries, including Britain, failure to protect subordinates from too much stress will leave your company vulnerable to expensive legal claims for negligence.

> More and more employees are receiving handsome settlements for stress-related injuries. In August 2000, Leslie North, a financial adviser at Lloyds TSB, received a £100,000 settlement to compensate for psychological damage caused by the bank's poor management. He was suffering from post-traumatic stress disorder after being given extra responsibilities when his staff was cut from 14 to five.
>
> Source: 'Business health and safety'. *Financial Times Guide*, 16 October 2000

The organisation

Apart from any legal implications from handling stress badly, its impact across the organisation can be damaging both in the short run and to profitability. For example, people under stress affect others, leaving vital safety or other important processes at risk. Not dealing with one case of stress can mean that you have many others waiting to surface.

Longer term, a damaging outcome may be to reduce the organisation's ability to compete and hence its profitability. For example, because of stress, people may resist change, reject new ideas without proper consideration, miss important market opportunities and so on.

Stress also spills over to clients, customers and other important relationships, such as working closely with suppliers. Wherever stress arises you can be sure that, while there are some positive benefits, it is far more likely to cause damage.

Audits

Good managers anticipate problems rather than waiting for them to surface. Legally it also makes sense to protect yourself and the company from compensation claims by conducting a stress audit.

Audits assess the situation and are usually conducted by an independent assessor using a standard way of measuring stress. Such an audit would normally cover:

- people
- processes
- environment
- culture and other influences.

The audit may reveal invaluable information about what people feel about their jobs, their managers and the organisation. It should also identify peaks in demand and areas with a potential for stress.

Adverse management behaviour

How are you handling stress at work? Sometimes the way managers personally cope with stress works for them, yet causes damage elsewhere.

For example, if under stress you start working excessive hours, others may feel compelled to copy you, and soon overwork starts to become addictive. The cumulative effect may reduce everyone's efficiency, not just yours.

There is also evidence that stress can lead you to behave badly towards others. Could you be starting to bully people or cause more conflict than necessary? Studies in the UK show that around 11 per cent of people say that they have been bullied at work in the previous six months.

You probably would not bully someone deliberately. But if you are under stress it might come out as excessive monitoring and fault finding. One managing director of a leading garden centre went round the store every day with a clipboard listing everything that was wrong and handed it to his retail manager. When the team worked with him on the issue, the main solution was to make sure he took at least two skiing holidays a year.

Causes of stress

It is hardly surprising that stress remains an issue for many companies and their managers since there has been a steady increase in working hours. Over the last 20 years, for example, hours worked have risen in the USA by the equivalent of one extra month a year. A similar pattern is emerging elsewhere.

These extra hours often stem from flatter organisational structures. Fewer managers work with reduced resources and people are expected to be more productive than ever. Line managers also increasingly take responsibility for the development of their subordinates when previously this was left to personnel experts.

The impact of information technology and the reduced need for middle managers, the pace of change and growing complexity are all additional factors behind problems arising from stress.

Stress generators

- changing management roles
- new requirement to handle interpersonal relations
- organisational structure and climate
- career prospects
- work and home interface
- conflicts between being a specialist and a generalist
- tension from being an individual and a team player
- inadequate support and recognition from one's boss
- relentless work pressure and low personal discretion
- poor work equipment and premises
- excessive organisational change
- job insecurity.

We all have tolerance to stress and the point at which we start suffering from it varies across individuals. How stress affects you depends on whether you are flexible or inflexible, introverted or extroverted and how well you fit into your job.

Consequently, it will always be your responsibility to learn how to spot the signs and act. Yet, some signs may be hard to catch early. These include:

- tension
- fatigue
- irritability

- emotional detachment
- withdrawal
- cynicism
- rigidity.

Good managers know the importance of watching for the signs. In PricewaterhouseCoopers, for example, senior managers have established a monitoring system to scan people's time sheets to identify anyone who is working excessive hours. They will have their workloads adjusted or be told to take a holiday.

One way to stay alert to the dangers to yourself and others is:

- Have a regular health check.

Many companies now arrange this as a matter of routine. It is also important evidence that the company cares about stress and reduces its vulnerability to legal damages from negligence around employee health.

The CBI has estimated that stress costs UK employers over £4bn a year. Studies in the early 1990s by the Massachusetts Institute of Technology suggested that depression at work was costing the USA billions of dollars – much the same as heart disease.

How we interpret events around us may entirely determine whether we react to them in a stressed way or not. For example, suppose you are summoned to see the chief executive, having just made a mistake; you are unlikely to see this as an occasion for rejoicing. When you get there, however, you may learn that the reason for the summons has nothing to do with the mistake at all.

We view the world through our own filter, which is affected by our own beliefs. It may not even be a particular event that causes stress, only our interpretation of it. The chart on page 276 demonstrates this effect.

The ABC of stress and distress

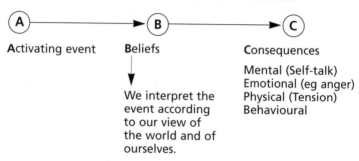

Activating event   Beliefs   Consequences

We interpret the event according to our view of the world and of ourselves.

Mental (Self-talk)
Emotional (eg anger)
Physical (Tension)
Behavioural

The above shows the role of interpretation in stress. While A is the stressful event situation, B is how we view it. C shows the mental, physical, emotional and behavioural consequences. Adverse consequences might be anxiety, sweaty hands, smoking more than usual. Favourable consequences might be positive anticipation, a feeling of being stimulated and facing an exciting challenge.

Event A does not directly cause C. Instead B, consisting of beliefs about ourselves and other people, intervenes. How we see the world may be just as important as how the world actually is.

The consequences of stress

When you are overstressed you become less effective as a manager. For example, when you are tired, just to keep functioning you start trying to make everything simpler. Issues get polarised into black or white, right or wrong.

Under stress, you are likely to start stereotyping people and situations, forcing them into familiar boxes that you understand how to deal with. Your recruitment decisions, for example, may prove faulty. Or you may begin to shorten your time horizons and postpone all difficult decisions until another day.

When you are overtired, to keep yourself awake you may tend

to do more talking than listening. Emotion rather than reason is likely to take over. Or to keep going you may be tempted to resort to drink or other stimulants.

How you are affected by stress also depends on whether you are mainly responsible for things or for people. Accountability for people means constantly interacting with them, attending meetings and often working under pressure. This can lead to heavy smoking, raised blood pressure and so on. Managers who are mainly concerned with things, on the other hand, seem to be less affected by stress.

Are you a type A or B?

Psychologists who have studied stress have identified two distinct types of people:

- Type A is typically extremely competitive, strives for achievement and may be aggressive, hasty, impatient, restless, very alert, with explosive speech and tense facial muscles, and may feel under pressure of time and the challenge of responsibility.
- Type B tends to be more easy-going, takes difficulties in their stride, spends time on what they do, and maintains a careful balance between events and actions demanding their energy.

Type A is more likely to suffer heart disease than a Type B person.

While you cannot readily alter your whole personality, you can at least be aware which type you tend towards and watch for the danger signs.

For instance, Type A people seem less interested in exercise and their general lifestyle leads to ill-health.

Combating stress

It is stressful having to deal with stress! While you cannot always minimise it, you can certainly start to manage it by taking an active, assertive and informed approach to it.

For example, while you should certainly resist excessive amounts of work for yourself or your subordinates, it is even more important to insist on working regular hours. This can be hard if your entire company culture approves of excessive hours. Such approval is sometimes based on the rather spurious grounds that if you love what you are doing, there is no separation between work and play.

> BT, GlaxoSmithKline, Marks and Spencer, Littlewoods, Sainsbury's, KPMG, Lloyds TSB, Shell and Unilever are just some of the UK companies now claiming to help employees find a balance between private lives and professional responsibilities.
>
> At BT staff are warned that working too many hours has a 'damaging effect' on them and their families and their communities. Managers at GlaxoSmithKline are now expected to tell staff who continually stay late that they must go home.
>
> Developing a work–life balance can encourage employees to participate more fully in company development.

Your job as a manager is to ensure good work arrangements and not connive at ever-lengthening hours in the chase for ever-expanding objectives.

As a result, handling stress is closely linked to:

■ assertive objective-setting
■ good time management.

You can raise your own productivity by as much as a quarter if you apply these principles to yourself.

An important part of handling stress at work is:

■ Do not rely on calling in the stress experts. Although a stress audit and coaches can be helpful interventions, it is a management responsibility to tackle organisational sources generating stress.

The same people you may call in to run stress reduction sessions may, for example, later appear in court as hostile witnesses talking about traumatic stress caused by your work environment.

Objective-setting

Chapter 1 deals with part of this management skill. However, it is not enough to set objectives well. To avoid unhealthy stress, effective managers resist unacceptably stressful goals and are ruthless at prioritising them. That way *you* do the driving, not the goals.

While deadlines attached to objectives are a healthy stimulus, they can also be stress inducing unless you:

■ set attainable deadlines
■ review deadlines regularly
■ change deadlines when the situation dictates
■ are flexible and willing to adjust objectives.

Setting impossible or hugely demanding goals runs through the mythology of motivation, managing teams or building outstanding companies. For example, in their book on long-lasting companies, *Built to Last*, James Collins and Jerry Porras talk of the importance of 'big hairy audacious goals'. Give people a huge challenge, goes the theory, and they respond by making enormous efforts to win.

Good managers, though, set attainable goals that are worth striving for. For themselves they learn which goals to accept and which to resist. For example, if a business goal threatens your health or your family life, it is worthless.

Be willing to regularly review and, where necessary, negotiate your goals. Do not wait until it is clear that you are going to fail to deliver.

David McMurtrie is managing director of the fast-growing dot.com company Real Media. He works long hours, partly because he enjoys it and because he is still settling into the job.

Despite his responsibilities, though, David remains a dedicated runner and keep-fit enthusiast. He commits himself to covering over 20 miles a week and enters both the London and New York Marathons. Running is David's way of keeping excess work at bay, of ensuring that work is simply not allowed to take him over completely, and of enabling him to cope with the pressures of the working day.

In the Real Media offices, there are various staff distractions such as a tabletop football game and a golfing fairway.

Time management

Anything upsetting the all-important balance between work and private life is likely to be an important stress factor. For example, are you or your subordinates taking work home several nights a week? Are you frequently working more than 60 hours a week? If so, it is time to act. You could be even more productive if you found better ways to take a break.

When you personally work long hours, it may initially send a message that you are committed, yet it soon suggests that you are not being particularly productive. There is no evidence, for example, that long working hours mean a successful career, company or even economy.

If someone you are leading consistently works late, what is your reaction? Are you obsessed with 'presenteeism' rather than actual effectiveness? In Germany, for example, the response that someone is working long hours is that this person is not coping. They are seen as either not managing their time properly, or as overworried about their job. Cancelling holidays is regarded as seriously delinquent behaviour.

It is not having an outside life if you return home and dump your stress on a partner who may also be facing pressures, or if you simply slump in front of the television or computer. Brooding about work does not contribute to reducing stress – it merely adds to it.

> Some people actually want to work long hours. 'We love what we do,' says Michael Smith, 25, co-founder and chief executive of Internet business Firebox.com. He reckons he works an average of 90-100 hours a week. 'It's almost impossible to separate work from play.'
>
> Several of Firebox's 10 staff share a flat, and all are young and single. Hours are not formally set, but 'presenteeism' is not a problem. 'No one raises an eyebrow if someone comes in at midday, or decides to take the afternoon off to sit in the park,' says Smith. There are also many office distractions, such as Sony Playstations.

Watch out for the warning signs of a lack of concentration, irritability, aggression and a failure to retain a sense of humour. These are all indications that either you or a colleague may be crossing the divide between healthy pressure and damaging stress. This is the time to fight the urge to go into the office at weekends and instead take a day off.

Well-being days

In some companies, the need for a mental break is built into the culture. For example, at Maynard Leigh Associates employees can take up to four 'well-being' days a year. These can be used whenever the person feels a need to get away, to drop out for a while.

There is no need to justify your well-being day to anyone. Instead, you just announce that you would like the time off and check that it will not cause serious work problems for others. One result of this approach is that people seldom phone in 'sick' when what they really want is a day in the country.

A board meeting at pharmaceutical giant GlaxoSmithKline was rescheduled at the last minute because two people could only attend part of it.

It was nothing to do with an important customer or a vital meeting in America. It was simply that the meeting clashed with the two people's children's nativity plays. The meeting was brought forward a few hours and the agenda adjusted so that the pair could leave early.

Stress-busters

There are numerous personal and organisational strategies to eliminate or reduce stress to manageable levels, such as:

- empowering others
- diet watch
- local community projects
- relaxation strategies.

Empowering others

Focus on helping those you lead to extend their range of work. For example, maybe you can let go of some of your own regular responsibilities so that they can acquire them.

When you empower others, you do more than just delegate. You relinquish control and accept that people will make mistakes. You simply trust that people 'don't come to work to screw up'.

If you have previously mainly managed things rather than people, this is a good time to seek some training. For example, consider asking for help in learning how to:

■ unlock people's motivation
■ deal with difficult employees
■ cope with the resistance arising from managing change
■ be a more effective communicator
■ understand how to pass on work and issue instructions
■ encourage participation.

Diet watch

Stress often affects people's eating habits. For example, when you are stressed you may tend to eat too much, or too little. You start to skip breakfast, miss lunch and grab snacks along the way. Many managers, for example, enjoy feeling so busy that they cannot spare the time for lunch. If this is happening to you, take action.

■ Count the number of times you have forgotten to take lunch in the last two weeks.
■ If you have missed more than three or four lunch breaks, you have the first signs of serious stress.

Dietary habits combined with smoking have long been important factors behind stress. The smoke-filled room, with plenty of pastries or biscuits and endless supplies of coffee, for example, is potentially damaging.

Local community projects

At the Body Shop, employees are actively encouraged to start local community projects. Apart from any team-building benefits, this takes staff away from becoming too obsessed with the work situation.

Getting involved with a charity, such as accepting a challenge to raise money by a certain date, matched by a contribution by the company, can stimulate you and others to put work back in perspective.

Relaxation

The harder you work the more important it is to use relaxation techniques to take off the pressure. One way is to schedule an instant break when you focus on specific relaxation methods.

For example, if you have your own office, try closing the door and posting a notice saying you cannot be disturbed for 15 minutes. If possible, lock it too. Switch off phones and anything else that could disturb you. Carry out the 10 steps to relaxation below and give yourself a break.

---

10 steps to relaxation

1 Sit in a comfortable chair, feet flat on the floor, with your eyes closed.

2 Become aware of your breathing.

3 Take in a few deep breaths. As you let out each breath, say to yourself mentally, 'Relax'.

4 Concentrate on your face. Feel any tension in your face and

---

eyes. Make a mental picture of this tension – it might be a knotted rope or a coiled spring. Picture this relaxing and unwinding, growing looser and more comfortable, like a sack of wet sand.

5 Experience your eyes and face becoming relaxed. As they relax, feel a wave of relaxation spreading though your whole body.

6 Tense your eyes and face, squeezing them tightly, then relaxing them. Feel this same relaxation throughout your body.

7 Do the same with other parts of your body, squeezing and relaxing each part from your head to your toes, in this order:

jaw	chest
neck	abdomen
shoulders	thighs
back	calves
upper arms	ankles
lower arms	feet
hands and fingers	toes

Do this until every part of your body is relaxed. For each part of your body, mentally picture the tension, see it melting away.

8 When you have relaxed each part of your body, rest quietly in this comfortable state for two to five minutes.

9 Let the muscles of your eyelids slowly lighten up, become aware of your surroundings again, and prepare to open your eyes.

10 Now open your eyes. You are refreshed, and ready to resume your usual activities.

Maynard Leigh Associates regularly invites in experts to conduct 20-minute massages for staff, and other companies have experimented with meditation sessions and aromatherapy.

Meditation

This is now increasingly accepted as on of the most powerful and easily learned weapons for countering the effects of stress. This is not something adopted by just Indian gurus or adherents of strange sects. Anyone can meditate and it is easy to learn.

Meditation sessions can vary according to your particular need. A few minutes during the day could transform the way you handle your work. Fifteen minutes at the start of each day can alter your life. It is so effective that many companies pay their managers to learn how to do it.

External relaxation also includes sport, hobbies and other non-work activities that absorb your time and interest. What is important is eliminating work from your mind for long enough to provide a real break. When you do so, your productivity is nearly always enhanced.

Underminers

If you have trouble unwinding, there may be several areas of your life to consider:

- **Television (or sitting at a computer)** – this can be relaxing, but a well-known effect is to excite certain parts of the brain to be more active. By watching TV late into the evening you may be unwittingly making it harder to relax at night and simply let go when you finally get to bed or try to sleep.
- **Sleep** – lack of sleep can also be an aggravating factor causing stress, rather than just a consequence of it. If you suspect that stress is starting to get to you, make sure that you have some early nights.
- **Late eating** – if possible avoid eating your evening meal

much after 9 pm. It takes several hours to digest food and doing so uses up energy. Try to eat earlier so that when you get to bed your body has less to do.

■ **Lack of holidays** – according to a study by Totaljobs.com, around 60 per cent of UK workers do not use their full holiday entitlement. About half of these felt guilty about leaving work. If you feel unable to take a long holiday, at least keep taking short breaks. You may feel as if you have never been away but your body will have recharged its batteries and you will be better able to cope.

Helping others

Help those you manage to tackle stress by being willing to discuss with them personal strategies for dealing with it. The fact that you are prepared to spend time doing this sends an important message about you as a manager. If you do it in a genuinely interested way – having a conversation between two human beings, rather than as manager to subordinate – you will make a considerable impact.

Women in particular can benefit from receiving help in realising how much they may be falling victim to stress. Often this stems from feeling a lack of control over their work environment. The box below offers some specific suggestions for Type A women managers.

Reducing stress for Type A women managers

■ Try to control your obsessional time-directed life by making yourself aware of it and changing the established pattern of behaviour.

■ Restrain yourself from trying to be the centre of attention by not constantly talking, particularly when there is no real need to do so.

- Develop reflective periods in your self-created hectic pro-gramme for life and assess the causes of your 'hurry' sick-ness.
- Most of your work does not require immediate action. Tell yourself at least once a day that no enterprise ever failed because it was executed too slowly, too well.
- Indulge in outside activities, theatre, reading, etc, to lessen obsessional, time-oriented behaviour.
- Try not to make unnecessary appointments and impossible deadlines.
- Protect your time; learn to say 'no'.
- Take as many stress-free breathing spaces during the course of an intensive working day as possible.
- Try to create opportunities during the day or night when you can entirely relax your body and mind.

The first step in helping a subordinate to handle stress at work is you being willing to:

- discuss it openly
- make it a team issue – others may be suffering too
- insisting they have time out
- offering support through coaching or counselling
- explore relationships and whether these are contributing to stress.

If, having tried to help, you feel that the person needs more support, they may benefit from attending a short course on stress management.

Team it

Teams are a great way to reduce stress through sharing anxieties and peer group support. If stress symptoms seem to be arising, put it on the team agenda. Encourage everyone to discuss what is happening and what might be done about it. Just the openness of the discussion can be an important contribution to tackling the issue.

Watch for signs that a team member:

■ argues with you more than usual
■ is unusually quiet, from previously being normally assertive
■ starts smoking when normally does not do so
■ begins having an excessive amount of sick leave
■ suddenly begins to perform less well.

You may be unwittingly an important cause of other people's stress because dealing with a manager can be stressful for some people, no matter how caringly you go about it.

If you are restructuring, reducing the numbers employed or changing people's roles, you may lose sight of how much this affects people. To you it all may make perfect organisational

---

Reducing stress during major change

Staff development
■ Help people adopt realistic goals.
■ Encourage people to choose new objectives that give alternative sources of satisfaction.
■ Provide opportunities for in-service training designed to increase role effectiveness and adapt to change.
■ Monitor stress levels, either in management supervision sessions or some other way.
■ Offer work-focused counselling or coaching for those experiencing serious stress.
■ Encourage the development of mutual support groups or networks.

Jobs and roles

- Review workloads and priorities.
- Where relevant, reduce workloads, temporarily or permanently.
- Spread difficult or unrewarding work equitably.
- Increase opportunities at every level to exercise judgement, enhancing people's feelings of competence, ability to cope and use of skills to make decisions.
- Structure roles and team arrangements to allow 'time out' sessions to occur.
- Use extra personnel to ease pressures during the transition phase.
- Insist that people take their holidays.
- Discourage frequent weekend and regular late-night working.
- Check how much people with subordinates are delegating.
- Build career ladders.

Management development

- Develop training that focuses on current major problems.
- Monitor performance and give regular feedback.
- Watch for stress and intervene when strain is excessive.

Organisational mechanisms

- Do not change everything at once; leave a stable and secure base from which new arrangements can be explored.
- Give adequate time and resources to project teams and their leaders charged with implementing change.
- Create formal ways to ensure group and organisational problem-solving.
- Promote involvement by maximising people's autonomy and participation in the change process.
- Formalise ways of handling conflict.
- Ensure adequate and direct feedback about new methods.
- Develop clear organisational goals and distinct values.

sense – these things need to happen. You help those on the receiving end if you try to:

- minimise uncertainty
- clarify work objectives
- redefine roles quickly.

Try to be a model for other people in handling stress. When people see you refusing to work excessively long hours, valuing your own personal time, making space for non-work activity, not being rushed, they realise that you are handling stress. They may soon find ways to do the same.

Call in the coaches

Increasingly managers are turning to coaches or counsellors to help them cope, either with their own stress or when their subordinates are suffering from it.

Coaching can be a powerful tool for helping someone change their way of behaving (see Chapter 4), but it is no substitute for managers being accountable for the work environment. Sending someone off for coaching can merely create a victim culture in which people are made to feel it is their fault that they are stressed.

Coaching can help when, despite a good working environment, someone still does not seem to cope.

Further reading

'Business health and safety'. *Financial Times Guide*. 16 October 2000.

CIPD. 'Stress at work'. www.cipd.co.uk, originally issued in October 1998; minor revisions July 2000.

Cooper C. and Palmer S. *Conquer Your Stress*. London, CIPD, 2000.

LAZEAR J. *Meditations for Men Who Do Too Much*. Wellingborough, Aquarian Books, 1992.

PRIEST S. *and* WELCH J. *Creating a Stress-Free Office*. Aldershot, Gower, 1998.

SCHAEF WILSON A. *Meditations for Women Who Do Too Much*. London, Harper & Row, 1990.

SUTTON J. *Thrive on Stress: Manage pressure and positively thrive on it*. Oxford, How To Books, 2000.

TIME MANAGEMENT

Chapter 17

John Spencer runs his own company, is an accountant, a world authority on UFOs, author of management books, happily married and leads successful workshops on time management.

Buzzing with ideas on how best to use time, what makes him so effective is his clear sense of purpose. He knows what he is trying to achieve, when he needs to complete his goals, and plans accordingly. With John there are few wasted seconds, let alone minutes, in his day.

John knows that goal-setting is one of the most fundamental secrets of managing time. Get the goals identified, sorted and prioritised and, like him, you will almost certainly find it easier to make sense of available time.

It is not just goal-setting that enables John to thrive and fit more into his average day than most managers do in a week. He is terrific at handling paperwork, great at delegating, knows about dealing with stress and is assertive about the nature and amount of work he undertakes.

> The greatest problem with doing things efficiently and promptly is that it leaves acres of empty time in which you feel obliged to do still more. It is an invitation to walk faster and faster on the treadmill. What most of us really need are tips on how to be less busy, less efficient and less productive. The really hard thing is to learn to stop charging around doing 16 things at once, and instead slow down and waste a little more time.
>
> KELLAWAY L. 'Inefficient and happy with it'. *The Financial Times*. 2 November 2000.

People like John Spencer seldom talk of time management. They see time management as an issue in its own right. They have found by experience that it is inextricably bound up with other important aspects of effective management, including:

■ objective-setting, which we look at in Chapter 1
■ assertiveness, which we look at in Chapter 16
■ dealing with stress, which we explore in Chapter 15
■ having effective meetings, which we explore in Chapter 7.

Cash-rich but time-poor people are busy, busy, busy. Yet often they have lost sight of what matters. Many complain of being under pressure and experience stress, often without knowing it. The point about good time management is not that you become so obsessively organised that you can then do a million more things. It is that using your time well enables you to lead a balanced lifestyle where you are not constantly rushing around trying to beat the clock.

Increasingly in the media we see articles and books devoted to issues around leading a balanced lifestyle. This is not merely a current fad. It is becoming important because so many people find it so hard to manage their personal time well, so that they lead a really satisfying life.

Hoarder or chucker?

Are you a hoarder or a chucker? Hoarders save files, paperwork and miscellaneous trivia because one day they might need them. To find some obscure piece of information, a lost contact and a stretchy bit of green rubber that fits around a milk carton, try contacting your local office hoarder.

Hoarders stuff filing cabinets, computer disks and offices with increasingly useless information. The trash they accumulate clogs shelves, overflows onto the floor and if allowed will gradually fill an entire office or even a whole floor of a building.

Without such people, though, companies would probably lose track of all sorts of useful material. Hoarders are natural archivists, though the worst of them can never find anything when you really need it.

Chuckers also live up to their name. Almost everything is 'rapidly dumped quickly' and their desks are predictably pristine, devoid of clutter and pending trays. Even their computer directories are sorted neatly and material disgorged into cyberspace at regular intervals.

The trouble with chuckers, though, is that they frequently end up searching for what was discarded only last week. Yet companies need their ruthless attitude to the bric-a-brac of daily business life. Without them the filing cabinets or hard drives would escalate to infinity.

It is tempting to believe that chuckers must be terrific at managing time. In fact they may spend a disproportionate amount of it searching for what was once readily to hand. Nor is it true that all hoarders are terrible at personal time management. What they lose in being swamped with excess material they may gain in having an impressive retrieval system.

Review your natural tendency towards hoarding or chucking. This can be a helpful guide for how you might improve your time management.

Are you surrounded by large amounts of paper, files or reports? While these may provide a certain sense of security, they may also be putting an invisible pressure on you. It is like having a constantly annoying hum in the background.

For you a useful guideline is:

■ 'If I haven't used it in the last 18 months – it goes!'

If your natural tendency is to be a chucker, then review how this might be reducing your efficiency. Are you letting material go because you cannot readily find a sensible home for it? Is your constant urge to houseclean making you dump items that may indeed be useful in the foreseeable future?

For you a useful guideline is:

■ 'If I chuck it now, how difficult or costly will it be to obtain if I need it again within six months?'

Time bandits

If someone tried stealing your handbag or wallet, you would surely try to stop it happening. Yet at work we constantly encounter time bandits who try extorting precious time without our permission.

Beating the time bandits

My five most demanding time bandits are:
1...
2...
3...
4...
5...

Now try taking these apart.

■ How much time does each tend to waste in a week?
■ When does each tend to occur most?
■ Who seems to be behind them?

Only by identifying and analysing your time bandits can you expect to start policing them.

Time bandits include useless phone calls, conversations that get nowhere, excess paper and e-mails, futile meetings and so on. To identify your most demanding time bandits, complete the audit below.

Most managers spend less than 3 per cent of their time focused on the future of the organisation. Most of it goes on running the business on a day-to-day basis. Researchers also estimate that one can increase personal productivity by as much as 20 per cent through better personal time management.

Log it?

Some time management experts urge you to keep a time log. They argue that by recording and classifying all the different actions taken, over several weeks you can make better sense of your time usage.

If that works for you, fine. In our workshops, though, we have met far too many people who have simply found time logs boring and hard to maintain. Most people abandon them long before they yield enough reliable data to analyse.

Anyway, you probably already know that you waste a fair amount of time, and you may even know why. It is doing something about it that can prove tricky.

Try calling your wasted time Red Time, and your efficiently used time Green Time. The point of good time management is learning to convert Red into Green Time.

Red Time happens anywhere. It is also highly personal. For example, some people find staring out of the train window enjoyable, and worthwhile – it may be the only opportunity to think creatively about certain issues. Others regard such periods as wasteful when instead they could be bashing away at a laptop or networking on their mobile.

Can you identify your Red Time, and how much there is of it during a day or a week?

- Identify examples of your Red Time.
- See what imaginative ways you can find to convert it into Green Time.

When you are using your time appropriately it becomes Green Time. For example, if you enjoy eating, ensure that you really do enjoy it and do not rush the experience. Similarly, if you think watching television is mainly a waste of time, identify those few programmes that are worth viewing. Give yourself permission to sit and enjoy them.

In converting Red to Green Time, a useful tool is the classic 80:20 rule. There is a common tendency to devote 80 per cent to the trivia and only 20 per cent to what really matters. We need to learn to do it the other way around, with 80 per cent of our time devoted to activity that we consider central to our aims.

Body time

Your body has its own version of Red and Green Times. Natural biorhythm means that we are at our peak only during certain periods of our waking lives. Treating every hour of every day as of equal importance is a sure way to minimise, rather than max-imise, your use of time.

Instead, try and identify when you really are at your best, when you operate with full energy and involvement. If the answer is never, it is time to rethink your job!

So, when do you best:

- think?
- work creatively?
- handle boring tasks?
- use lots of energy?

Each of these might be at different times during the day or night. Knowing *when* you function really well and at what makes your time management easier.

Internal Green Time may only be an hour or so. This is when it pays to concentrate on those vital tasks you must do quickly and that give you the biggest return.

Think of it as 'making a profit'. When you really use your internal Green Time well, you keep adding value – to yourself, your life, the job, a task, the company, a client, a customer and so on.

For example, you might realise that you make decisions more easily first thing in the morning, finding it harder as the day wears on. Good time management, therefore, means allocating as many important decisions as possible to the early part of the day.

Protect this precious internal Green Time from attacks by the time bandits. To get the message across that 'I'm now in my Green Time, please leave me alone', some people wear a special cap, place a stuffed animal on their desk or put up a flag! In the extreme case, where you have a private office you simply shut the door and stick a notice on it explaining when or under what circumstances you can be disturbed.

Jealously protecting your Green Time soon gets noticed and you may find others start copying you. Carefully limit, though, how much Green Time you claim for yourself and exclude others. As a manager you need to be available and not hide behind an impenetrable Green Time barrier.

Equally, you are entitled to have your limited Green Time respected, since this is when you are most productive.

The ego trip

Many managers love to look busy. They happily complain of being swamped by e-mails, meetings, reports or other paper work. Being seen to be busy is used as a signal that:

- 'I am important'
- 'I am working hard'
- 'I am committed.'

Becoming a good time manager includes tackling any ego issue about being 'busy'. Why, for example, do great time managers always seem to have space for people? Simply because they refuse to allow the paperwork or time bandits to detract from their core purpose of:

- managing and motivating others well.

Your aim is not to look constantly busy, or even actually be busy the whole time. It is to get the trivia sufficiently under control to allow ample time to devote to interacting with those you manage or lead.

Paper

At the end of a working day in some companies every desk must be completely cleared. This may be for security reasons, including industrial espionage, bombs and terrorist activity. When you are forced to clear your desk daily it imposes a discipline on any hoarding.

Two powerful paperwork principles worth adopting are:

- Take an overview first.
- Handle each piece of paper once only.

Overview

It is hard to make sense of the paperwork when you deal with every item in isolation. That way you hold all your priorities in your head, possibly ignoring the changing nature of the bombardment.

Instead:

■ Choose a fixed time every day to review your paperwork, rather than constantly trying to keep up with it.

If only a few pieces of paper hit your desk daily then it hardly matters if you dealt with it at the time. But if like many managers you face a constant stream, then sticking to a definite time to deal with paperwork imposes a useful discipline and makes time management easier.

If you have an assistant or secretary, then all paperwork should reach you sorted and labelled. You may have to coach your colleague on organising material so it arrives in the most useful form. If you have no one to do this for you, make sorting the material the first task – *before* tackling the individual items

The overview means you whiz through every item to decide initially what to do with it. This lets you prioritise material so that you:

■ only tackle important items and delegate the rest
■ tackle important items first, not last.

Sort it
Sort paperwork items into:

■ for action
■ ones addressed to you personally
■ non-routine communications
■ material for signature
■ background reading.

Once only

Managers using their time well invariably adopt the principle of only handling each paper item once or twice. While in practice this may be hard to achieve, it can rapidly force you to change wasteful habits, such as allowing material to mount up in pending trays.

Pending items soon accumulate into a depressing pile that you know needs attention, yet never seems to lessen. Is this happening because you want to look busy?

As part of the 'handle it only once' method, try these simple guidelines:

- dump it
- devolve it
- do it
- direct it.

Dump it

On his travels, Ulysses stopped the ears of his crew to prevent them from hearing the fatal songs of the Sirens. Meanwhile he listened while lashed to the ship's mast. You may not have heard his particular brand of Sirens, yet you have probably already encountered the:

- Storage Sirens.

The Storage Sirens have equally diverting music. Their tunes can seriously distort your time management. For instance, one song repeats the hard-to-resist message: 'Someday, somebody may want this bit of paper – save it.' Invariably this proves irresistible to anyone with even a hint of the hoarder gene in their DNA.

A subtler Siren song tells of your need for a system to contain your papers. This particular temptation goes: 'Create a complete system – expand it, expand it, expand it.' Even devoted chuckers can fall for this one as they fight their natural tendency to sweep everything away.

Like Ulysses, part of you will undoubtedly want to obey the Sirens, because the sounds are so compelling. They make such sweet sense, why risk problems by ignoring their commands? Resisting them, though, is essential for taking charge of your own time.

The success of the Storage Sirens explains why even quite small companies possess filing cabinets packed with dead paper. Most of it conforms strictly to the 80:20 rule, that is, 80 per cent of the work done by the organisation is handled by around 20 per cent of the papers on file.

How can you counter the effects of the Storage Sirens? The first step is to take a personal interest in your own filing system, insisting that it remains as simple as possible. The more elaborate the structure, the harder it is to maintain or to keep under control. If you cannot quickly check through the entire contents in a few hours it is probably not serving you well. A simple structure means you or your assistant can rapidly:

- navigate around it
- weed out dead material.

Some managers regard half a dozen bulging filing cabinets in or just outside their office as a sort of virility symbol. For others it is a security blanket. It implies that they are busy, important people. Yet these same systems can seriously impinge on their personal efficiency, wasting time, not merely because items are hard to find, but because they are a burden to maintain and make everyone feel weighed down.

Delegate it

Ruthlessly pass unwanted paper to someone else. Much of the material coming your way either has little real value or requires only a brief response.

Do not prepare a memo to send the thing on its way, just scribble a legible note on the original material indicating your response. Or add a post-it note to the item and get rid of it!

Put each item through a simple filter by asking:

■ Can someone else deal with this apart from me?

This check question forces you to consider how to pass work on to others, enlarging their jobs at the same time.

Do it

Some papers require action and these are ones that you really want to identify from the daily bombardment.

How do you decide what needs your immediate attention? A useful tool is the urgency/importance guide shown on page 309. This helps you decide whether you take action personally, or hand it on to someone else to see through.

Papers demanding action could be consigned to a tray for attention later. This is fine if you only have a few such items. But with dozens, the mounting pile soon has an adverse effect on your time management.

The time management tip here is to make a start on the action in some form, if only to open a file, make a call, or add it to your 'to do' list.

The investigation of the famous near nuclear disaster at Three Mile Island nuclear plant in America examined the company's filing system. Amongst the many papers were ones predicting the crisis and demanding action. Yet the managers had either failed to get around to reading them or not taken action.

Does your business or job have the equivalent of a Three Mile Island incident waiting to happen? Good time management means handling all the papers that reach you appropriately and expeditiously. You can only do that if you are properly organised.

Paper tips

- Make a decision.
- Do not let paper stand still for long – files soon make piles.
- Know how to find what you file, which means regularly clearing obsolete files.
- Be driven by the 'one contact only' guide – ie process each piece of paper only once or at most twice.
- For papers in a pile, work one day from the top downward, and the next day work from the bottom upwards.
- Avoid pending trays with papers hanging around for attention, with no set date for processing.
- Consign current papers that you are not working on at this moment to a 'bring forward' file divided into useful time periods such as daily, weekly or monthly sections.

Direct it to filing

Keep only a few essential files in your own desk or personal filing cabinet – highly confidential ones and those you are working on currently. You should know what they are and expect to use them regularly.

Send all other papers to either a central filing system or an archive facility.

E-mail

The equivalent of having a tidy desk for computers is having regular clear-outs of files, and dealing effectively with electronic bombardment. Unless you have a restriction on data storage, for example, it is tempting to file absolutely everything, including back-up copies of countless versions of material. Similarly, you may be tempted to read all your e-mails in strict order of appearance on the screen, which may be as unproductive as reading all your hard copy as it piles up in an in-tray.

Some useful electronic guidelines include:

■ Clear all inbox e-mails before closing down for the day. This allows you to start each new session with a fresh, empty inbox. It contributes to feeling more in control and less cluttered.

■ Delete all previously 'sent' items using a personal time frame. This means choosing a time after which you do not retain a record of 'sent' items. It might be after two days, a week or monthly. What counts is consistently and regularly deleting to a standard time frame.

■ Every file needs to be within a folder (or directory) – no miscellaneous items. This encourages you to regularly make decisions about what goes where. More than a couple of dozen items in a miscellaneous category is a sign you need to create a new folder (directory) heading.

■ Delete old back-up copies of documents. This reduces the sheer number of items as you open the file. You can sort through the contents quickly, rather than scroll past countless items that are long since dead and gone.

■ Read through all topic headings first before opening up any particular item. Move items that have a high priority rating to form a group at the top of the screen. Delete items that are clearly junk mail. Save items with attachments for later.

Sorting

A widely used time-saver is dividing all incoming hard-copy material into three broad categories:

- **A items** – these must be done, no matter what happens.
- **B items** – you should probably deal with these but are uncertain what needs to happen next.
- **C items** – things it would be nice to read or do.

Put all C items into a drawer. If you deliberately ignore this material until you are forced to dig into the drawer and relocate it, most of it will simply wither away.

The 'C drawer' seldom demands attention. Most items die a natural death and can be dumped permanently after a few days or weeks. Occasionally something forces its way out of the C drawer and demands your attention. This might be when you move into the A or B list.

Be careful with your C drawer. While it can make you feel more secure about not throwing things away, it only works well if you regularly weed out dead stuff.

Lists

Ask any really successful person 'do you keep lists?' and invariably the answer is 'yes'. Lists are an essential way of using your time well, no matter how good your memory.

If you do not have a formal action list, it is time to start one!

Two kinds worth trying are:

- the master list
- the daily list.

The master list

Here is a challenge! Spend 10 minutes now writing down absolutely everything you think you need to do at work. Do not be general, such as describing your entire job description.

Instead be specific by listing as many tasks or activities that you know demand your regular current attention.

Do not worry if the initial list runs to two, three or even more pages. If you prefer, create it on a computer screen.

Master lists can be daunting and are often wrongly used as a regular daily guide to action. Their real value is to provide guidance about the broad range of activities you see as important. To really be in charge of your time you need to:

■ prevent the master list from ruling your life
■ create a much shorter daily task list.

Daily task list
Your 'to do' list is kept on a pad, in a notebook, on a computer or anywhere that you can quickly find it. The important thing is to have one! A piece of loose paper is not an effective daily 'to do' list as it can soon be lost or mislaid.

Keep your 'to do' lists short. The danger of computer-based 'to do' lists is that you keep adding to them and they gradually convert into master lists.

There are not enough hours available to deal with a long list, no matter how hard you work. Also, in most managerial jobs you need to respond to the unexpected. So even a short daily 'to do' list may become unachievable. A list extending to more than 10 items is probably too long.

If there are more than 10 items on your daily list, look closely at each one. Will it:

■ add value to the company
■ be a creative contribution
■ help others to be more effective
■ help move towards a key target?

What do you do with the uncompleted items? It seems to make sense to simply move them onto the next day's list. However, this will soon clog it up and turn it into yet another master list. Instead, adopt a personal guideline, such as uncompleted items appearing more than three times on the daily 'to do' list will be:

- dumped
- allocated serious time
- delegated.

Prioritising

Lists capture how you might spend your time and generally need constant refining. A time management tool that many people swear by is the urgency/importance grid.

This analyses your potential activities so that you can decide:

- when to do it
- whether you do it
- whether someone else should do it.

Urgency/importance grid

High

Ask someone else to do it, *now*	You do it *now*
Ask someone else to do it, *later*	You do it *later*, scope for passing it on

URGENT

Low   IMPORTANT   *High*

You personally spend time on items that are both urgent and important. These are ones where you cannot afford things to go wrong and where there is clearly a tight timescale for completion.

All the other items, though, can either be devolved or offer some scope for handing on to others.

More time management tips

- Dial your own calls; it is generally quicker.
- Ensure phone messages are on proper message pads and message-takers are trained.
- Keep delegating until people say they are overloaded and then review their priorities.
- If you spend more than 10 per cent of your total work time travelling, rethink your working methods.
- Explain to people that when your door is open you welcome callers and when it is shut you can only be disturbed in an emergency.
- If you must meet a deadline, be willing to spend time away from the office to work in a quiet place.
- Insist that all reports to you start with a one-page summary.
- Except as a last resort, do not personally progress-chase.

Ask colleagues to assess how effectively you use your time. Get them to mark you on a six-point scale of 1 (= poor use of time) to 6 (= excellent use of time). Invite these colleagues to offer suggestions on how you might use your time more effectively. It is often surprising how others can spot what you may be missing.

Finally, try sharing with colleagues your own tricks and techniques for maximising your time. It will encourage them to share theirs, and you will both find some highly practical ideas you can use.

Why do certain methods seem to work for them? For example, some people swear by leather organisers while others rely on a spiral-bound daybook, and yet others cannot be parted with their laptop or hand-held personal assistant. How do they use these day-to day? Be curious and you may uncover some terrific time-savers.

Further reading

Amos J. *The Things That Really Matter About Making the Most of Your Time.* Oxford, How To Books, 1999.

Lakein A. *How to Get Control of Your Time and Your Life.* London, Mass Market Paperback, 1996.

Maitland I. *Managing Your Time.* London, CIPD, 1999.

Roberts-Phelps G. *Working Smarter.* London, Thorogood, 1999.

Smith J. *How to be a Better Time Manager.* London, Kogan Page, 1997.

LISTENING

Chapter 18

'I listen . . . I hear . . . I will act,' declared Prime Minister Tony Blair in a fighting speech at the 2000 Annual Labour Party Conference. Business leaders and managers likewise have to listen, hear and act.

It is not enough just to be a good listener. Nor is it sufficient to show that you are absorbing what other people are saying. To be an effective leader or manager you need to be seen to act on the feedback.

Most managers are good talkers, though not always good listeners. The more successful the manager, the better the communicator. Yet we often think of communication mainly in terms of speaking rather than effective listening.

Listening is not merely staying silent. For managers there are several sorts of listening. You can do it to:

- monitor the environment
- take in someone's messages
- promote communication.

Monitoring the environment

A listening manager is constantly monitoring the work environment, that is the organisation's climate. This means staying alert for signals, absorbing information, hearing messages about the big picture.

When you are listening strategically, you stay sensitive to anything that might determine how the organisation achieves its strategic intentions. It means being hungry for information that will help the organisation transform itself.

For example, when you hear on the morning radio as you are preparing to leave for work that some change has occurred that could affect your business, this is building the big picture. When you attend a conference and someone talks about a new technological development that could radically alter some aspect of how your organisation functions, that too is adding to the big picture.

Listening to build the big picture is an essential management skill. Gradually you filter out irrelevant sounds and messages. Some of this filtering is unconscious, done instinctively without planning. However, there is also active listening to identify the information that can sharpen or change the big picture. For this you need to develop a sense of what you are listening for and why.

Active listening to enhance the big picture becomes easier when you have a clear sense of your current priorities, when you know what your organisation, division or section is trying to achieve. You can then listen in the correct frame of mind.

Within your organisation, you might listen in order to discover:

- what customers you are now serving
- through what channels customers are reaching you
- who your competitors are today
- what the basis of your current competitive advantage is
- what skills or capabilities make you unique today.

Actively listen to people talking about what is happening to discover these things.

In listening to build the big picture of the future, you try to discover:

- what customers you will be serving in the future

- which channels might reach your customers in the future
- who will be your future competitors
- what skills or capabilities will make you unique in the future.

These help you to think strategically.

Taking in someone's messages

You depend on influencing others and need to make conversations work for, rather than against, you. It matters:

- what you say
- how you say it
- the way you listen.

These affect how you produce results through others. The more you learn about your personal impact, the more you can adapt and develop your approach.

You do not control conversations, although with practice you can certainly control your side of them. When you do so, you automatically start influencing other people and their response to what you want.

Conversation skills effective managers develop include:

- handling personal criticism
- making proposals
- registering a protest
- disagreeing without aggression
- responding creatively
- negotiating
- acting assertively
- giving reassurance
- offering recognition
- using humour appropriately.

What do these mean in practice? What would you actually do during a conversation to put these into action? Although each conversation situation is unique, your listeners would expect you to:

- listen in a positive way at the right time
- talk meaningfully when it is your turn
- alter the direction of the conversation in acceptable ways
- keep the communication moving at a comfortable pace
- build on other people's key points
- deal with differences of opinion
- learn what people think
- provide positive feedback
- use the right word for the right occasion.

We spend 80 per cent of our waking lives communicating and the biggest slice (40 per cent) is devoted to listening. Despite this, few people receive training in it. Managers who have discovered the power of listening, for instance, have mainly done so through trial and error.

Many organisations now recognise the importance of learning to listen, and some even train their employees so that they can do it better.

Ideally, colleagues and subordinates should regard you as someone who understands them, is sensitive to their feelings and what they say. Those reporting directly to you want to see you genuinely interested in helping them perform well. It is not enough just to listen; they want you to absorb what they say and respond to it.

Selective hearing

Marks and Spencer had the evidence right before it. The company was losing its premier place in shoppers' hearts. Yet managers failed to respond until matters deteriorated so much that there was even talk of a hostile takeover in this once invulnerable icon of business excellence.

Likewise, there were ample warnings about the intentions of the Japanese to bomb Pearl Harbor in the early stages of World War II, yet somehow those in charge did not seem to hear. Mrs Thatcher, the UK prime minister, received overwhelming evidence that the poll tax threatened her entire political existence. Yet she too seemed immune to the facts.

It seems to happen so often. In business, managers and leaders receive difficult or unwanted information and fail to act. This includes warnings about their company's environmental impact, faulty products launched despite the danger signs, advance signs of impending competitor action, employee dissatisfaction leading to loss of hard-to-replace talent.

We tend to hear what we want to hear. Selective hearing explains why managers consistently ignore information that might otherwise help them avoid important mistakes. Selective hearing is comfortable, unchallenging and does not demand real action. Instead phrases like 'we'll monitor the situation', 'let's keep an eye on this', 'that's not really how we see it', prevail.

Sexual or racial discrimination, for example, is frequently 'tuned out' until either legal action or publicity forces the item back on the company agenda. For example, Ford UK faced a much-publicised court case before its management finally acknowledged there was a problem, flying in the company's global president to admit that no one had been listening.

Financial crises are a significant reason why organisations are forced to face up to reality and make major changes in direction or policy. Yet often the financial facts have been previously presented in various ways, including in writing. When you take the trouble to really listen to other people's messages, you:

- discover what is happening and the nature of current problems
- learn how problems have altered
- realise how to deal with people, how their minds work and how they approach problems
- access a rich source of ideas for improvements
- convey the message: 'I care'
- gain clues as to how to avoid future problems
- give people a chance to express their feelings about their jobs
- increase the chances that other people will listen to you.

So often managers prefer talking and pontificating to listening, reflecting and acting.

You cannot become a great management listener overnight. Being aware of your natural tendency towards selective hearing – all human beings suffer from it – is the first step towards countering the damaging effects.

It is important to practice your management listening skills daily. For example, when you are engaged in a conversation with someone, do you tend to wait for your turn to speak? By doing that you are not devoting your full attention to listening. People soon realise that you are listening merely so as to know when you can speak next.

What do we actually do while we are listening, apart from all the usual body language signs that we are paying attention? We listen to:

- understand
- remember
- recall.

Understand

Three powerful listening questions you can keep asking yourself are:

- What does this person mean?
- What does this person feel?
- What is this person not saying?

The average person talks to you at around 125 words a minute. Yet you think at up to 500 words a minute. You are therefore operating with plenty of spare capacity. You can either use these spare resources to get frustrated with the other person, or more profitably to mentally review the sorts of questions suggested here.

Remember

Most of the time, instead of active listening, we become distracted, pass superficial and rapid judgements, or silently concentrate on preparing our own response. If we are to remember what someone is saying we cannot just sit passively, hoping it will be absorbed. Instead, we need to listen hard for words and phrases that will tend to fix the information in our minds.

Recall

To recall what someone has said can be hard if you try to remember it in isolation, unconnected with anything else. A useful technique for remembering is to consciously make associations between a person's message and something that will make it easy to bring the information to mind later.

For example, if someone tells you that their department has increased its output by 31 per cent, you may not easily recall this precise percentage. However, by imagining them standing on a giant apple sliced into thirds, you may implant the image and fact indelibly in your mind until you later need to recall it.

Bad listening habits

Anti-listening behaviour is not simply talking when you should be silent. It is also:

- branding the subject as uninteresting
- criticising a speaker's delivery or mannerisms
- getting overstimulated by what the speaker says
- listening only for facts
- faking attention
- becoming distracted
- avoiding difficult material
- allowing emotion-laden words to arouse personal antagonism
- daydreaming and wasting the benefits of thought speed.

You enhance your listening by allowing adequate time to hear. When you are rushed or force someone else to hurry with their communication, you immediately reduce your chances of hearing well.

When people describe their contacts with really successful managers, they often say things like, 'She always seems to have time for me', 'When she listens to me I feel as if I'm the most important person in the world for her at that moment', or 'He really seems to be interested in what you have to say.'

There is no magic in acquiring such a reputation. You merely have to start taking the listening role seriously. For instance, do you really encourage people to take their time talking to you? Do your words and actions convey that you are ready to devote your whole attention to them?

Try the demanding exercise of having a conversation in which you never terminate it, leaving the other person to end it.

Do you eliminate interruptions when listening to someone in

your office or workspace? Are you constantly answering the phone, dealing with people popping their head around your door, signing letters and so on while the other person waits? If so your message is unmistakeable: 'I'm busy and haven't really got the time for you or your message.'

Sometimes the actions you can take to show that you are listening are simply good manners. For example, by clearing surplus papers off your desk, making a 'clean space' around you can convey that you are ready to listen and will not allow anything to distract you.

Energy

When you listen actively, you show it with your whole body. It is clear to the other person that you are focused. It takes energy to do this, including where you put your hands, how you hold your body, how you walk from one place to another.

Energised listening means staying awake both mentally and physically. This can be hard if you are tired, so having enough sleep and staying fresh is an important part of being an effective listener.

Even small signs can reveal that you have no energy to listen – for example, if you try to disguise tiredness by holding your body upright, while your eyes give you away by gradually closing or taking a long time to complete each blink.

Promoting communication

Three other essentials for enhancing your listening capabilities are:

- attending
- making requests
- expressing understanding.

Attending

Use non-verbal methods to help show that you are giving the other person the attention they deserve. Different national cultures have their own body language requirements. Generally, in the developed world, these are signs of attending:

- **Eye contact** – hold this for at least 70-80 per cent of the time; more can make the other person feel uncomfortable. When breaking contact, avoid looking all over the place or darting your eyes from side to side.
- **Position your body** – lean slightly towards the other person, and nod regularly to show that you either agree or are paying attention. Slouching does not necessarily convey that you are relaxed.
- **Use facial muscles** – these express interest and other emotions. Avoid folded arms, as this places a barrier between you and the other person.
- **Mirroring** – imitating the body position of the other person is another way of signalling that you are listening to what they are saying. For example, if the other person crosses their legs, you might do the same; if they place their hands in a steeple shape, you might do so too.

Making requests

Another indication that you are listening is asking relevant questions, seeking more information or demanding clarification. Ask open-ended questions as part of your listening strategy. These encourage the other person to continue talking, and cannot be answered by a straight yes or no. Use expressions like:

- 'I'd like to hear how things went while I was away.'
- 'Tell me about . . .'
- 'What do you feel about . . .'
- 'That is interesting, can you elaborate a bit further?'

Try posing fact-seeking questions. You ask the person to give you information while also showing that you have heard what they have said so far. Use these sparingly and in an encouraging way, rather than as conducting an interrogation.

Probing shows that you are listening by encouraging the person to become more specific. Do it in a patient, neutral way, for example:

■ 'In what ways are pressures on the team increasing?'
■ 'Can you give me an example?'
■ 'Tell me how I could do what you suggest.'
■ 'Would you like to explain how I could help?'

Verbal signals like 'mm', 'I see', 'really', are the oil that keeps a conversation moving along its track. Even when you merely nod your head in a positive way you are helping to push the conversation on further.

Other non-verbal messages that show that you are listening include nodding, eyebrow raising, quizzical but interested looks, leaning forward and smiling. These small signs are important, easy to do and needed. When you fail to use them, people soon stop in their speaking.

Expressing understanding
Listening is not enough; it is also important to show that you have understood. Ways to do that include:

■ reflecting back feelings
■ paraphrasing
■ summarising.

Often it is more important to respond to how someone is feeling than to their actual words. For instance, the person may talk in a calm way, yet be bubbling over with enthusiasm, anxiety or anger.

Try to detect the underlying emotion that the words may not be conveying. If you consider that the feelings are more important than the words, demonstrate your ability to 'hear' what is being said by reflecting back with expressions like:

- 'It seems you are feeling . . .'
- 'It sounds to me as if . . .'
- 'You must be really . . .' (angry, pleased, worried etc).

Another clear sign of understanding is repeating back to the person what they have said in your own words. Paraphrase the content of their communication, not their emotions.

Paraphrasing also allows the other person to correct misunderstandings and shows that you are listening with care.

Key word repetition is part of the technique of paraphrasing in which you pick out particular words or phrases to encourage the speaker to explain in more detail. These key words almost jump out at you if you are listening carefully for them.

Part of paraphrasing is adding to a person's theme or argument, rather than taking it apart in a critical fashion:

- 'What makes you say that? Is it for example . . . ?'
- 'What are you thinking of specifically?'
- 'This seems important. Do you think that . . . ?'
- 'Yes, I can see that, though can you clarify . . . ?'

When you summarise what someone has said, you again convey the extent of your active listening. You condense the information into brief points or themes and focus rambling remarks into crisp phrases. Like paraphrasing, this technique demonstrates that you are taking in what the person is saying.

You might for example say:

- 'As I understand it . . .'
- 'If I've got it right . . .'
- 'So what you are saying is . . .'

Group listening

Much of your daily listening probably occurs in a group setting, such as a team, a meeting, a conference, a sales presentation. During these, it is usually easy to switch off, either permanently or temporarily, and hardly absorb anything of value.

Listening actively in a group shows that you are alert and interested in what is happening. To counter any tendency to doze,

---

Techniques for listening in a group

- Check what new ideas, goals or solutions are emerging. Can you write them down in order of importance?
- Identify what facts need further clarifying, and how.
- Define the missing information.
- What opinions, judgements, values or convictions come to mind?
- Take an idea expressed by someone else: mentally explain it, elaborate it, analyse it. Invent some examples, illustrations or explanations.
- What is the relationship between the facts you are hearing? Try moulding them into a single theme, argument.
- What might prod the group to greater activity, such as reminding it of the importance of the task, its limited resources or its deadlines?
- Keep your own set of written records to serve as the group memory.
- Watch to see whom to encourage to speak next.
- Who is talking too much? Find a way to reduce this behaviour.

---

listen selectively or lose concentration, listen with some specific aims in mind. When you listen with a clear aim it helps you concentrate on some mental gymnastics. They make your mind do the equivalent of press-ups or running on the spot.

Listening techniques keep you mentally active, rather than passively allowing the sounds to flow over you. For example, if you attend a conference or a large meeting, it is easy to sit back and let the words of each speaker wash over you without ever fully paying attention.

Try disciplining yourself to either take notes of the main points, or better still start drawing a mind map. Mind maps can keep you awake, even alert, during the most boring situations since creating them is a creative challenge. You can become so involved with drawing the map that the time simply flashes by. Use note-taking judiciously so that you avoid note mania. For example, it is not good listening technique to be absorbed tapping the notes into a laptop computer. Writing excessively while listening can also convey the message: 'I'm recording this for the record, so watch what you are saying.'

Further reading

HAMILTON C. and PARKER C. *Communications for Results: A guide for business and the professions*. Belmont, Wadsworth, 1997.

MACKAY I. *Listening Skills*. London, CIPD, 1998.

BETTER READING

Chapter 19

How is your in-tray? What is the state of your e-mail inbox? Like most managers you probably find them full much of the time. KPMG research found that its UK directors spent 11 per cent of their time reading and answering e-mails. Managers returning from holiday can face over 1,000 e-mails and dozens of reports and papers to process. It soon puts an end to that holiday feeling.

You need to develop into an expert reader, not just a competent one. The higher you go in an organisation, the more material you will have to handle, even if you can afford a bevy of personal assistants. No wonder that some companies have insisted on keeping all reports and memos to a single A4 sheet.

The ease with which people can send multiple copies of e-mails creates a barrage of literature demanding more than an ability to read fast. You need an intelligent reading strategy, one that protects you from sheer overload and a sense that you can never keep up.

Think strategically

How you tackle your reading can influence how quickly you get through the bombardment. Basic approaches can help you do it better.

- Read with a definite purpose in mind.
- Think about the future as you read.
- Use rapid scanning techniques.
- Learn to skim at lightning speed.

Reading with a purpose

When you have a definite purpose you can whiz through a vast amount of material. Your brain has a superb ability to filter out unwanted items and focus on only what is essential. If someone told you, for example, that a novel contained your name in it, you would almost certainly find it within minutes, simply because that was all you were looking for.

Think about the future

Try and read while thinking about the wider context of the organisation's strategic intentions. This means that your reading is future-directed. This is a leadership rather than a managerial focus. It will tend to set you apart from other managers who may lose sight of what their job is really about.

To treat the reading task as a low priority is usually a mistake, since it allows you to absorb far more information than you can through oral means and at your own pace. You, rather than someone speaking, control the communication process.

Scanning techniques

This is when your eye glances over text to find particular information. You get better at this the more you practise and the faster you go. Although there are some clever artificial devices to promote scanning, they tend to be rather cumbersome. A simple sheet of paper that you pull down over a page of text, revealing each line as it descends, is an effective way of practising scanning.

Skimming

This is more complex and takes scanning to a far higher level. Your eye covers selected sections of material so as to gain an overview. A good way to practise this technique is to set a stopwatch going and give yourself increasingly shorter times to read roughly the same amount of material.

You need to develop your reading skills if you:

- read everything – you always start at the beginning of the text and diligently read everything to the end
- sub-vocalise – you move your lips even slightly when reading
- read fewer than 350 words a minute
- have difficulty in scanning quickly and obtaining salient points
- experience poor recall and comprehension
- tend to reread words or sentences you have just read
- feel impatient, bored or unable to concentrate when reading
- often puzzle over the meaning of words
- feel pressured, with insufficient time for reading
- have difficulty coping with incoming paperwork.

Skimming involves going through reading material incredibly fast, not taking in everything. Instead you read selectively, seeking signs that it is time to slow down and pay attention to the content.

Experienced managers can skim vast quantities of information in minutes and still find the salient points. For example, next time you pick up a business magazine or a report look first at the content list, titles, subheadings, illustrations, words in italics, in fact anything that stands out from the mass of words. Try finding the pattern or structure of the material before plunging into it.

Similarly, concentrate your attention on nouns and verbs rather than on adjectives or prepositions.

Searching

One of the most powerful means of speeding up your reading is to develop greater clarity about the purpose behind each reading task. Try approaching the material by asking yourself:

■ What information am I seeking?

Rather than wandering around the text in a leisurely way, savouring writing style or contents, you read for results.

While speed is important, it is unlikely to be the only reason for developing better reading techniques. You may also benefit from organising your reading material so that it best suits your needs.

■ Sort reading material before even attempting to tackle it.

Do you have a pile to which you consign all trade journals and other magazines? Or do you read them all in bits and pieces during the day? It is generally more effective to set yourself a definite time slot to deal with them. Better still, have you tried an abstracts service to cut down on much of your professional reading?

How does your reading material reach you? Can any preliminary sorting be conducted on your behalf? For example, you may be able to get someone else to cover certain publications and incoming material, so that you receive only relevant items, or ones for decision.

Environment

You cannot expect to read well in a hot, stuffy room with lots of noise, or when you are cold. Yet it is surprising how often managers attempt serious reading when the conditions are working against them.

Make sure the environment is comfortable and supports you when concentrating. It may be tempting to slump in your chair when reading, yet this too can prevent good reading technique.

For example, if you read while looking downwards onto your lap, your eyes are more likely to start to close than if you keep material and yourself fully upright.

How fast do you read?

Most people believe that they read faster than they do.

- Count the number of words on three pages of a book; choose a relatively easy one. A quick way is to count the number of words in several lines and use the average, multiplied by the number of pages.
- Time how long it takes to read three pages of the book.
- Divide the number of words by the number of minutes it takes to read them.
- The formula is:

$$\text{Words read per minute} = \frac{\text{Number of pages read} \times \text{number of words per page}}{\text{Number of minutes spent reading the words}}$$

You can almost certainly handle more reading. Even if you increased your present weekly bombardment of material by 20 or 30 times, you would still have plenty of spare mental capacity. Your brain is equipped to deal with vast amounts of extra information so why not start exploiting it?

We tend to think of reading as merely understanding what the writer intended. It is far more than that. By reading well you:

- assimilate the information
- integrate it with existing knowledge and experience
- retain it for later use
- recall it when needed
- communicate.

Reading technique

Most reading happens at a surprisingly relaxed, almost lazy pace. So there is ample scope for speeding up, while still maintaining or improving comprehension and retention.

Here is something to try right away. Use your forefinger to trace what you believe to be the movement and the speed of your eyes. Start on the left of this paragraph and move your finger now, to show how you think you read.

When asked to do this most people trace a smooth path from left to right, with a quick jump from the end of one line to the beginning of the next. This zigzagging movement usually takes between a quarter to one second for each line.

This seriously underestimates what happens with even the slowest reader. If your eye moved at just one line a second, you would still cover over 600 words a minute. Yet most people actually handle easy-to-read material at around only 250 words a minute. Our eyes can potentially cover the words far more quickly than we realise.

Rather than moving in smooth lines, our eyes really move in a series of short, quick jumps and stops – see below.

Eye movements

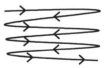
How most people think the
eye moves when reading text

words
How the eye actually moves
Eyes jump in a stop/start way

words
Eye movements of a faster reader; more words
are read in each jump, with no skipping back

While these jumps take hardly any time, the pauses can absorb from a quarter to one and half seconds. If you are a slow reader you will tend to read one word at a time, skipping back over words and letters. Your stops will also tend to be longer. The result? You have a much slower reading speed than you are capable of achieving.

Speeding up your reading depends on:

■ expanding the number of words read during each eye jump.

The more efficient you are as a reader, the more words you cover with each eye movement jump. For example, slow readers cover only one or two words in a single eye jump. Slightly faster readers cover four or five words at a time. Still faster ones take in a whole line in one jump, without skipping back.

Super-fast readers force their eyes to make big jumps right across an entire line. Eventually, they can run their eyes rapidly down the centre of a page and still understand what they are reading.

Slower readers therefore do more work. Smaller jumps make it harder to comprehend material. Faster, smoother readers acquire the meaning of text and do not need to understand every word.

■ You do less work as a quicker reader because your eyes are stopping and starting less per page.

Schools seldom teach you good reading techniques and few people are trained to understand how the eye traverses the page or the techniques for reading material, sifting, recall, note-taking, concentration, handling boredom and so on. Consequently many managers are both slow at reading and do not particularly enjoy it.

Fast-reading facts

- Your present average reading speed is not necessarily ideal; you may simply not be using the best reading strategy.
- You can easily learn to read more than 500 words per minute. With practice you can reach 1,000 words or more.
- Even when you read fast, you can still expect to understand material, since you are concentrating on it more and have more time to return to areas of special interest.
- The faster you go, the more impetus you gain and the more you tend to concentrate.

Since you are reading this part of the book, you are at least sufficiently interested to want to do it better. Motivation is a critical success factor in most learning, but particularly so with faster reading.

The basics of speed
Use a guide
Help your eye move faster by using a finger or a pen, as this helps your focus and concentration.

Get comfortable jumping
The bigger the jump, the more words you traverse.

Hold the text at distance
The further away the material, the more you use your peripheral vision. If you start straining, it is too far; if you start squinting, it is too close.

Scan the entire e-mail list
Before starting on your e-mails, scan the topics to see which ones are worth reading first. Do not just plunge in at the top and work down.

Create a store box

In your e-mail inbox, create a store folder for dumping e-mails in that you either have not got time for or are clearly low priority. Drag the low-level items into this store and then concentrate on the rest.

Read it all at once

Practise 'taking in an entire e-mail' in one complete glance. You can almost certainly do this with material that does not extend beyond the bottom of the screen.

Trace a question mark

Use a pen or finger to trace a question mark from the top to the bottom of the page. Read as you trace the shape. This develops eye and hand co-ordination. Soon you will be able drop the guide and let your eyes do the movement by themselves.

Double-line sweep

Use a card or a blank page to uncover two lines of text at a time. With your eyes make a smooth, gentle movement to take in both lines simultaneously. With practice you will soon be reading these pairs of lines in one clean sweep. Try extending to three or more lines at a time.

James Bond style

This is when you take in a whole page in one rapid glance. The secret is to start at the top in the middle and weave your way down the middle section of the page while simultaneously running your eye from left to right of centre. It takes practice but it works!

Backwards reading

Try reading a magazine from back to front. You tend to go faster and somehow it all makes more sense! You can even do that on a single page.

Training

Speed-reading classes can raise your reading speed, often to impressive levels, but these tend to be only temporary gains. Speed courses merely use your new motivation to read better. Because you want to improve, you do. After the course, however, the discipline it imposes ends, and the experience seldom permanently changes your whole approach. You can usually do just as well without a course by practising at home.

Set a rhythm

- Use a musical metronome to increase your reading speed.
- Set it ticking at a reasonable pace, with each beat indicating a single sweep of your eyes. This helps to acquire a smooth, steady rhythm. It counteracts the natural tendency to slow down after a while.
- Once you have found a comfortable rhythm, increase your speed by gradually adding an extra beat per minute.
- Use the machine to pace yourself so that eventually each beat represents one page you are sweeping.

Other practice techniques you can use at work or home include:

- **Rush** – read as fast as possible for one minute, without bothering about comprehension.
- **Page turning** – practise turning 100 pages at roughly two seconds for each page, moving the eyes very rapidly down the page; do this in short sessions of about two minutes.
- **Find it** – ask a friend to select a paragraph or sentence from a book without you knowing where it comes from. Try finding the chosen text, giving yourself first five minutes, then four minutes and so on. Now try the same approach with the main idea behind an article.
- **Scan** – look for themes and major lines of arguments in a business or professional magazine. Try reading the first

sentence of each paragraph and perhaps the last one. See how much you can absorb of the whole text from just this sampling.

■ **Instant novel** – read a whole book in two minutes. Turn the pages as fast as you can, absorbing as many words as possible without stopping. Force yourself to race through the material. When you return to ordinary reading, your average reading speed will be higher, perhaps twice as fast as before.

Blockages

Anxiety may be one reason for being a slow reader. You may be worrying about whether you will find what you want, understand the material or remember it. You may also be concerned about whether you really can improve your reading ability.

Yet to read better you do not do anything differently; you just do it more efficiently. It is about practice and motivation.

■ Give yourself a series of rewards for completing reading tasks such as speed exercises.

Memory

Most people assume that the faster they read, the less they will retain. Speed, though, is not the most decisive factor governing what you recall. Remembering depends on:

■ context
■ understanding
■ memory traces
■ reinforcement.

Context

You need to be able to put your reading material into a frame of reference. This is why all of those e-mails can seem so daunting. You do not really know how to view them; you have no immediate context except the name of the sender and a short topic heading.

You can be halfway through the second page of a report before you grasp the context in which it is written unless you make this the first priority for your reading purpose.

Memorising depends on being able to classify and analyse the material in a recognisable way. Right from the start, therefore, you should be looking to establish the context. In which 'box' does it fit within your whole range of responsibilities? Become clear on the context and you will more easily remember the contents.

Understanding

Knowing the context is only helpful if you can also understand the material. So much written for managers seems unnecessarily complicated and long. While you will not have much control over how people outside the organisation write, you will certainly be able to influence what is sent to you from within it:

■ Insist on material being presented in summary form and in short paragraphs and sentences.
■ Wage a war against jargon. Even when you know what it means it can still slow your comprehension.

Memory traces

Material that you want to memorise needs a memory trace attached to it. The strength of this trace governs how much you recall. The trace lets you recall the material because your mind can literally 'find' what you are seeking. For a trace to have strength, you rely on:

■ association
■ motivation.

You tend to remember something you have read when it is also strongly associated with a memorable picture, idea, pattern, arrangement, event and so on. So, for example, you may have trouble remembering a complicated telephone number as a straightforward sequence of numbers:

0488717588

By making it into a different pattern it becomes easier to memorise:

04 88 71 75 88

Or an item of information may be more memorable because it is associated with something not easily forgotten. For instance, in a report to a senior company team, a manager described what could go wrong as the 'Humpty Dumpty effect'. People remembered the material associated with it long after the report itself had been forgotten.

Reinforcement
You cannot assume that one reading alone will commit a piece of material to memory. You may need to reinforce your recollection in various ways until the information 'sticks'.

In the early stages of memorising something you may rapidly forget material unless it is reinforced in some way. You may need to return to it at quite short intervals initially to strengthen the memory. Gradually, however, the gaps between the different reinforcements reduce until the memory becomes permanent.

There will be vast amounts of material that you do not need to memorise at all, so that reinforcement is not necessary. However, when you have identified the information that you want to remember, you can improve your chances of being able to recall it later if you consciously set to reinforce it several times.

Further reading

LEWIS D. *Information Overload: Practical strategies for surviving in today's workplace.* London, Penguin, 1999.

Redway K. *Beat the Bumph! Cut the clutter, read rapidly and succeed in the information jungle.* London, Nicholas Brealey, 1995.

ASSERTIVENESS

Chapter 20

Grace Hopper, the first woman US Admiral, was once asked how she had succeeded in such a difficult and male-orientated organisation. With all her considerable gravitas, she growled: 'Do it first, apologise later.'

Are you a victim or a chooser? Victims tend to say things like 'I'm powerless', 'It doesn't affect me', 'I can't because . . .', 'There's no way to . . .'

The trouble with being a victim is that it creeps up on you. You do not mean to be negative or cynical about what is happening around you, it just somehow happens. It could be because you have been involved in too many change initiatives that never come to fruition, or because you have tried to make things happen but run up against too many obstacles and resisters.

Burnout, stress and overwork tend to breed a victim mentality. You find yourself rejecting changes, not being proactive or creative in your work, and simply unable to say 'no' to demands for new bits of work. Equally, it stems from frequent rejection of your ideas and suggestions, a lack of respect from colleagues, senior managers and so on.

Being a victim is seldom either enjoyable or productive. As a manager, you simply cannot afford to act the victim for long. People around you will first find that it is not much fun being around you, then later they actively avoid you. Longer term, it can mean a sad end to a job for which once you, and they, had high hopes.

It is about opportunities
Victim managers tend to deny or ignore opportunities, often when these are staring them in the face. Often such opportunities are relatively minor affairs – an invitation to a meeting, a

chance to see how someone else is tackling an important issue, a refusal to believe that a new task is possible or even desirable.

When victim behaviour becomes really serious you start closing off important options, making decisions without really exploring the alternatives and generally seeing the down side of every situation rather than its possibilities.

Like the frog that boils to death because he does not notice the water slowly heating in the pan, victim managers do not so much manage change as allow it to happen to them. They are constantly surprised at what pops up and impacts on their role; they feel 'done to' rather than 'doers'.

The opposite of a victim is a chooser. Someone who says things like: 'What I want is . . .', 'There must be a better way . . .', 'I can have an effect', 'I intend to . . .'.

Choosers manage change, they take and seek opportunities. Ultimately, really effective choosers do more than grab opportunities, they actively create them. The chart shows the various forms of behaviour we are discussing here.

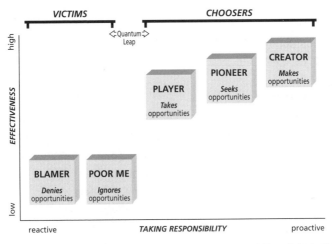

© Maynard Leigh Associates

Taking opportunities is still fairly reactive; it is a rather passive response compared to the more positive form of chooser behaviour – actively seeking opportunities. This is when you are constantly searching for ways forward, solutions and gaps in the market, new products and fresh ideas. People like being around this kind of chooser. They begin to feel that anything is possible and it is the kind of leadership that makes things happen.

The ideal form of chooser behaviour is when you use your creativity and drive to make new opportunities. This can be a lonely road to travel, since you are pioneering, going where others have not been, or taking risks that others have avoided or not even seen.

Choosers are assertive. Their behaviour underpins their management role and if you are to manage better, you need to hone your assertiveness so that it serves both you and others.

Non-assertive behaviour means you:

- find it hard to say no
- accept requests for additional work when you are not coping now
- feel unable to explain why you must get home early tonight
- find it hard to manage time and goals
- accept stress as part of the job.

No one listens?

You are in a meeting with some important people and want to make a point. Every time you start to say something, someone gets in first. When you finally get a word in, someone says that they have to leave and their departure is the cue for everyone else to depart. Before you know it, the meeting is over.

Furious, you walk back to your office wondering how it happened. How was it that you never really made your presence felt? Why did you never manage to get your point across, especially as it was a good one?

While you are ruminating on these events the person chairing the meeting catches up with you. She says that she missed hearing your comments. She wonders if there was anything you wanted to say. Still annoyed with yourself for not speaking up, you retort that if the meeting had been managed better you would have been asked for your views. The chairperson mumbles a half-hearted apology and soon walks away.

Not speaking up during a meeting is an example of being unassertive. Being angry with the chairperson and putting her down is an example of aggression. To manage better you need to learn how to use assertiveness rather than aggression. Generally the more successful the manager, the more assertive they tend to be.

Assertiveness is about speaking your mind openly and objectively, without being overemotional or using emotional blackmail. If you are overemotional, your words may be so charged with feelings that people may find it hard to disentangle important issues from your emotive communication.

Being assertive is saying no (or yes) clearly and firmly, without causing unnecessary offence. Being aggressive is a form of attack on the other person, however carefully this is wrapped up in polite language. Many managers grow adept at what psychologists call passive-aggressive behaviour. They are not openly rude or abusive; indeed they may be the epitome of politeness. Yet underneath the honeyed words is an attitude that reeks of aggression or victim behaviour.

Chooser and victim behaviour

Chooser	Victim
A chooser:	A victim:
■ works harder – and has more time	■ is always too busy
■ goes straight to the problem	■ goes around the problem and never solves it
■ makes a commitment	■ promises too readily
■ knows when to fight hard and when to give way	■ gives way on important issues or holds on to things that are not worth fighting for
■ feels strong enough to be friendly	■ is rarely friendly and at times can be a petty tyrant
■ listens	
■ respects other people's strengths	■ waits for his or her turn to talk
■ learns from others	■ focuses on others' weaknesses
■ explains	■ is resistant to others
■ feels responsible for more than just his or her work	■ makes excuses
	■ says, 'That's not my job!
■ sets his or her own pace	■ has only two speeds: full speed ahead or dead slow
■ uses time to improve	■ uses time to avoid criticism
■ is not afraid of making mistakes	■ is afraid of making mistakes and of what others will say
■ focuses on possibilities and solutions.	■ focuses on problems and unsolvable issues.

Victim remarks and behaviour tend to lead to no reward. The best comment is no comment.

The more you talk and act like a *chooser*, the more chooser-orientated you will become. Just like a favourite music cassette, the more you play it, the more you know about it and the better able you are to hum the tunes and recognise the rhythms and harmonies.

In every situation, you are directly responsible for the tapes you play!

Why assertiveness matters

Apart from the obvious desirability of managing your life and job so that it is enjoyable, an important reason why you may need to develop your assertiveness is because of the need to show strategic thinking.

As you learn to think strategically, you will start asking important questions about the future of the organisation. This may not make you particularly popular with colleagues who are more obsessed with the day-to-day. You will need to be able to stand up for your right to speak about the longer-term future. So in essence, assertion is about:

- standing up for your rights
- expressing your needs, preferences and feelings without threatening or punishing others
- acting without undue fear or anxiety
- acting without violating the rights of others
- direct, honest communication between individuals interacting equally and taking responsibility for themselves.

You need to be assertive because you often face tricky situations at work. These may require you to deal with issues without being disrespectful or making the other person feel humiliated. For example, you might:

- be asked to do something unreasonable by your boss
- feel angry about a lack of co-operation from other people
- need to communicate an unpopular decision
- wish to challenge the view someone senior to you is expressing
- deal with an angry customer without losing valuable business or making promises that are hard to keep
- make a presentation to an important audience with little time to prepare.

Non-assertive behaviour means:

■ having difficulty standing up for yourself
■ voluntarily relinquishing responsibility for yourself
■ inviting persecution by assuming the role of victim or martyr.

Aggression

It is easy to allow assertiveness to slide unnoticed into aggression. In your determination to speak up and be heard, to go after important opportunities, you allow yourself to become verbally violent.

You are being aggressive when you:

■ stand up for your rights yet violate the rights of others in the process
■ promote yourself by putting down or humiliating others
■ manipulate people and situations using subterfuge, trickery, seduction and subtle forms of revenge.

Many managers rely on aggression to deal with difficult situations or resort to passive-aggressive behaviour, which is less noticeable. Neither of these ways is likely to enhance your career in the long run.

Many managers think that to be successful they must be aggressive. Sometimes this is because they have seen apparently successful senior people behaving that way. Usually such managers have succeeded despite their aggression. People have tolerated it only because they have other valuable talents.

People who act aggressively at work usually obtain some kind of direct or indirect reward from it. For example, they see people caving in to their demands or failing to argue. In some way the person concludes that it pays to be aggressive. But does it? Aggressive managers may temporarily get people doing what they want but it seldom lasts. Aggression seldom gains true commitment, and without that you can never get the best from people.

You may tend to act aggressively for a variety of other reasons, for example because you:

- see situations or other people as threatening
- have previously been non-assertive and are reacting against this
- are responding with emotions left over from a previous incident
- need to develop your assertiveness skills.

While aggression can certainly work in some situations, there is usually a high price to pay through poor relationships and your own well-being. It often leads to stress, lack of rational thinking and ultimately poor decisions.

Signs of aggression:

- constantly using 'I' statements
- offering opinions as facts
- using threatening questions
- issuing requests as instructions or threats
- giving advice in the form of 'ought' or 'should'
- putting the blame on others
- making assumptions
- using sarcasm or put-downs.

Anger

Managing anger is essential for any successful manager and if this is one of your issues, it is time to learn some new ways to deal with it. For example, consider some personal coaching or even attending a programme that deals with anger management.

The equivalent of road rage is certainly happening at work. Suddenly someone loses their cool and all hell breaks loose. In an age when people have been constantly told it is right to speak their mind, aggression can become a substitute for rational argument.

It is not that you should never get angry. The trick is to be angry in the right way at the right time with the right person. Get colleagues to warn you when your anger seems to be escalating, so that you receive direct feedback when it happens.

Shouting

It is said that the person who shouts has already lost the argument and if you are a shouter, then it is time you tackled this tendency. Otherwise you will be modelling some poor management behaviour that others may also feel free to copy.

Shouting may make you feel better but the cost is high and will ultimately do your career harm. Of course some people would try the patience of a saint. No one is expecting you to be an absolute paragon of patience, though top managers are often just that.

While shouting and 'letting go' may prove a release of long pent-up emotions, the management issue is why such feelings have so long been suppressed. What stopped people speaking out before now?

If you find that you are shouting a lot at work, it is time to take a step back and ask:

- What is happening to me?
- Am I trying too achieve too much?
- What are my true priorities?
- Is this a good time to talk to a management coach?

Persistence

Persistence underpins all assertive management behaviour. Rather than merely wishing things were different, you keep on trying to make them so. Rather than giving up when you do not immediately get what you want, you keep on demanding.

Valuable though persistence can be, it may not immediately get what you want. This does not necessarily mean that you should resort to aggression. Assertive people can be surprisingly unaggressive yet still obtain the most wonderful results.

One famous public speaker invited to attend an international conference, for example, was coming through passport control and was told that he could not enter the country. Patiently he explained that he had flown several thousand miles to the country so as to speak at an important conference.

But the official refused to believe him. The speaker showed the man the conference papers but these cut no ice. After trying to achieve what he wanted through persistence, the speaker finally just shrugged. 'I suppose I had better just get on another plane and go home then.'

The official was astounded. 'You mean you are just going to turn around and go back?' 'Of course,' came the reply. 'It's not the end of the world if I don't attend this conference.' Faced with such equanimity and lack of confrontation, the official softened and soon allowed the person through. He even offered apologies for the delay!

You can be persistent and assertive without aggression by simply stating what you want and how you feel. An important principle here is:

■ self-disclosure.

When you are willing to share how you think and feel, you naturally make yourself vulnerable. This is powerful leadership behaviour and as a manager you need to practise it regularly.

Proactive

Assertive managers say what they think and tend to be proactive. They are willing to be out in front, taking a public position. This requires you to use your personal power. Unlike power that stems from your formal position, personal power depends on how you use your personality, persuasion skills and networking talents. The proactive manager:

- sets an example
- experiments
- gives feedback
- initiates
- leads
- makes things happen
- puts personal reputation on the line
- questions assumptions
- responds
- shows self-reliance
- shows the way
- takes risks
- takes certain actions without requiring approval
- takes responsibility.

Inexperienced managers often complain of having insufficient authority. For example they ask, 'How can I be persuasive when I have so little power?' This confuses formal power with the informal kind.

Talk to most senior managers in any organisation and they will usually reveal that they have severely limited powers. No matter how important you become in an organisation, you never really seem to have enough power.

Being proactive, therefore, involves taking enough power to achieve what you want. When you do that you acquire authority, merely because others end up willing to let you exercise it.

Your management power can stem from:

- **coercion** – getting what you want through fear, threats and punishments
- **expertise** – your superior knowledge or skills
- **role position** – your job or location in the organisation
- **rewarding** – your ability to reward emotionally or financially
- **connections** – your access to networks, groups and hence social power.

All but the last tend to be under attack in organisations that are changing at Internet speed, where who you know is as important as what you know.

Increasing assertiveness

An important step towards becoming more assertive is recognising when you are being non-assertive. Like any skill, from riding a bicycle to public speaking, you can develop your assertiveness and reduce aggressive tendencies by practice.

Being assertive as a manager means that you:

- make requests without apologising for them
- are direct about what you want, without wrapping it up in long sentences or convoluted ideas
- do not take refusal personally
- respect the other person's right to say no
- refuse unwanted requests by saying no
- disagree by stating your own views
- give praise without being apologetic about it and without hesitation

- avoid giving excessive praise and be sure that it comes from the heart
- accept praise without shrugging it off or offering praise in return
- receive praise without aggression such as boasting: 'Thanks, of course it was a good presentation, I always do them well'
- give bad news without delay or being overapologetic.

Assertion techniques

Three useful ways to enhance your assertiveness are:

- the broken record
- fogging
- counter behaviour.

Broken record

You repeatedly say what you want, calmly and quietly, until the other person finally hears it. You do not repeat all the arguments or share angry feelings. Instead, you just stick quietly to your point, saying it in various different ways. The broken record is particularly useful for when someone refuses to accept your instructions or tries to give you a task you do not want to do.

The broken record becomes annoying if you merely repeat your response in identical words. Instead, be creative. Find ways to vary the message so that each time it comes across in a slightly different way. For example, suppose someone wants you to prepare a report for their project group and you simply do not have the time. Instead of giving an aggressive refusal, you might offer the same message in a variety of more acceptable ways:

- 'I'm really pushed for time. I won't have space to meet your deadline.'
- 'I have some other pressing priorities; it will have to wait.'
- 'No, I can't do it by Tuesday. I have no free time until Friday.'
- 'I'd love to help; I just can't fit it in right now.'

Fogging

Use this to deal with manipulative criticism, the kind where someone says, 'You didn't do that too well, did you? What I want is better results.' Instead of being aggressive back, you calmly acknowledge the likelihood that there may be some truth in the criticism. But you remain in charge of yourself and the judgement about what you do. It allows you to receive criticism without being anxious or defensive.

You respond by agreeing with the person, wrapping up your agreement in constantly changing ways. 'Yes I could certainly have done that better', 'Yes, I agree, I'll really have to try harder to get it right next time', 'It's awful – I got it so wrong.'

Counter behaviour

We tend to mirror other people's behaviour, often quite unconsciously. By becoming more aware of this tendency, you can be more assertive and avoid aggression. For example, suppose someone is acting aggressively towards you, pointing a finger, talking in a loud voice and waving their arms. Rather than doing the same you consciously choose to relax, breathe deeply and talk in a calm manner.

Another use of counter behaviour is adopting the guideline:

- When people talk about feelings, ask for facts.
- When people keep referring to the facts, ask about feelings.

Again, you are doing the opposite of what others are doing, so as to transform the situation.

Praise and criticism

An important part of being an assertive manager is being able to offer praise and constructive criticism. You are not alone if you feel slightly uncomfortable with doing either, since the reaction to both can often be quite emotional. You may therefore be tempted to shy away from these two important management responsibilities.

It is all too common for managers to fail to give praise. Endless surveys confirm this tendency, right across the Western world. The result is that people often feel unappreciated and insufficiently recognised for their efforts.

Successful top managers seem to know how to hand out praise in a way that is genuine and unforced. Being able to praise someone honestly without doing it grudgingly is good management and means that you are being assertive. When you offer genuine praise you sound authentic and tap into your own humanity.

Similarly, people are entitled to know when they are not living up to your standards. You cannot expect them to somehow guess this; you need to tell them. However, it also matters the way in which you convey that information.

Faced with someone who is not performing well, you are being non-assertive if you either avoid raising the issue or do so in a tentative, apologetic manner. Equally, you are being aggressive if you work yourself up into an angry state and then raise the issue in an abrupt, heavy-handed way.

For criticism to be offered assertively, it needs to be specific, preferably with examples, and not made as a personal attack on the other person. Much the same applies to praise. Ill-defined praise is too diffuse to sound convincing.

Meetings

How assertive are you in meetings? (See also Chapter 7.) In meetings you have certain basic rights that you are entitled to assert regularly. For example, to:

- state your opinions and make suggestions
- be listened to and receive a response
- understand what is being said
- disagree
- make your contribution without being interrupted.

You are also entitled to know how long the meeting will last. Being 'called to a meeting' by a senior manager is a common experience. Never accept the demand in isolation; always enquire how long the meeting is likely to last. This is an important way of asserting that your time is also important.

Being assertive in meetings is not merely about speaking up. It involves obtaining what you need to make an effective contribution. No one has the right to make you ineffective in a meeting. So, for example, apart from knowing how long the meeting will last, your are entitled to know:

- Is there any preparation required?
- Is there an agenda?
- Who else will be there?

Other assertive meeting behaviour includes:

- helping the meetings along
- suggesting the use of a flipchart
- asking for a few minutes to study information that has been provided
- requesting a summary when you feel the meeting is getting bogged down
- seeking other people's reactions
- saying you agree with other people.

There are also non-verbal ways of being more assertive in meetings that are worth using:

- give good eye contact
- make above-the-table hand movements to emphasise your point; use body movements such as sitting forward or sitting back in your chair to signal your involvement.

Further reading

BACK K. *and* BACK K. *Assertiveness at Work: A practical guide to handling awkward situations*. Maidenhead, McGraw-Hill, 1999.

GILLEN T. *Agreed! Improve your powers of influence*. London, CIPD, 1999.

GILLEN T. *Assertiveness*. London, CIPD, 1998.

ROGERS J. *Influencing Skills: The essential guide to thinking and working smarter*. London, Marshall, 1999.

WEBSITE RECOMMENDATIONS

Many websites you could visit around the topics of *20 Ways* are glorified advertising pages. Here are some sites that you might find useful and that are likely to be around by the time you get your hands on this book!

www.inst-mgt.org.uk
Institute of Management
Extensive links, summaries of publications, career development, qualifications and courses.

www.anbar.co.uk
Anbar International Management Database
A management abstracting service for international management journals. It is expensive but the service covers many of the chapter areas in more depth.

www.cranfield.ac.uk
Cranfield School of Management
Part of Cranfield University. Offers short and tailored courses, management, development and related research.

www.bized.ac.uk
A business and economics service for students, teachers and lecturers offering links and learning resources.

www.employment-studies.co.uk
The Institute for Employment Studies
Research, links and publications.

www.dfee.gov.uk
Department for Education and Employment
Links and publications.

www.scottish-learning-network.co.uk
Learning opportunities, courses, and links.

www.indsoc.co.uk
The Industrial Society
Training courses, information, Campaign for Leadership.

www.dti.gov.uk
Department of Trade and Industry
Links and news.

www.ipma.co.uk
International Professional Managers Association
Qualifications, research and links.

www.psi.org.uk
Policy Studies Institute
Publications and links.

www.cipd.co.uk
Chartered Institute of Personnel and Development
Training, resources and courses.

www.mindtools.com
Simple summaries of management tools, including goal-setting
and decision-making.

CHAPTER-SPECIFIC

Coaching

www.coachingnetwork.org.uk
The Coaching and Mentoring Network
An independent site for coaching and mentoring – information,
resources and links.

www.oscm.co.uk
Oxford School of Coaching and Mentoring
A virtual organisation – links and resources.

Decision-making

www.decision-making.co.uk
A private organisation – links, courses.

Project Management

www.apm.org.uk
The Association for Project Management
Publications, qualifications and links.

www.projectnet.co.uk
Project Manager Today magazine
Events and publications.

Presenting

www.bizpresenting.com
Business presentations, tips and information

Force field analysis

http://panoramix.univ-paris1.fr/CRINFO/dmrg/MEE98/misop016/
More practical detail on using force field analysis.

With over 100,000 members, the **Chartered Institute of Personnel and Development** is the largest organisation in Europe dealing with the management and development of people. The CIPD operates its own publishing unit, producing books and research reports for human resource practitioners, students, and general managers charged with people management responsibilities.

Currently there are over 150 titles, covering the full range of personnel and development issues. The books have been commissioned from leading experts in the field and are packed with the latest information and guidance to best practice.

For free copies of the CIPD Books Catalogue, please contact the publishing department:
Tel: 020 8263 3387
Fax: 020 8263 3850
E-mail: *publish@cipd.co.uk*
Web: *www.cipd.co.uk*

Orders for books should be sent direct to:
Plymbridge Distributors
Estover
Plymouth
Devon PL6 7PY
Tel: +44 (0) 1752 202301
Fax: +44 (0) 1752 202333
E-mail: orders@plymbridge.com

Chartered Institute of Personnel and Development

Customer Satisfaction Survey

We would be grateful if you could spend a few minutes answering these questions and return the postcard to CIPD. Please use a black pen to answer. If you would like to receive a free CIPD pen, please include your name and address. IPD MEMBER Y/N

....

1. Title of book ....

2. Date of purchase: month .... year ....

3. How did you acquire this book?
   ☐ Bookshop   ☐ Mail order   ☐ Exhibition   ☐ Gift   ☐ Bought from Author

4. If ordered by mail, how long did it take to arrive:
   ☐ 1 week   ☐ 2 weeks   ☐ more than 2 weeks

5. Name of shop .... Town.. Country............

6. Please grade the following according to their influence on your purchasing decision with 1 as least influential: (please tick)

	1	2	3	4	5
Title					
Publisher					
Author					
Price					
Subject					
Cover					

7. On a scale of 1 to 5 (with 1 as poor & 5 as excellent) please give your impressions of the book in terms of: (please tick)

	1	2	3	4	5
Cover design					
Paper/print quality					
Good value for money					
General level of service					

8. Did you find the book:
   Covers the subject in sufficient depth   ☐ Yes   ☐ No
   Useful for your work   ☐ Yes   ☐ No

9. Are you using this book to help:
   ☐ In your work ☐ Personal study   ☐ Both   ☐ Other (please state)

Please complete if you are using this as part of a course

10. Name of academic institution...

11. Name of course you are following? ....

12. Did you find this book relevant to the syllabus? ☐ Yes ☐ No ☐ Don't know

Thank you!
To receive regular information about CIPD books and resources call 020 8263 3387.

1795/05/00

Publishing Department

Chartered Institute of Personnel and Development

CIPD House

Camp Road

Wimbledon

London

SW19 4BR